Engines
of the Mind

JOEL SHURKIN

Engines
of the Mind

The Evolution of the
Computer from
Mainframes to Microprocessors

W · W · NORTON & COMPANY

NEW YORK · LONDON

THE TEXT OF THIS BOOK *is composed in VIP Baskerville, with display type set in Windsor. Composition and manufacturing are by the Maple-Vail Book Manufacturing Group. Book design by Marjorie J. Flock.*

First published in an updated paperback edition 1996

Library of Congress Cataloging in Publication Data
Shurkin, Joel, 1938–
    Engines of the Mind
    Includes index.
    1. Computers—History.   I. Title.
QA76.17.S49   1984   001.64'09   83-11433

ISBN 0-393-31471-5

W. W. Norton & Company, Inc., 500 Fifth Avenue, New York, N.Y. 10110
W. W. Norton & Company Ltd., 10 Coptic Street, London WC1A 1PU

1 2 3 4 5 6 7 8 9 0

Contents

	Introduction	9
	Acknowledgments	13
1.	One, Two, Many	19
2.	Sir Alphabet Function	37
3.	Hollerith	66
4.	Dinosaurs and Flip-Flops	93
5.	Eckert and Mauchly	117
6.	ENIAC	139
7.	Von Neumann	173
8.	UNIVAC	209
9.	The First Dwarf	248
10.	Bleak House	280
11.	The Revolution	300
	Epilogue	323
	Glossary	339
	Bibliography	345
	Index	349

ILLUSTRATIONS *appear following page 158.*

For my mother

Introduction

THIS BOOK IS ABOUT PEOPLE, not machines. The machines are interesting, but the people are fascinating and their story should be told. They changed our world.

I think the three most important inventions of the twentieth century are the atomic bomb, the computer, and the transistor. They have had the greatest effect on our lives. The marriage of the last two, the computer and the transistor, has brought about a transformation unmatched since the Industrial Revolution of the nineteenth century.

Historians have expended considerable energy telling the story of the atomic bomb and of the people who created it. The development of the transistor did not take much time or involve many people, and perhaps historians have believed it was therefore not worth much of their attention. But the computer's antecedents go back to the early ages of humanity; involved in its evolution have been hundreds of men and women, some of them quite extraordinary.

It is hard to know why historians have not been drawn toward the story, for it contains virtually every human trait: genius, stupidity, generosity, avarice, integrity, dishonesty, daring, caution. The people currently involved with computers have probably been too busy building and playing with their machines to pay much heed to the origins; engineers are not noted for their sense of history. But why historians have tended to ignore the story is curious. Maybe they all thought that others had already told the tale. Maybe they have been put off by the bitter men and women, some of whom are still alive, and very angry.

The reader should be forewarned: much of what follows is still hotly debated by the surviving participants. It is no exaggeration to say that some of them continue to be so bitter almost forty years later that they will not even appear in the same room together.

There are several controversies confronting anyone telling this tale. The first concerns an inventor whose claim to priority is recent, John Vincent Atanasoff. Atanasoff has been named by no less than a federal judge as the real inventor of the computer, and his claim is supported by two of the men who participated in the later, more famous events. Atanasoff's story is dealt with in great detail because if he is really responsible for the computer, a grave injustice has been done.

Another, greater controversy is over the role of one of the century's most esteemed scientists, the mathematician John von Neumann. To most people, von Neumann is responsible for the logic that went into the electronic computer as well as for the computer's capacity to remember or alter instructions—in short, for the modern computer. If this is not his work, another injustice may have been committed.

Finally, our story is about two men, J. Presper Eckert and John Mauchly, who seem to have gotten little more than a footnote in the history of the modern world. Both men staunchly believe that they are the inventors of the computer and that they have been grossly mistreated. We shall see whether that is true.

This book, I expect, will not be the final word on the subject. Many of those involved will not like its conclusions and will wish to say more. I hope they do; their contributions to the modern world are so great that they should get no less than our full attention and respect. I have done the best I can.

JOEL N. SHURKIN

Palo Alto, California
April 1983

Acknowledgments

No one writes a book of this size in a vacuum. One has to have a lot of help. I did.

Many people wanted the story told. Some of them probably wish it had been told in a different way because the book cannot please everyone. For things that they find to quarrel with, the author claims sole responsibility.

The bibliography lists the people who sat for an interview. I greatly appreciate their kindness and their taking the time. A few, however, should get special mention. One not listed in the bibliography, Paul Armer, led me to Hank Tropp, who is listed. Dr. Tropp, in turn, told me whom to see and gave me some warning about what I was going to run into. The kindness and hospitality of Dr. Tropp and his wife, who live in bucolic, if somewhat insular, splendor at Humboldt State University, near Arcata, are very much appreciated.

The initial interviews with Eckert, Mauchly, and Brainerd were done as part of a story I wrote when I was on the staff of the *Philadelphia Inquirer*. By the time the book was being written, John Mauchly had died; I could therefore not go back and ask him further questions. Fortunately for me, Esther Keenan Carr and James B. Schoedler had spent roughly nine hours videotaping an interview with Mauchly about a year before he died. They have kindly granted me permission to quote from those tapes, which have been of inestimable value.

Kay McNulty Mauchly spent a considerable amount of time with me. Her husband had the admirable trait of never throwing anything out, so Mrs. Mauchly had a great deal to show me. Her kindness, and that of her family, was quite special.

The most complete account of ENIAC is in the doctoral dissertation, which was later published as a book, called *From ENIAC to UNIVAC: An Appraisal of the Eckert-Mauchly Computers,* by Nancy Stern, now of Hofstra University. Portions from it are quoted with her permission and that of Digital Press. I have also quoted from Herman Goldstine's fine book *The Computer: From Pascal to von Neumann,* with the permission of its publisher, Princeton University Press.

John Atanasoff and his wife were most hospitable, as were Pres Eckert (who sat through a second interview) and Mrs. Eckert.

Saul Gorn was my guide at the Moore School and helped me find people and things there. Marshall Ledger of the *Pennsylvania Gazette,* who wrote several stories about the ENIAC controversy, also gave assistance and moral support.

The people at the Stanford University Libraries were wonderful. The reader can only imagine what it is like to work as a writer at a university with libraries and librarians like those at Stanford. I also have fond thoughts about the Research Libraries Information Network computer, which got me a number of references I would not have been able to find on my own, particularly the article by Hollerith.

Lisa Sonne read most of the manuscript with orders to pick every nit, and she did. Her talent as a copy editor was infuriating; she was almost always right, and writers hate that. She greatly improved the product. Paul Kaufman also read the manuscript with orders to be thoughtful and kind. He knows no other way.

For the technical-minded, an acknowledgment to the machinery. The book was written on a Radio Shack TRS-80 Model

III, using Scripsit and, at the end, Superscripsit, both word-processing programs, all by Tandy. I also used Aspen Software's Proofreader and Grammatik, which arrived when the manuscript was about half completed. The whole damn manuscript fit on five 5¼-inch floppy disks. Frightening.

Bows also go to Jonathan and Michael, as usual.

Finally, and absolutely not least, they go to Bob Beyers, whose patience was beyond description. The same for the rest of my colleagues at Stanford University News and Publications Service.

Readers wishing more information will not have a great many choices, but four books were of particular help to me, and I recommend them: Robert Sobel's history of IBM, *I.B.M.: Colossus in Transition*, Katharine Davis Fishman's *The Computer Establishment*, and the books by Goldstine and Stern.

The *Annals of the History of Computing*, where most of the battles are now fought, is great fun and highly recommended. Watching academics spit venom is always a treat, but besides the venom, the quarterly publication is full of matters cosmic and trivial in the history of the computer. I would have been lost without it.

*There is perhaps in every thing of any consequence, a secret
history which it would be amusing to know, could we have it authentically
communicated.*

JAMES BOSWELL

1. One, Two, Many

An honest man has hardly need to count more than his ten fingers, or, in extreme cases he may add his toes, and lump the rest. I say, let our affairs be as two or three, and not as a hundred or a thousand; instead of a million count half a dozen, and keep your accounts on your thumbnail.

THOREAU

FOR MOST OF HUMAN HISTORY counting was scarcely necessary; computing was irrelevant. It did not matter much if there was one wolf outside or if there were seven; one saber-toothed tiger was as necessary to avoid as four. At one time or another, however, some of our ancestors began to notice little things.

They noticed, for instance, that one elk and one daffodil had something in common: each was alone, and there was only one of them. One. That recognition was a giant step for mankind because it was the first number. It followed, of course, that something else was required; there might be more than one daffodil, perhaps a field full of them. So the first counting system probably consisted of two numbers—one and many. Later many societies apparently added a second number—two. For thousands of years one, two, or many described the quantity of daffodils in a field. A few groups have never progressed beyond this stage. Like the society that Thoreau idealized, they need nothing more.

Given five fingers on each hand, communicating quantity was not difficult if the numbers were small. How many wolves were out there? Four fingers might relay the message. It was easy to handle numbers up to ten. Aristotle was the first man to note that the base-10 system (or, in a few places, the base-5), which eventually evolved in most societies, derived from the simple fact that human beings had five fingers on each hand.[1] In order to count more than ten, a man could call in a friend and his ten fingers. Now he had twenty different numbers he could deal with. Or his friend's fingers could count for something else; they could count for an aggregate, usually ten each. The number 12 would be one finger on a friend's hand, two on yours. There are societies in Africa that still compute things that way. Two concepts were at work in this method: the decimal system (base 10) and the idea of group numbers, the notion of combining more than one number to produce a needed value. When fingers (and toes) were insufficient, an external method might serve, often a pile of stones, which were usually piled in groups of fives.

It is not clear to historians whether advances in mankind's ability to compute numbers were caused by the pressures of increasingly complex societies or whether the advances were the stimuli for the complexity. Changes, when they occurred, were a long time in coming.

Cutting notches into a stick or a bone was easier and more useful than piling stones. In Czechoslovakia, anthropologists found the jawbone of a young wolf containing fifty-five marks arranged in two clusters, twenty-five in the first, thirty in the second. In each case the clusters were arranged in groups of five to make it easier to read.

---

1. A number of societies adopted other bases, or radices, for their mathematics. The Babylonians used base 60. The Mayans used 360 (derived from the number of days they computed for one year), including a figure for the zero. A few societies utilized a rudimentary binary system, just 1 and 2.

The use of written numbers is generally believed to have preceded the use of words for numbers. Numbers were communicated either by gesture, by artifact, or by some form of symbology long before the language caught up. Very possibly mathematics had become quite complex by the time there was a language to express it. One impetus in the development of a language of numbers could have been religious rituals or military activities in which words for ordinal numbers were needed. Something had to serve for such commands as "You go first, you go second, you third." Some experts have suggested, in fact, that ordinal numbers preceded cardinal numbers (one, two, three) in the language.

By the time agrarian societies formed, about 11,000 years ago, the use of numbers had gone far beyond the mere reporting of mundane situations. The use of numbers to explain astronomical events, beginning with the seasons and the changes in the moon, had become common, and this relation produced the first science. The relation between numbers were also beginning to interest people, and from that awareness the mathematical sciences evolved.

A piece of bone found in Africa and dated at around 8,500 B.C. has engraved markings containing what appear to be representations of the numbers 11, 13, 17, and 19, all of which are prime numbers (they can be divided only by themselves and by the number 1), a somewhat advanced mathematical exercise. But by that time life had become considerably more complicated and perhaps there was a need to understand more about the structure of numbers and even to compute them.

An economic system had been developed; governing systems were being formed; the beginnings of architecture and geometry existed. More complicated forms of mathematics were needed to cope with these changes. Adding and subtracting were imperative; multiplication and division, and geometric concepts such as pi, were quickly becoming vital.

There was, however, a serious problem: keeping track of written cardinal numbers was extremely cumbersome. They could be written down, but they could not be manipulated with ease. Each culture had developed its own, unique method of writing computations. Some of these methods were excruciatingly com-. plicated. The Egyptians, for instance, had a system in which the numbers 1 to 9 were depicted by one to nine vertical lines. A 10 was a U or a circle, 100 was a coiled rope, 1,000 was a lotus blossom, 10,000 was a pointed finger, 100,000 a tadpole, and 1,000,000 was the picture of a man with his arms stretched toward heaven in astonishment. The historian G. C. Chase points out that the Egyptians would have to depict the number 3,647,543 by three amazed men, six tadpoles, four pointed fingers, seven lotus blossoms, five coiled ropes, four circles, and three vertical lines. Chase wonders how many men standing in amazement would be necessary to depict the U.S. national debt.

Multiplying six tadpoles by five coiled ropes is unthinkable. Some evidence indicates that the Egyptians also evolved a method of computation on papyrus using dots and lines. One papyrus, kept in the British Museum and dated at around 1500 B.C., has a dot diagram on the back that seems to have no relation to what is on the front of the papyrus (the ancient equivalent to the back-of-the-envelope computation) and that consists of ten rows of ten dots with a line drawn underneath the fifth row. An incomplete vertical row runs alongside it. Egyptologists have figured out several ways in which this system could have been used for performing mathematical functions, but how the Egyptians used these doodlings is still unclear. The Egyptians also employed stone counters.

The wise Greeks and the powerful Romans did not have a much easier time of it by using letters for numbers. It is not convenient to multiply CLXXIII by XVII, a basically simple computation. The Roman system, which in Europe lasted almost until the Renaissance, kept mathematics out of the hands of all but a small elite. Fortunately for that elite, they had the use of history's first digital computer, the abacus.

Early societies had undoubtedly developed some mechanical methods for aiding them in simple addition and subtraction. They might have marked units on two pieces of wood and then added the lengths of the wood, a crude form of slide rule. A clay tablet in the British Museum dated at 2300–1600 B.C. and coming from Senkereh, in Babylonia, contains the squares of numbers up to

24. The tablet apparently served as a reference table with which Babylonian mathematicians could look up squares, a function that is useful in geometry. The importance of the Senkereh tablet is that whoever calculated the squares probably had some mechanical assistance, perhaps in the form of small polished stones used as counters.

The use of stone counters is universal in primitive societies, even to this day, and was common all through history. The shepherd in Shakespeare's *The Winter's Tale* laments trying to count his sheep (called "wethers") and figure out his income from their wool (measured in "tods" of twenty-eight pounds each):

Let me see. Every 'leven wether tods; every tod yields pound and odd shilling; fifteen hundred shorn, what comes the wool to? . . . I cannot do't without counters.

Even in the late sixteenth century, the counters he would have used were counting stones, and he would have used the system of group numbers, probably in base 10, to compute how much he would be paid for his wool.

The evolution from stone counters to an abacus is a simple one. Simply take the pebbles, put them in an enclosed area in an ordered pattern in groups of base 5 or 10, perhaps connect them with wires or hair, and you will not find it difficult to work out a method of adding and subtracting (and, by repeating the steps, of multiplying and dividing). The ancient Greeks clearly had abacuses by 500 B.C., but they just as clearly did not invent them; the Babylonians are generally credited with the invention. The word itself comes from the Phoenician word *abak*, designating a flat slab covered with sand on which figures are drawn.

The first abacuses probably used an *abak* with pebbles placed on lines in the sand. Herodotus mentioned pebble abacuses in the fifth century B.C., and even left behind calculations performed on them. One calculation was of the interest on a loan of 766 talents, 1,095 drachmas, and 5 obols over 1,464 days at the rate of one drachma a day for each 5 talents. Such a calculation could have been performed on an abacus and would have been a very difficult chore without one. In the third century B.C., Eytocious of Ascalon could find the square of 3,013 3/4 and come out with the right answer. Again, he almost certainly needed mechanical help to do that. There are references to pebble abacuses in the writings of Demosthenes in the fourth century B.C., in the plays of Alexis (fourth to third century B.C.), and both Diogenes and Polybius alluded to them.

The word *calculus* stems from the Latin word for pebble. The Romans used several different types. A Roman abacus might be a smooth board or table with places on which to mark units; several stone abacuses of this kind have survived. Another form is a small rectangular board with two rows of eight slits, each slit containing beads. Some are small enough to be held by hand— the first hand calculators. The markings indicate Roman money values, including fractions, a concept that was fairly recent in human history.

In the Roman abacus each wire holds ten or more "calculi" denoting units, tens, hundreds, and so on. When the number of "calculi" on one wire exceeds ten, one is "carried" over to the next wire on the left. The Chinese used bamboo rods instead of beads or pebbles.

The abacus underwent several changes through history, the major one being the addition of a crossbar separating two zones in the frame—one zone called "heaven," the other "earth." The heaven section contains two beads, the earth section five. Each heaven bead counts as five, the earth beads are one each.[2]

The abacus, in the hands of a skilled operator, is amazingly fast. On November 12, 1946, the U.S. Army staged a contest between its fastest mechanical adding machine operator, Pvt. T. N. Wood of the finance disbursing section, and Kiyoshi Matsuzaki, of the savings bureau of the Ministry of Postal Administration. Matsuzaki used an abacus. There were five types of calculations; Matsuzaki won four of them. According to *Stars and Stripes*, the abacus's victory "was complete."[3]

2. The modern Japanese have eliminated one of the heaven beads, since it is not necessary. The operator slides the beads along the wires. Every bead touching the crossbeam or connected directly to that bead counts.
3. Historians frequently refer to that contest as a demonstration of the abacus's speed, but there is some reason to think that Matsuzaki was one of those calculating geniuses who can do whole columns of figures in their heads and that he was using the abacus as a prop. Nonetheless, abacuses are very fast.

Between the first and second century A.D., the Hindus had developed a nine-digit numbering system. It was not until much later that they added their most remarkable invention, the zero, which represented the empty column in the abacus. There was now a method of notation in which any number could be represented in base 10 by an ordered sequence of numbers. The zero is one of the most important inventions in human history. The French scientist Laplace wrote in the eighteenth century:

It is India that gave us the ingenious method of expressing all numbers by means of ten symbols, each symbol receiving a value of position as well as an absolute value; a profound and important idea which appears so simple to us now that we ignore its true merit, but its very simplicity, the great ease which it has lent to all computations, puts our arithmetic in the front rank of useful inventions; and we shall appreciate the grandeur of this achievement when we remember that it escaped the genius of Archimedes and Apollonius, two of the greatest men produced by antiquity.

The exact date of this development is not known, but the first unquestioned use of the zero that historians agree on occurred in A.D. 876. By adding the zero to a decimal system, the Indians began a shining era of mathematics that lasted until around 1200 and led to major advances in algebra.

The Arabs had considerable commercial dealings with the Indians and adopted both the decimal system and the zero from them. Indian astronomy tables using the decimal system were brought to Baghdad as early as 773 and translated. The Arab mathematician al-Khowarizmi visited India around 830 and wrote a book entitled *Al-jabr wa'l muqabalah*. The word *algebra* evolved from the title.

The Arabic genius for mathematics is just one aspect of what is widely known as the golden age. All the arts and sciences flourished. In fact many of those who contributed most to this golden age were not Arabs at all; many were Jews, others were Persians. Nonetheless, they attained heights of intellectual glory in the warm and stimulating culture of the Arabs. One man who participated in this glory was the Persian Jamshid ben Mas'ud ben Mahmud Ghiath ed-Din al-Kashi (1393–1449). He was the head of an astronomical observatory in Samarkand that the grandson of Tamerlane set up.

Al-Kashi was probably the first mathematician to use decimal fractions, adapted, perhaps, from the Chinese. He also computed the value of 2pi (6.2831853071795865) with an accuracy unmatched until the late sixteenth century. He made major contributions in trigonometric calculations. Indeed, Al-Kashi took enormous pleasure in performing huge computations, making use of some mechanical devices, many of which he invented. He devised a mechanical "plate of conjunctions," which could determine when two planets would come close to each other. Al-Kashi also created a mechanical computer that could predict lunar eclipses. Another of his devices calculated the longitudes of the heavenly bodies. Mostly, his computers involved sliding disks, a simple form of an analog computer.

Eventually, all this knowledge and skill found its way to Europe. According to most historians, the path was through Spain and the Moorish occupation. The Arabs did their best to keep infidel Christians from learning their secrets, but around the year 1120 a monk named Adelard of Bath (not Heloise's Abelard) infiltrated the University of Cordova disguised as a believer. He translated al-Khowarizmi's *Al-jabr.* Within twenty years, the use of the Arabic notation had spread throughout Europe. A Sicilian coin of 1134 contains Arabic numbers.[4]

The Arabic form of notation was called "algorism," a corruption of the name al-Khowarizmi.

Another major proponent of the use of Arabic numbers was the Italian Leonardo Fibonacci (b. 1175). His father sent him to be a commercial agent on the Barbary coast of North Africa, where he became acquainted with Moslem culture. Back in Italy in 1202 he wrote *Liber Abaci,* which explains the Arabic system so "that the Latin race might no longer be deficient in that

---

4. Other historians credit the mathematician Boethius (ca. A.D. 475–524) with introducing the Arabic system, but most do not. The first European mathematician to come into contact with the system might have been Gerbert (940–1003), who became Pope Sylvester II, but he did not succeed in convincing many to use it. He may, moreover, have introduced the abacus to Europe. John of Seville, a converted Jew and a contemporary of Adelard, has also been credited with the introduction.

knowledge." Among the problems the book uses is the following: "How many pairs of rabbits will be produced in a year,
beginning with a single pair, if in every month each pair bears a
new pair which becomes productive from the second month on?"
He helped push the Italians to the forefront of the new wave of
Arabic numbers, although considerable resistance persisted for
centuries. In 1299 the city of Florence called Arabic numbers
the work of infidels and banned their use by Florentine bankers.
But by 1400 the numbers were being used universally in European science.

The invention of the printing press made it possible to teach
both the algoristic system and the abacus to the common man,
particularly the merchant. In 1478 a book printed in Treviso,
Venice, explained that the five main forms of arithmetic were
"numeration, addition, subtraction, multiplication and division."

Numeration is the representation by numbers by figures. This is done
by means of ten letters as shown, 1, 2, 3, 4, 5, 6, 7, 8, 9, 0. Of these the
first figure, 1, is not called a number, but the source of number. The
tenth figure, 0, is called cipher or "nulla" i.e. the figure of nothing, since
by itself it has no value, although when joined with others it increases
their value.

The change from Roman numbering to Arabic took a very long
time in England. Evidence of the common use of Roman numerals goes well into the seventeenth century. The mayor's audits
for the city of Bristol in 1635 show two pages of Arabic numerals, but the audits for 1636 were completely in Roman numerals.
A young, progressive clerk apparently supervised the pages in
1635, but a more conservative clerk won out the next year.

The English used the abacus, but during Tudor times a dot
system, something like the system found on the back of the
Egyptian papyrus, was sometimes used for computations in the
Exchequer. The British also computed with an exchequer table.
The table used squares of alternating colors, like a chess board,
to do sums of taxes. In fact the name Exchequer comes from
that board. Eventually the board was replaced with "tally sticks,"
sticks cut in such a way that they could act as totalizers and receipts.
The British clerks probably employed a paper backup, as well.

The stick system was used until 1783. In 1834 the government ordered the destruction of the cellar full of tally sticks, but the fire flared out of control and the House of Commons burned down.

Modifications of the Arabic system in the sixteenth and seventeenth centuries included the use of the addition sign (+) and of decimal fractions. Decimal points are attributed to Palazzi of Nice, at the very end of the fifteenth century.

Herman Goldstine (about whom we shall hear much more later) has written that a watershed was reached around the year 1600. When Galileo married mathematics to the physical sciences, his genius made it possible to quantify and even prove physical principles; at the same time, he created for mathematicians previously unimagined worlds and needs. Both mathematics and the physical sciences flourished. It was necessary, however, for mathematics, particularly the computation of figures, to advance if the study of the other sciences could go forward. In a thirty-year period around 1600, this happened.

Galileo served as professor of mathematics at Pisa and Padua. Mathematics at universities really consisted of physics and astronomy, but Galileo did perform complex mathematical computations because the physics and astronomy he studied required it. He devised a number of computational techniques, and in 1597 he invented and marketed "geometric and military compasses." The compasses consisted of two arms joined at one end with a pivot. Each arm contained equidistant markings with numbers up to 250. Galileo's compass could not be used without a conventional compass, or calipers (the device used to measure distances on maps), with one measuring against the other. His compass performed crude calculations without great accuracy, but Galileo made a great deal of money selling it. Engineers and architects needed something, and Galileo's geometric compass was the best they could get.

Galileo's invention was hardly his major contribution to mathematics (he toyed, for instance, with the nature of infinite numbers), but the compass's success pointed out the increasing gap between scientists' need to understand natural phenomena and their ability to perform the mathematics necessary for that understanding. Other mathematicians soon jumped into the breach.

Instruments such as abacuses adequately handled the need to add and subtract, but they were fairly cumbersome in division and multiplication. A Scotsman, John Napier, devised a method to perform these calculations arithmetically. Napier, the laird of Merchiston, dabbled in theology, finance, and, often, mathematics. Although he was hardly a professional mathematician, the idea of making mathematics easier fascinated him. He wrote that there was nothing worse than "the multiplications, divisions, square and cubical expansions of great numbers, which, beside the tedious expense of time, are subject to many slippery errors."

He claimed that the idea for logarithms first came to him in 1594. He was considering the various patterns made by the products of numbers multiplied by themselves, called powers of numbers, an idea that goes all the way back to Archimedes. One variation on that idea was a formula for making use of arithmetic products called prosthaphaereses. One day in 1594, a friend, John Craig, physician to James VI of Scotland, called on Napier. Craig said that he was on the royal party to Denmark in 1590, when James went to pick up his intended bride, Princess Anne. Their ship had been hit by fierce storms, and they had to seek shelter on the Danish coast near the astronomical observatory run by the astronomer Tycho Brahe. While they waited for the storms to abate, Brahe amused the party with a tour of the facilities and mentioned that computations were being made using prosthaphaeresis. That encouraged Napier to think that the study of patterns of products and powers was of considerable value.

The system Napier produced in 1614 is based on the geometric progression of powers relative to the number 1. Each power was assigned a number, which Napier called a logarithm. The log of 1 was eventually determined to be 0, and the log of 10 to be 1. If a chart could be produced listing the logarithms of every number, all that would be required to multiply or divide given numbers would be to add or subtract their logarithms; multiplication and division was reduced to addition and subtraction. Squaring and cubing was also greatly simplified.

Napier was too busy to make up such a chart. Three years

after he published his logarithm idea, he invented a series of cylinders called Napier's Bones, which contained a series of squares with numbers on them. By adjusting specific squares next to other squares, one could multiply and divide the numbers. It was not a very good system.

But an Englishman, Henry Briggs, a professor of geometry at Oxford, was working on the idea of logarithms and had actually produced a chart with the logarithms of the numbers 1 to 1,000 to fourteen decimal places, a job of excruciating tedium.

According to legend, when Briggs and Napier first met, they stood in silent awe of each other for fifteen minutes before friends could break the trance.

Finally Briggs said, "My Lord, I have undertaken this journey purposely to see your person, and to know by what engine of wit or ingenuity you came first to think of this most excellent help unto astronomy; but my Lord, being by you found out, I wonder nobody else found it out before, when you know it is so easy."

Napier died shortly after Briggs's first book was published, in 1617. Later, in a continuation of work that would take him the rest of his life, Briggs printed logarithmic tables for numbers all the way up to 20,000 and from 90,000 to 100,000, all to fourteen decimal places.

The idea of using logarithms in mathematics was accepted almost instantly, and the slide rule, one of the most important offspring of logarithms, lasted for more than 300 years, until solid-state electronics finally replaced it as the symbol of the engineer and mathematician.

The world certainly needed the slide rule. Even in that relatively enlightened time, well-educated men found calculations an obstacle. On July 4, 1662, the estimable Samuel Pepys, in charge of the contracts division of the Admiralty, reported:

Up by five o'clock, and after my journal put in order, to my office about my business. . . . By and by comes Mr Cooper, of whom I intend to learn mathematiques, and do begin with him today, he being a very able man. After an hour's being with him at arithmetique (my first attempt being to learn the multiplication table); then we parted till tomorrow.

Pepys, a very well educated man who held an extremely responsible position, needed tutoring in mathematics.

An English clergyman, William Oughtred, was the inventor of the slide rule. The device he produced in 1621 had two flat pieces of wood fixed so that they slid against each other. On each piece of wood was a scale on which the numbers were arranged at a distance from the end relative to their logarithms. In order to multiply, one merely puts the number to be multiplied (the multiplicand) opposite the number 1. One then looks for the multiplier. The answer is the number opposite the multiplier. Division is merely the reverse of that process.

Oughtred's slide rule was an immediate success. A few months after Pepys made his sad entry in the journal, he bought a slide rule and gleefully reported that it was "very pretty for all questions of arithmetic."

The slide rule was a simple device, but it was not very accurate. Still, as long as the user kept track of where the decimal points went, the slide rule gave a good approximation of the answer to any problem of multiplication and division. The slide rule's longevity certainly attested to its usefulness.

The slide rule, however, does not count anything; it measures a physical property that is analogous to a number. Such a device is called an analog computer, and analog computers remain in use in some fields to this day, although they are probably electronic, not physical. The abacus, on the other hand, actually counted discrete units, or digits, and can be called a digital computer. The distinction between analog and digital computers is important. Both have advantages and disadvantages. Some functions, such as computing measurements of electricity, are better performed by analog computers. Most analog computers, however, cannot add or subtract; the slide rule is an example. But other mathematical functions, such as multiplying or dividing large numbers, are better performed by digital devices. The slide rule was an extraordinarily useful device, but the future lay with digital machines.

Many mathematicians tried other mechanical ways of computing; indeed the problem absorbed some of the finest minds of the seventeeth and eighteenth centuries. Not all of them were successful. Some were. One machine that probably worked was designed by the German astronomer and mathematician Wilhelm Schickard, a friend of the great astronomer Johann Kepler. In 1623 he built a machine that could add and subtract mechanically and could perform multiplication and division with a little help from the operator. In 1624 he wrote to Kepler telling him that the machine "immediately computes the given numbers automatically, adds, subtracts, multiplies, and divides. Surely you will beam when you see how [it] accumulates left carries of tens and hundreds by itself or while subtracting takes something away from them. . . ." Schickard ordered one for Kepler, but when it was half finished it "fell victim to a fire which broke out unseen in the night." He took the loss "very hard" because it would be a long time before it could be replaced. It is not clear whether Kepler ever actually received a Schickard machine.

No copy of a genuine Schickard machine exists, but he left behind enough notes to permit others to build some working models. They performed as advertised.

The next to try to build a computing machine was Blaise Pascal, mathematician, scientist, philosopher, and, apparently, part-time mechanic. He produced a computer in the years 1642–44, when he was a teenager. According to the legend, he developed his machine to assist his father, a tax collector. In his advertisements for the machine he wrote:

I submit to the public a small machine of my own invention, by means of which you alone may, without any effort, perform all the operations of arithmetic, and may be relieved of the work which has often times fatigued your spirit when you have worked with the counters or with the pen.

All mechanical digital calculators face one difficult problem: How do you carry numbers automatically? The best way uses two gears with a gear ratio of ten to one. When the first counter gets to $9 + 1$, the second counter goes from 0 to 1 and the first goes back to 0. That is 10.

This method makes it possible to accumulate numbers, but something else is needed if addition is required: the calculator must have two counter systems (one or more counters in each system geared to handle carries). Both systems are set to 0. Next, the first number is set on the first system. The number being added to it is then set on the second system, which is connected by gears to the first. The first counter, which contains the first number plus the second number, records the result of the addition.

Pascal's machine made use of a complex version of these counter systems with a series of eight setting wheels divided into ten parts (0–9). Each wheel could be turned with a stylus. Equal numbers of result wheels turned with the setting wheels and showed their numbers through a slit on the top of the machine. There was one wheel for units, one for tens, and so on. Pascal devised a weighted-ratchet system to connect the counters to the result wheels. As each counter turned, the ratchet was raised. As soon as the counter passed nine, the weight tripped and the next result wheel to the left turned to 1 as the first one went back to 0. This method made it "just as easy to move one thousand or ten thousand dials, all at one time, if one desired, as to make a single dial move, although all accomplished the movement perfectly."

Pascal's machine did subtraction by a method using the complement of a number. He could subtract by adding complements, the relationship of that number to 0. The advantage here was that the wheels turned in the same direction whether the operator was adding or subtracting, which not only made it easier for the operator but also made the design of the machine much simpler than it would otherwise have been. Multiplication and division were performed by repeating the adding and subtracting. Like computers of the future, Pascal's machine was as accurate as the numbers that were entered on it.[5] It was described by Diderot in his *Encyclopédie,* and several machines are extant in museums in England and France.

Pascal's calculator was essentially an adding machine. The German Baron Gottfried Wilhelm von Leibniz actually produced a mechanical multiplier. One of the central figures in sev-

---

5. In modern computer jargon: GIGO—garbage in, garbage out.

enteenth-century science, Leibniz invented the calculus while
Newton independently did the same. He strongly advocated the
binary numbering system (the use of 0 and 1 for doing calculations), which would become one of the cornerstones of computers.

Leibniz was well aware of the difficulty scientists were having
in coping with the advances in science because of their inability
to compute quickly or accurately. The hardship of doing those
calculations, he said, was deterring many scientists from carrying their experiments to conclusion, from correcting tables, "from
working from hypotheses, and from discussions of observations
with each other. For it is unworthy of excellent men to lose hours
like slaves in the labor of calculation which could safely be rele-
gated to anyone else if machines were used."

In 1673 Leibniz constructed his first machine.

In the first place it should be understood that there are two parts of the
machine, one designed for addition (subtraction) and the other for
multiplication (division), and they should fit together. The adding
(subtracting) machine coincides completely with the calculating box
of Pascal. Something, however, must be added for the sake of multiplication.

Special wheels handled the multiplication. Although Leibniz
called them wheels, they were in fact, not wheels at all but rods
with teeth cut into them. The teeth interacted with other gears
that were set parallel against them in what Leibniz admitted was
a "peculiar arrangement."

The wheels, known as Leibniz stepped wheels, were crucial
to the whole design. Each wheel was a drum containing nine
teeth of varying length, one for each digit. The longest tooth
represents 9, the next longest, 8, and so on. A rod parallel to the
stepped wheel contained a small geared pinion wheel. A pusher
moved the pinion wheel up and down the length of the stepped
wheel. The pusher determined which of the teeth would be
engaged by the pinion wheel, the equivalent of a gear wheel with
a varying number of teeth. A complex series of these pinion wheels
and stepped wheels moved in and out, depending on the numbers and the functions.

The wheels which represent the multiplicand are also provided with ten teeth which, however, are movable so that at one time there should protrude five, at another six teeth, etc., according to whether the multiplicand is to be represented five times or six times, etc. For example, the multiplicand 365 consists of three digits 3, 6, and 5. Hence the same number of wheels (three) is to be used. On these wheels the multiplicand will be set, if from the right wheel there protrude five teeth, from the middle wheel six, and from the left wheel three. In order that this could be performed quickly and easily a peculiar arrangement would be needed, the exposition of which would lead too far into details.

The results were transferred to the addition wheels, which acted as result registers.

With a somewhat gratuitous dig at Pascal, Leibniz added:

Pascal's machine is an example of the most fortunate genius but while it facilitates only additions and subtractions, the difficulty of which is not very great in themselves, it commits multiplication and division to a previous calculation so that it commends itself rather by refinement to the curious than as of practical use to people engaged on business affairs. And now we may give final praise to [my] machine and say that it will be desirable to all who are engaged in computations which, it is well known, are the managers of financial affairs, the administrators of others' estates, merchants, surveyors, geographers, navigators, astronomers, and those connected with any of the crafts that use mathematics.

Leibniz's method was elegant and generally foolproof. He sent a copy of the machine to Peter the Great with the request that Peter send it to the emperor of China. He hoped it would encourage the emperor to increase trade with Europe.

His machines were custom-made and rare until the early part of the nineteenth century, when Charles Thomas of Alsace went into the business of manufacturing them for merchants. Thomas produced approximately 1,500 in a sixty-year span. His machines used the Leibniz stepped wheel, but the figures were set using numbers in slots. Another variant was patented in 1875 by F. J. Baldwin, and machines using that patent were manufactured by W. T. Odhner. They became the most popular business calculators for years. The system of stepped wheels can be found in many mechanical calculators manufactured until the electronic revolution of the 1970s.

But Leibniz's machine could not handle the steady expansion of mathematical tasks that confronted scientists. By the nineteenth century the ability to perform computations lagged behind the demand. The problem still challenged some of the finest minds of the time.

The next attempt at providing adequate computing ability came in the middle of the nineteenth century, a time in Britain when science, genius, and certainly eccentricity flourished. The main attempt was made by one of the brightest and perhaps the most eccentric of them all.

2. Sir Alphabet Function

Sir Alphabet Function, a knight much renowned,
Who had gained little credit on classical ground,
Set out through the world his fortune to try,
With nought to his pate but his x, v and y.

CHARLES BABBAGE

BRITAIN, in the years between 1820 and 1880, was an astonishing place. This period not only marked the zenith of the empire; it also saw an extraordinary intellectual and artistic explosion probably unmatched since the Renaissance. The sciences, arts, and letters flourished, seemingly nurtured by the ferment of the Industrial Revolution, then in its second, most productive phase. The fruits of invention and innovation had produced a large, striving middle class, a meritocracy of daring, foresight, and sometimes simple genius that was replacing the hereditary aristocracy in economic and political power.

The middle of the nineteenth century was the true beginning of modern technology, when men embraced the machine as the heart of economic expansion, the engine of empire. A whole class of technocrats—some firmly based in science, others brilliant economic opportunists—assembled and designed ever more complex machines that created entire industries from cottage crafts, mechanized transportation, and developed the greatest commercial nation of the time.

Among these innovators was a man who seemed to straddle perfectly technology and science—the peculiar, tragic engineer, mathematician, and inventor Charles Babbage. One writer has suggested that Babbage "raised personal eccentricity to heights that have not since been exceeded in the field of computing, though there have been some splendid tries."

Babbage conceived the idea that mathematical computations, logic, and even analysis could be mechanized. Despite the innovative fertility of his time, he failed. To a large extent he was responsible for his own failure. Yet Babbage, a character who seemed to have stepped out of the pages of *The Pickwick Papers,*[1] and the remarkable young woman who became his disciple developed the techniques and the methods that men and women one hundred years later would have to rediscover. Quite famous in his time, Babbage went through a century of obscurity before he would become the earliest folk hero of the computer age.

Babbage was born in Devonshire on December 26, 1791. His father, Benjamin, was a managing partner in Praed, Mackworth & Babbage, a London bank. The family line is believed to have been an old one: mainly goldsmiths, Charles Babbage wrote, but generally undistinguished. The family lived above the bank for four years, but Benjamin, a wealthy man, finally sold his partnership and moved to the country.

Charles came by his eccentricities honestly. Benjamin was haunted by the "visions" of three women in white most of the later years of his life. He was very calm about it, not frightened, somehow bemused. He knew that the ghosts did not exist, but they just would not go away. His father eventually "assigned the facts to some derangement of the optic nerve and these visions

1. England was small enough that many of the leaders of this ferment knew each other, socialized, and corresponded. Babbage and Charles Dickens were friends. It is doubtful that Dickens drew on Babbage for the famous Pickwick Society, but he probably used Babbage as a model for Daniel Doyce in *Little Dorrit,* the inventor who runs into the "How Not To Do It Office" of government bureaucrats.

gave him no further uneasiness," Charles wrote in his autobiography.

His mother was anything but eccentric, and Babbage was devoted to her. The young Babbage was full of curiosity and would wander off whenever something provoked his curiosity, getting lost more than once.

From my earliest years I had a great desire to inquire into the causes of all those little things and events which astonish the childish mind. . . . My invariable question on receiving any new toy, was "Mamma, what is inside of it?" Until this information was obtained those around me had no repose, and the toy itself, I have been told, was generally broken open if the answer did not satisfy my own little ideas of the "fitness of things."

Babbage remembered in his old age one scene from his childhood that probably had more of an influence on him than he might have admitted. It involved his first experience with automata—delicate, complex spring-operated robots that were the rage in the early nineteenth century. He and his mother had gone to the workshop of a man who called himself Merlin.

There were two uncovered female figures of silver, about twelve inches high.

One of these walked or rather glided along a space of about four feet, when she turned round and went back to her original place. She used an eye-glass occasionally, and bowed frequently, as if recognizing her acquaintants. The motions of her limbs were singularly graceful.

The other silver figure was an admirable *danseuse*, with a bird on the fore finger of her right hand, which wagged its tail, flapped its wings, and opened its beak. This lady attitudinized in a most fascinating manner. Her eyes were full of imagination, and irresistible.

These silver figures were the chef-d'oeuvres of the artist; they had cost him years of unwearied labour, and were not even then finished.

Babbage would eventually buy one of those figures and make it the centerpiece of his home. He would also understand the sadness of unfinished labor.

Although he was physically fragile as a child, he was extremely bright. He performed experiments on his school chums and dabbled in the occult. He tried to raise the devil one night. On another occasion, he made a death pact with a friend, the son of Admiral Richard Dacres: whichever of them died first would pledge to return to the other and tell him what death was like. Dacres died at the age of eighteen, after a hard voyage on a prize ship. On the night of Dacres's death, Babbage waited in his room for his friend to appear. "I passed a night of perfect sleeplessness," he later wrote. "The distant clock and a faithful dog, just outside my own door, produced the only sounds which disturbed the intense silence of that anxious night."

In the school library, he ran into his first advanced text in mathematics, Ward's *Young Mathematician's Guide.* Babbage had found his milieu. He would awaken at 3 A.M., make a fire in his room to keep the morning cold away, and work until 5.

He also tried his hand at inventing, producing two hinged boards that, when attached to his feet, were supposed to help him walk on water. He nearly drowned when he tried them out.

Babbage entered Trinity College, Cambridge, in October 1810. There he immediately fell in with a circle of bright young men, including John Herschel, the son of the great astronomer Sir William, and George Peacock. The three remained friends for the rest of their lives; Herschel became a renowned astronomer, famous for plotting the southern sky, and Peacock, after a career in science, became dean of Ely. The three vowed "to do their best to leave the world wiser than they found it."

Herschel and Peacock were every bit Babbage's intellectual equals; Babbage was so sure they would place first and second in their Trinity class that he eventually transferred to Peterhouse College, where he was assured of being top ranked.

But Babbage quickly became dissatisfied with the state of mathematics education at Cambridge.

. . . I went to my public tutor Hudson, to ask the explanation of one of my mathematical difficulties. He listened to my question, said it would not be asked in the Senate House, and was of no sort of consequence, and advised me to get up the earlier subjects of the university studies.

After some little while I went to ask the explanation of another difficulty from one of the lecturers. He treated the question just in the same way. I made a third effort to be enlightened about what was really a doubtful question, and felt satisfied that the person I addressed knew nothing of the matter, although he took some pains to disguise his ignorance.

I thus acquired a distaste for the routine of the studies of the place. . . .

One of his goals was to get British mathematicians to adopt the scientific notation developed by Leibniz. The system then in vogue in Britain used Newton's dots to denote mathematical concepts. The difference stemmed from the dispute between Newton and Leibniz over who invented the calculus. British mathematicians naturally sided with Newton and used his symbols. Babbage felt this was one of the reasons British mathematicians were behind their Continental counterparts. Leibniz's method, common in Europe, used letters like *d* for notation. He thought this more sensible. Tongue planted firmly in cheek, he wrote:

I then drew up the sketch of a society to be instituted for translating the small work of Lacroix [a French mathematician] on the Differential and Integral Calculus. It proposed that we should have periodical meetings for the propagation of d's; and consigned to perdition all who supported the heresy of dots. It maintained that the work of Lacroix was so perfect that any comment was unnecessary.

The principles of the group, the Analytical Society, he reported, were "The Principles of pure D-ism in opposition to the Dot-age of the University."

The Analytical Society actually succeeded in dragging British mathematics into the nineteenth century. Babbage, Herschel, Peacock, and others translated Lacroix's treatise on the calculus from the French and helped write a textbook, *Examples to the Differential and Integral Calculus*. One historian has written that the Lacroix translation "broke down barriers of national prejudice" in mathematics "and created an epoch of thought which in a few years entirely revolutionized the ancient system of University teaching." Presumably no other students would meet the kind of incompetence that had so bothered Babbage when he entered Cambridge.

During his time at Cambridge, Babbage may have first conceived the notion of a mechanical calculating machine. There are two stories concerning the origin of the idea. In his autobiography Babbage says he was sitting in the rooms of the Analytical Society sometime around 1812 or 1813, daydreaming over a table of logarithms.

"Well, Babbage, what are you dreaming about?" asked another member.

"I am thinking that all these Tables might be calculated by machinery."

Historians, who do not seem to trust Babbage's autobiography, because of the advanced age at which it was written (he was in his seventies), have accepted an earlier explanation as more likely. In this version, Herschel and Babbage were checking some calculations made for the Royal Astronomical Society, which they had helped found in 1820. It was accepted in those days that any tables of calculations would be rife with errors. Both young men became exasperated with the task.

"I wish to God these calculations had been executed by steam," Babbage exclaimed.

"It is quite possible," said Herschel.

Babbage had met his life's obsession.

It was a worthy obsession. The state of science and mathematics was now quite complex. Much of it relied on interminable tables of calculations, produced by hand by people called "computers." Not only did the human computers make mistakes—it was inevitable, considering the length and complexity of the tables—but the copying and publication of their tables inevitably introduced further mistakes. None of these tables could be trusted, and many an experiment was undermined when the scientist discovered an error in a table he had relied upon. One writer of the time, Dionysius Lardner, discovered that mistakes originally committed by European mathematicians in 1603 cropped up 200 years later in Chinese manuscripts. Government tables used for accurate navigation had more than 1,100 errors and seven folio pages of corrections. The corrections needed corrections.

The tables involved everything from astronomical charts to tables of multiplication, logarithms, trigonometric functions such as sines and cosines, air density, and gravity. If Babbage, or anyone else, could succeed in eliminating the hand calculation and copying mistakes in these tables he would be a savior to contemporary science. Babbage proposed to be nothing less.

Life, science, and academic politics intervened before Babbage could do anything about producing a computing machine.

In June of 1814, when Babbage was twenty-three, he married Georgiana Whitmore. She was a lovely, tolerant, patient woman with golden brown hair.

She had to put up with a demanding, somewhat cold, obsessive, unusually energetic husband, who could spend hours poring over mathematical formulas or run off to perform scientific observations and experiments. She had to tolerate a mother-in-law who was enormously possessive. Georgiana was perpetually pregnant and frequently in mourning. She bore eight children, only four of whom approached adulthood: one daughter (her namesake and Babbage's favorite), who died a teenager, and three sons who actually survived adolescence. Babbage was not a warm or helpful father. One surviving son, Henry, tells of running from the house when his father came home so he would not have to meet him. When Babbage was working at his desk, children were to be neither seen nor heard. Babbage's biographer Maboth Moseley writes that it was clear that Babbage adored his wife "and was utterly unaware of the unhappy impression he was creating" with his children. When Georgiana died, at the age of thirty-five, after her eighth childbirth, Babbage was shattered.

Babbage was forever dabbling. Upset at the cost of shipping parcels through the mail, he designed a system that would enable the post office to cut costs and make a healthy profit. His follow-up study showed that the cost of actually transporting the mail was quite negligible; it was collecting and delivering the mail that ran up costs. He suggested flat-rate charges. The result of this study was the penny post.

I then devised means for transmitting letters enclosed in small cylinders, along wires suspended from posts, and from towers, or from church steeples. I made a little model of such an apparatus, and thus transmitted notes from my front drawing-room, through the house, into my workshop, which was in a room above my stables.

In 1818 he submerged in a diving bell made of cast iron. That experience later led him to do a study of submarine navigation.

In 1824 he was asked to open a life-insurance office. He studied the matter and produced the first statistically sound actuarial table. He pointed out that all previous tables were based on insufficient data, which angered the insurance industry. His insurance office was never opened, but his tables were used in Germany for fifty years.

Throughout this period he was still totally dependent on his father. He applied for teaching jobs at least twice and both times was denied them for political reasons. This was only the beginning of a long life of frustrations in which Babbage, who publicly eschewed reward and recognition, would grow increasingly bitter when he failed to get the honors.

In the meantime, he contributed to dozens of scientific journals and was elected a fellow of the Royal Society, the greatest honor that could then be given a British scientist. He wrote papers on the knight's move in chess, and on games of chance. He also made a scientific study of beggars, in an effort to find a way of determining which ones were frauds.

Through all of this he never forgot the notion of a mechanical calculator. Some time after the conversation with Herschel, he built a small model of what he called a Difference Engine, constructed from his own design. It had six wheels.

The name requires an explanation. The Difference Engine was based on the "method of differences," a way of solving certain mathematical equations by means of the relations that numbers have with each other.

The following chart shows a method for calculating the cube of a number. The cube is any number multiplied by itself twice. The cube of 3 is 27 ($3 \times 3 \times 3 = 27$).

Column A contains the numbers to be cubed. Column B contains the cubes of those numbers (e.g., the cube of 2 is 8). Column C contains the differences between the cubes in column B. For example the difference between the cube of 1 (1) and the cube of 2 (8) is 7, shown in column C. The difference between the cube of 2 and the cube of 3 (27) is 19, the next number down in column C. The difference between the cube of 3 and the cube of 4 (64) is 37, the next number down.

Column D consists of what are called the "second differences," the differences between the differences in column C. For instance, the difference between 7 and 19 in column C is 12, that between 19 and 37 is 18, and so forth.

There is one more column, E, presenting the "third difference," that is, the difference between the numbers in column D. In this chart it is always 6.[2] This is the key to the method of differences: sooner or later one of the columns produces a constant number, such as 6 in the example above. That column must contain only that number; if something else appears, an arithmetic error exists somewhere in the other columns. That makes the calculations easy to check.

A	B	C	D	E
1	1			
		7		
2	8		12	
		19		6
3	27		18	
		37		6
4	64		24	
		61		6
5	125		30	
		91		6
6	216		36	
		127		6
7	343			

It now becomes possible to figure out the cube of any number, by simply reading the chart backward. All that is required is adding, something Babbage knew machines could be built to perform. For instance, by working right to left from column E, we can calculate the cube of 8. It works the following way.

By adding 6 (always the content of E) to 36, the last number in D, we get 42. This is added to D. The 42 is then added to the last number in C, 127, and the result is 169, which is added to the last number in B, 343, and the result is 512, the cube of 8.

This procedure can be carried on infinitely once the pattern is established. It is only necessary to add the differences.

Babbage did not want to produce a machine that could just calculate cubes. He wanted his first Difference Engine to work

2. The entries in the next column would therefore always be 0.

out more complex equations, called polynomials.[3] But the procedure was the same. On June 14, 1822, before the Royal Astronomical Society, Babbage proposed building a giant Difference Engine. His presentation is generally considered to be the first scientific paper on mechanical computing.

I considered that a machine to execute the mere isolated operations of arithmetic, would be comparatively of little value, unless it were very easily set to do its work, and unless it executed not only accurately, but with great rapidity, whatever it was required to do.

On the other hand, the method of differences supplied a general principle by which *all* Tables might be computed through limited intervals, by one uniform process. Again, the method of differences required the use of mechanism for Addition only. In order, however, to insure accuracy in the printed Tables, it was necessary that the machine which computed Tables should also set them up in type, or else supply a mould in which stereotype plates of those Tables could be cast.

Babbage's idea, then, was a machine that did the calculations and also printed the tables, leaving little room for error. One could check accuracy by merely looking at the column with the difference constant, making unnecessary the kind of laborious hand checking that so bothered Herschel and him.

My first plan was to make it put together moveable type. I proposed to make metal boxes, each containing 3,000 types of one of the ten digits. These types were to be made to pass out one by one from the bottom of their boxes, when required by the computing part of the machine.

He cut the numbers so that each number had a unique notch. Numbers with the wrong notch could not drop through the bottom of the box. This process prevented someone from putting the wrong number in a font. Wires were run through the fonts to make sure all the numbers belonged there.

He told the society that the small machine he had constructed successfully produced charts of squares, cubes, and the one polynomial. He explained that the machine worked almost

3. The equation he was after was $x^2 + x + 41$, a formula that contains a large number of prime numbers and that is of great use to mathematicians. Many mathematical functions can be expressed in polynomial equations, and Babbage assumed correctly that if he could get the machine to solve one, it would be able to solve most polynomials.

as fast as a manual computer, but was more accurate and had far more endurance than any human. There was no limit to the number of differences the machine could handle; the bigger the task, the more it would outstrip human computers.

"The whole of arithmetic now appeared within the grasp of the machine," he wrote later.

The idea of the Difference Machine was more important than that; it substituted a machine for the human brain in performing an intellectual process, which Moseley has correctly called "one of the most revolutionary schemes ever to be devised by any human being."

The Astronomical Society was also impressed. Knowing full well how much easier such a machine could make their lives, they rallied to his support in his plans to build a larger machine, one that would work to twenty decimal places and six order differences.

A process then began that would echo through the history of science: the dance of the government grant. Babbage turned to the government for financial assistance, believing his invention would help with ballistics and navigation. On April 1, 1823, the Lords of the Treasury asked the Royal Society to make a study of Babbage's plan in order to determine whether public funds should be expended, one of the first instances of peer review. The Royal Society, with only one dissent, reported, "Mr. Babbage has displayed great talent and ingenuity in the construction of his Machine . . . which the Committee think fully adequate to the attainment of the objects proposed by the inventor." The chancellor of the Exchequer agreed to give Babbage 1,500 pounds for the building of a Difference Engine, one of history's first government research and development grants.[4]

Babbage believed that he could build the machine in two or three years and that he would be able to finish the task for about 5,000 pounds. He also believed that the government had orally promised him more money if he needed it. Whether such a promise was made became a point of bitter contention between Babbage and subsequent governments for the rest of his life.

---

4. The contract would produce another first: cost overruns.

He had seriously underestimated the size of the task. He had also overestimated the ability of the current technology to build a machine with the complexity and precision that would be required of the Difference Engine.

But for the time being, Babbage was a hero to all. The Royal Astronomical Society gave him its first gold medal.

Babbage went immediately to work. He hired Joseph Clement, the best toolmaker in Britain, to make the tools necessary to build the machine. Clement hired the best workmen he could find. His workshop was largely taken over by the Difference Engine project. The precision techniques developed in the process eventually spread to all the workshops of London—a spin-off of the project, which set yet another precedent.

Babbage started drawing the plans with C. G. Jarvis, a superb draftsman. The job was so complex that he had to invent his own notation system. He also determined that the best way to build a complex machine was to divide the functions into smaller parts; in this revolutionary modular system, the whole machine would be the sum of its parts, a technique reinvented in the next century by the first computer builders. In many cases each of the modules required innovation and invention, and Babbage went through them all one by one. He worked by trial and error and inspiration. Each piece in the device had to be machined to a degree of precision then unknown outside of watchmaking; Babbage was pushing the state of technology.

The work was slowed considerably, however, by one of Babbage's most serious character flaws—his inability to stop tinkering. No sooner would he send a drawing to the shop than he would find a better way to perform the task and would order work stopped until he had finished pursuing the new line. By and large this flaw kept Babbage from ever finishing anything, including the Difference Engine.

Long after he thought he should be done with the Difference Engine, he was still struggling with the technology. Rumors began to circulate that the project was a failure. Several of his enemies, particularly Sir George Biddell Airy, the current Lucasian Professor of Mathematics at Cambridge (the chair once held by Newton), publicly called the project "humbug."

In the latter half of 1827, Babbage lost his wife, two of his children, and his father to disease. He suffered a nervous breakdown, and while his mother jumped into the breach to care for what was left of his family, he went abroad for almost a year, where his fame was even greater than it was at home. Babbage hobnobbed with the Bonaparte family and met a number of prominent European scientists, including Baron Alexander von Humboldt.

He descended at the end of a rope into Vesuvius with a barometer. As a conversation piece he carried a set of gold buttons stamped by dies containing parallel lines 4/10,000 inch apart, a defraction grating. They glowed like golden rainbows. He helped one doctor design an improved stomach pump, and in Vienna designed a four-wheeled coach, complete with its own kitchen.

In Rome he was notified he had been appointed the new Lucasian Professor at Cambridge. His first instinct was to refuse petulantly, but two friends talked him into accepting. (He held the chair for years but never gave a lecture.) Babbage returned to England at the end of 1828.

Now thirty-seven, he had inherited his father's fortune— £100,000, enough to make him independently wealthy. But all was not well. While he was away, rumors about the misuse of public funds had been denied by Herschel but not stopped. Furthermore, Babbage had authorized the spending of another £1,000 of his own money on the machine, and it was clear this was not going to be enough. He decided to ask the government for more. It refused, claiming it had never agreed to provide more funds. Babbage went to see the duke of Wellington, a firm supporter of the Difference Engine, and then the prime minister. Wellington asked the Royal Society for an appraisal, and a committee from the society, headed by Herschel, expressed admiration for how much Babbage had accomplished. They urged support. The government granted another £1,500. Babbage had already spent £6,000 of his own money on the project, and the new grant was clearly insufficient.

A group of Babbage's friends called a meeting on May 12, 1829, to see whether they could help. Firmly believing Babbage had acted honorably, they went back to Wellington, who inspected the machine and gave Babbage another £3,000. Babbage, feeling a precedent had been set, tried to get the government to put its obligations in writing. He offered to grant the government title over the machine, asked that independent engineers inspect the machine and the bookkeeping, and insisted that the government agree to defray all further costs of the work. The government hesitated, setting off a wave of correspondence. Finally it was agreed the government would provide another £3,000, send engineers to inspect the books, and discuss ownership of the machine when it was completed.

Meanwhile Babbage, who was active in the political reform movement of the time, had also declared war on the scientific establishment. He was offered a knighthood but turned it down, saying it was not a fitting reward for a scientist. There began a public debate over just how a country should reward its scientists, which gave little luster to Babbage. He also started a public battle with Sir Humphry Davy and Davies Gilbert over the operation of the Royal Society, a debate that was to divide that society for years. Babbage wanted serious reforms in the society; the current administration took his suggestions as the insults they were intended to be. He had succeeded in making scores of enemies, many of whom would exact revenge.

Babbage decided that the machine was too big for Clement's shop and that a separate building was needed.

In order to carry out my pursuits successfully, I had purchased a house with above a quarter of an acre of ground in a very quiet locality [Dorset Street]. My coach-house was now converted into a forge and a foundry, whilst my stables were transformed into a workshop. I built other extensive workshops myself, and had a fire-proof building for my drawings and draftsmen. Having myself worked with a variety of tools, and having studied the art of constructing each of them, I at length laid it down as a principle—that, except in rare cases, I would never do anything myself if I could afford to hire another person who could do it for me.

Work on the machine continued, as Babbage gave directions and Clement ran the shop. For a while the system worked well, but Clement began to balk at slow payments from the government. Babbage would send the bills to two engineers appointed by the government. If they approved of the expenditure—and they usually did—they forwarded the invoice to the Treasury, which would then issue the money. But the bureaucracy at the Treasury was very slow. Clement demanded immediate payment. Eventually he refused to pay his workmen unless he was paid; this forced Babbage to lay out the money from his own funds and await repayment by the government.

When the Dorset Street workshop was completed, Babbage prepared to move the Difference Engine and told Clement he would get paid when the government sent the money, not before. Clement, a scoundrel, countered with a series of preposterous demands that Babbage could not and would not meet.

Babbage had already spent £17,000 of the government's money and a like amount of his own. This began to drain the family fortune, but Babbage was encouraged by his mother, who told him to "pursue it, even if it should oblige you to live on bread and cheese."

The government tried to mediate. Clement would not budge. He quit the project and walked off with all the tools built for the Difference Engine, many of which Babbage had invented. Babbage, who needed the tools, tried to buy them back, but Clement refused. All work on the Difference Engine ended in 1833. The part of the machine that Babbage finished is now in the Science Museum in London.

A description of the machine found its way to Sweden in 1834, and an engineer named Georg Scheutz actually built a small Difference Engine, which was brought to England in 1854 and which Babbage's son Henry demonstrated. With the surprising support of the Babbages, Scheutz received a gold medal from the Royal Society; the machine was displayed in public and was later purchased by an observatory in Albany, New York. It and a later machine built by the British government worked exactly as Babbage had predicted they would.[5]

The death of the Difference Engine hardly meant Babbage

5. The performance of Scheutz's machine gives the lie to the oft-repeated theory that Babbage failed because the technology was not advanced enough to permit the building of his machine.

was idle. He set himself up as a consulting engineer and hired out to the railroads, working with the engineers Isambard Kingdom Brunel and Marc Isambard Brunel and with his engineer son, Herschel. They designed instrumented carriages that could measure the stress and forces at play when the carriage was moving on the rails. Babbage would take his instrumented train for a ride on Sundays when traffic was light, but he nearly killed himself when he found his train steaming head-on into another. His work led to the adoption of wide gauges on British rails. He suggested the cowcatcher and claimed to be the first man to operate a sail-powered train, an idea whose time never came.

He also invented the "occulating" lighthouse, in which the light went on and off in rhythm. He once walked into an oven to see what effects short exposure to a temperature of 265 degrees had on the human body. He ascertained that there were none, and left quickly.

In 1831 he published one copy of *Specimens of Logarithmic Tables,* in twenty-one volumes. The tables were not important to him; he wanted to find out which combination of paper color and ink was the easiest to read. The work used 151 different shades of paper and two shades of blue ink.

In 1832 he wrote a landmark book, *On the Economy of Machinery and Manufactures,* considered to be the beginning of the science of operations research, which influenced John Stuart Mill and Karl Marx. He worked on secret codes (a serious passion for the mathematician in him) and helped the Bank of England fight forgers of banknotes.

In 1833 he ran for Parliament from the borough of Stroud, on a reform platform heavily influenced by the utilitarian philosopher Jeremy Bentham. He came in a respectable third. He ran again the next year and finished fourth in a field of four, garnering 379 votes, to the winner's 2,514.

Meanwhile, Babbage was at the center of a social set that contained many of the prominent figures in the arts and sciences of the day. Darwin and Dickens might come to dinner on Saturday night. So might Thackeray, Herschel, and Longfellow. After he read a poem by Tennyson, which contains the lines "Every minute dies a man / Every minute one is born," Babbage wrote to the poet, an occasional guest at his famous dinner parties, and suggested a few changes.

I need hardly to tell you that this calculation would tend to keep the sum total of the world's population in a state of perpetual equipoise, whereas it is a well-known fact that the said sum total is constantly on the increase. I would therefore take the liberty of suggesting that in the next edition of your excellent poem the erroneous calculation to which I refer should be corrected as follows:

> Every moment dies a man,
> And one and a sixteenth is born.

I may add that the exact figures are 1.167, but something must, of course, be conceded to the laws of metre.

Tennyson changed the poem to read:

> Every moment dies a man,
> Every moment one is born.

His parties (called by guests "doing our Babbage") became a salon, and an invitation was highly sought after in the bubbling intellectual ferment of London. At the center of this salon were the little silver dancing lady and the Difference Engine, now in the workshop.

But Babbage was not finished with computing machines. Even before the Difference Engine was scuttled, Babbage had conceived of a device that far exceeded anything yet imagined, a machine that could do sixty calculations a minute and perform real mathematical analysis, issue commands, and alter its procedures according to the results of calculations. What Babbage now had in mind was nothing less than a modern computer. "I am myself astonished at the power that I have been able to give to the machine," he wrote.

On June 5, 1833, there was at one of his parties a guest who, almost alone in the world, could comprehend, explain, and inspire Babbage. She was an unlikely source of support—the slim, beautiful, seventeen-year-old daughter of the poet Lord Byron, Augusta Ada. The meeting altered Babbage's life and provided much of his later fame and the modern appreciation of his work.

In 1815 Lord Byron had married Anne Isabella Milbanke in an effort to defuse the growing scandal over his incestuous rela-

tionship with his half-sister, Augusta Leigh. The marriage did
not work, either as a marriage or as a distraction for the morally
outraged; Byron left Anne Isabella and England a month after
his only legitimate daughter, Augusta Ada, was born.[6]

Prohibited by Lady Byron to see his "Ada, sole daughter of
my house and heart,"[7] the poet sent presents and kept abreast
of her growth through his half-sister. When Ada was eight, Byron
wrote, "I hope the gods have made her anything save poetical—
it is enough to have one such fool in the family." He asked about
her character.

Lady Byron replied that Ada "preferred prose to verse" and
that her imagination "is at present chiefly exercised in connection with her mechanical ingenuity—her self-invented occupa-
tions being the manufacture of ships and boats. . . ."

Ada applied her father's artistic intensity to her music. As a
child she played the violin for hours, walking around a billiard
table rather than interrupt her practice for daily physical exercise. She also adopted many of her father's quirks: she never
slept in a bed and had "strange fancies about eating . . . and the
same love of startling and surprising people by her statements,"
according to a family friend. Like her father, she also suffered
from childhood migraines, which her mother diligently treated
with a "perpetual leech."

Her aptitude for mathematics may have been inherited. Before
he married her, Byron called Ada's mother the "Princess of Par-

6. Byron's prodigous sexual appetite lent one more, somewhat indirect, anecdote to the history of the computer. Pamela McCorduck has written that just
before he fled England he had another affair with Claire Clairmont, the stepsis-
ter of Mary Wollstonecraft Shelley. Through Clairmont, Byron met the Shelleys
and spent the summer of 1816 with them in Switzerland. It was in response to
Byron's challenge that the nineteen-year-old Mary Shelley wrote *Frankenstein*,
the world's first science-fiction novel and the first exposition of what modern
computer experts call artificial intelligence.

7. From the third canto of *Childe Harold's Pilgrimage*. The canto also includes
these lines: My daughter! with thy name this song begun!
                My daughter! with thy name thus much shall end!—
                I see thee not—I hear thee not—but none
                Can be so wrapt in thee; thou art the friend
                To whom the shadows of far years extend:
                . . . .
                A token and a tone even from thy father's mould.

allelograms" because of her mathematical prowess. Later he referred to her less flatteringly as the "Mathematical Medea."

When she was fourteen, Ada began the serious study of mathematics and astronomy because her legs became suddenly paralyzed, restricting her physical activities. No one knows where the paralysis came from, although there is some speculation it was a psychological escape from her hysterical, almost-always-neurotic mother. Several of her friends suggested that Ada was less an invalid than she pretended to be. Not until she was seventeen did the paralysis end.

Because of her father's peerage, Ada was presented at court and at various royal assemblages and balls. She was far more stimulated that season, however, when her mother took her to a party at Babbage's.

While the other guests were taken with the little silver dancing lady, Ada was awed by the Difference Engine. A friend wrote:

While other visitors gazed at the working of this beautiful instrument with the sort of expression, and I dare say the sort of feeling, that some savages are said to have shown on first seeing a looking glass or hearing a gun—if, indeed, they had as strong an idea of its marvelousness—Miss Byron, young as she was, understood its working, and saw the great beauty of the invention.

Ada returned to see Babbage and the Difference Engine time and time again, and attended lectures on the machine by Babbage's friends. Her mathematical genius easily grasped what Babbage was trying to do with the Difference Engine, and when he explained to her his newer idea, the Analytical Engine, she had no trouble in understanding that either.

She had, by this time, gone through several mathematical tutors and pleaded with Babbage to find another who could keep up with her. She would write mathematics to her friends, most of whom had no idea what she was talking about. Only Babbage and his mathematician friend Mary Somerville seemed to be able to provide her with the intellectual stimulation she craved.

Ada and Babbage began a voluminous correspondence. They flirted, cajoled, challenged, encouraged. For Babbage, Ada was in many ways a replacement for Georgiana, the daughter who died in her late teens; for Ada, Babbage was the father she had never known. Their letters sometimes had the proper passion of Victorian lovers, and theirs was clearly a profound relationship. How much she contributed to the design of the Analytical Engine is hard to determine. One of Babbage's biographers, Anthony Hyman, thinks she contributed nothing original, but others believe she helped design the method by which the machine was addressed, what in the modern sense is called programming. She was possibly the world's first computer programmer. But her main contributions included her providing the analysis and the description by which her contemporaries knew of the Analytical Engine, and her making sure that Babbage's huge leap in intellect would eventually be appreciated by those who followed him.

What Babbage was now proposing was an immense step forward, even from the Difference Engine. It was to cover an area of approximately ten feet by five feet, with concentric toothed wheels two feet in diameter. Power would apparently come from a steam engine, although Babbage never made that clear. Some parts of the machine he designed were so like the eventual design of the electronic computer as to be almost spooky. That those who followed Babbage were at the time unaware of his work and yet followed a similar design tells much about the logic behind this machine. Babbage wrote:

The Analytical Engine consists of two parts:—
    1st. The store in which all the variables to be operated upon, as well as those quantities which have arisen from the result of other operations, are placed.

That is now called the memory. Babbage's memory consisted of columns of wheels, each with ten engraved numbers. He wanted it to be big enough to hold 1,000 fifty-digit numbers, a larger memory than most of the first modern machines could handle and bigger than that of the average microcomputer of the early 1980s.

2nd. The mill into which the quantities about to be operated upon are always brought.

That is known now as the central processing unit (CPU).

Every formula which the Analytical Engine can be required to compute consists of certain algebraical operations to be performed upon given letters, and of certain other modifications depending on the numerical value assigned to those letters.

Those formulas are called algorithms by modern computer programmers.

There would also be a device, consisting of wheels and gears, that transferred numbers back and forth between the mill and the store.

There are therefore two sets of [punch] cards, the first to direct the nature of the operations to be performed—these are called operation cards: the other to direct the particular variables on which these cards are required to operate—these latter are called variable cards.

And indeed, they still are.

The use of punch cards is, in some way, the most uncanny coincidence associated with the Analytical Engine. Punch cards were not Babbage's invention; a Frenchman, Joseph Marie Jacquard (1752–1834), had used punch cards to control looms. "It is easier to punch pasteboard than to screw on a multitude of studs," Babbage explained. Each card was fixed with holes in a particular sequence. The cards were placed on a rolling drum. As each card rolled on the drum, a series of rods attached to the threads on the loom sought the holes. If a rod found a hole, the rod rose; if not, the rod remained stationary. This determined the throw of the shuttle. The punch card system was so good that Babbage owned a portrait of Jacquard that had been loom woven by 24,000 punch cards. Viewers had to stand very close to the portrait to realize that it was a woven pattern, not an engraving. As Ada wrote, "We may say most aptly that the Analytical Engine weaves algebraic patterns just as the Jacquard-loom weaves flowers and leaves."

The punch cards were not the only uncanny part of the design, however. The Analytical Engine would be able to anticipate carries, the jump from 9 to 10. This was much faster than the previous methods, in which each counter clicked off in sequence. Modern computers have the same ability. "I concluded . . . that nothing but teaching the Engine to foresee and then to act upon that foresight could ever lead me to the object that I desired," Babbage wrote.

The Analytical Engine is therefore a machine of the most general nature. Whatever formula it is required to develop, the law of its development must be communicated to it by two sets of cards. When these have been placed, the engine is special for that particular formula. The numerical value of its constants must then be put on the columns of wheels below them, and on setting the Engine in motion it will calculate and print the numerical results of that formula.

His machine would also be able to perform conditional operations, a function that modern computers require. The machine could be told to be ready for a number or value. If the number came up as a result of the calculations, then the machine would perform one function. If another came up, then the machine would perform a different function. The machine would make the decision on the basis of what it saw. Babbage described it as "the Engine moving forward by eating its own tail."[8]

The engine would have a library of its own. When a calculation called for a specific formula, "say the logarithm of a certain number," a bell would ring, the machine would stop, and the operator would have to fetch the cards containing that formula. He would place the cards in the machine, which would read the card to make sure he had used the right ones. If so, the machine proceeded to make the calculation. If not, it would stop and a louder bell would go off, urging the human operator to stop wasting the machine's time.

Anthony Hyman has written that Babbage never actually thought he would finish the Analytical Engine, that he doubted he would get the funding he needed. Nonetheless, he attacked the problem with his usual obsessiveness.

His colleague through most of this was Ada. On July 8, 1835, Ada married William King and briefly became Lady King. King soon became the earl of Lovelace, and Ada has ever since been known as Ada, countess of Lovelace. King appreciated his wife's genius and encouraged it. He frequently assisted in copying for-

8. Modern computer programmers will recognize that Babbage had invented the IF THEN statement—IF this happens, THEN do that.

mulas and helped keep communications between the countess and Babbage smooth when they fought, which they did frequently, and he tended the children while she worked.

She was a small, soft woman, with dark hair. Her husband and Babbage frequently used similar nicknames for her, especially "Lady-Bird." Indeed, they shared her. Both men recognized her intellect and her passion to use it. "Before ten years is over," she once wrote to Babbage, "the Devil's in it if I haven't sucked out some of the life-blood from the mysteries of this universe, in a way that no purely mortal lips or brains could do." She signed that letter "Fairy for ever."

In 1840 Babbage went to Turin, Italy, to give a paper on the Analytical Engine. In the audience was L. F. Menabrea, a scientist and a general in Garibaldi's army who later became prime minister of Italy. Menabrea was fascinated by Babbage's notion and published a detailed description of the talk in 1842. Ada decided to translate it.

What she eventually produced was a translation with copious editor's notes. The notes were far longer than Menabrea's original paper. Her work provided the best and most complete description of Babbage's Analytical Engine, both the mechanics and the mathematical logic of it. Babbage could not have done better.

The archives of the correspondence between Ada and Babbage grew as the manuscript grew. They ranged from gentle prodding to angry retorts and back to loving care. There were plenty of fights. He wanted her to take credit for her work, but women in midnineteenth-century England did not publish scientific papers.[9]

Messages flew by courier and post. Babbage visited the Lovelaces at their various estates. Ada was a constant visitor on Dorset Street. She worked almost as hard on the Engine as Babbage did. In order to describe the machine, she had to describe the programming, and that took up most of her time and energy.

9. She finally agreed to use her initials, A.A.L.; not everyone at the time knew it was she, although her husband and Babbage were not shy about leaking the information.

My Dear Babbage. I am working very hard for you; like the Devil in fact; (which perhaps I am). I think you will be pleased. I have made what appears to be some very important extensions & improvements. . . .

I am delighted with Note D. It is in your usual clear style and requires only one trifling alteration which I will make. This arises out of the circumstance of our not having yet had time to examine the outline of the mechanical part. . . .

Think of my horror . . . at just discovering that the Table & Diagram (over which I have been spending infinite patience & pains) are seriously wrong, in one or two points. I have done them however in a beautiful manner, much improved on our first edition of a Table & Diagram. But unluckily, I have made some errors.

Sometimes he would make an error, and she would gently chastise him.

It is quite evident to me that you have been looking over the superseded sheet 4, instead of the corrected one. All your remarks seem to apply to the former; & the latter is passed over without notice. Please be with me at half past nine o'clock tomorrow morning if you can; as I am exceedingly disturbed about it. Lord L—— is so vexed too . . . that I am half beside myself.

If he corrected her, he risked her wrath.

I am much annoyed at your having altered my Note. You know I am always willing to make any required alterations myself, but I cannot endure another person to meddle with my sentences. . . . I cannot agree to your having effaced the paragraph.

Babbage and Jarvis continued to work on the plans, drawn on huge sheets of paper that must have stretched across his shop floor. They were probably the most complicated set of blueprints attempted to that time. They absorbed him entirely. Solving difficult problems left him feeling exhilarated, he said.

One problem he could not solve was the funding. He had written to the government that he had a new idea for a machine to replace the Difference Engine, and asked whether he should finish the engine or drop it and go on to the new one. His letter was sufficiently ambiguous that the bureaucrats totally misunderstood his meaning, and the correspondence was tied up for years. Not even his acquaintance with Prince Albert seemed to save him. There was clear indication that his enemies, particularly Airy, had a hand in his troubles. Any work Babbage did on the Analytical Engine was at his own expense. His bitterness and frustration grew as the years went by.

In August 1843, Ada's translation of Menabrea was ready for publication. Not only had she translated perfectly, but her notes were brilliant. Babbage understood clearly what she had done for him and wanted her to get credit. He suggested she drop the Menabrea translation and write a scientific paper. They had a huge brawl. She was angry enough to threaten to end their relationship unless he met certain conditions.

Yours [she wrote to him] is to love truth & God (yes, deeply & constantly); but to love fame & glory, honours, yet more. You will deny this, but in all your intercourse with every human being (as far as I know & see of it) it is a practically paramount sentiment. Mind, I am not blaming it. I simply state my belief in the fact.

She wrote a friend that she was "harassed and pressed in the most perplexing manner by the conduct of Mr. Babbage."

We are, in fact, at issue; & I am sorry to have to come to the conclusion that he is one of the most impracticable, selfish and intemperate persons one can have to do with. I do not anticipate an absolute alienation between us; but there must ever be a degree of coolness and reserve I fancy in the future.

He was everything she said he was. But her long, angry letter to him, in which she gave him the chance to cut her off, ended with a query: "I wonder if you will choose to retain the lady fairy in your service or not?" Of course he did. In his reply to her, he called her the "Enchantress of Numbers" and invited himself up to her estate at Ashley to make peace. He ended the letter with the words "Fairwell my dear and much admired Interpretress." She was the only person who could tame Charles Babbage.

Their main efforts now were raising money for the Analytical Engine. Babbage was still fighting with the government, and any hopes he had of getting government aid were sabotaged by

some of the many enemies he had made in the scientific establishment. Babbage was bitter and frantic. Mary Somerville wrote:

> Mr. Babbage is looking wretchedly and has been very unwell. I have
> done all I could to persuade him to leave town, but in vain. I do fear
> the machine will be the death of him, for certain I am that the human
> machine cannot stand that restless energy of mind.

Ada and Babbage toyed for a while with the idea of creating
a robot tick-tack-toe machine to raise funds at carnivals. It would
consist of automata: two children playing the game accompanied by a lamb and a cock. "The child who won the game might
clap his hands whilst the cock was crowing, after which the child
who was beaten might cry and wring his hands whilst the lamb
began bleating." Producing such a machine, he finally concluded, would take too much time away from his Analytical
Engine. He applied for the job as master of the mint (which
Newton had held), but was turned down. He had hoped the salary would underwrite the machine.

By 1848, however, Babbage had decided he had mastered
the Analytical Engine. Typically, he abandoned it for yet another
project, the Difference Engine No. 2, which would draw on what
he had learned from the preceding two machines.

Meanwhile Ada was in serious trouble. She was a compulsive
gambler and was constantly in debt to various bookmakers. She
referred obliquely to her problem as "the book." According to
legend she hoped Babbage could compute a system for betting
on the horses, which he would never do. She drank and used
cocaine, the latter a not uncommon practice in Victorian England.
She had also become the mistress of a notorious womanizer and
gambler, John Crosse. Babbage and her mother knew; her husband did not. A public scandal was growing. Twice she had to
pawn her family jewels to pay off her debts. Twice her mother
bailed her out.

The story does not have a happy ending. By 1850 she was
quite ill, her "health . . . so utterly broken" that she could not
write her friend regularly. She had uterine cancer, and she lin-
gered too long. Her mother, a monstrous woman, withheld the
painkilling morphine for a time, the better to punish her errant

daughter. Eventually the walls of her room had to be lined with mattresses so that she would not harm herself when she thrashed about in agony. She wrote to Babbage asking him to take care of some personal tasks, which included paying off a particularly obnoxious bookie. Her wilful mother would not let Babbage see her at the end. Augusta Ada, countess of Lovelace, died on November 27, 1852. She finally joined her father, as she had requested, in the family crypt. She was thirty-six, the same age at which Lord Byron died.[10]

Babbage and Lady Byron immediately began a painful row, while the grieving husband, who by that time had learned about Crosse, tried to unsnarl his wife's affairs. Lady Byron dedicated herself to giving Lovelace as much pain as possible, turning his children against him and, eventually, leaving him a sad, lonely man.

Babbage remained active, working not only on the Difference Engine but also on his other inventions, including the ophthalmoscope, which physicians still use to examine the interior of the eye. He devised colored gels for colored stage lights and even wrote a ballet to show off his idea.

As he grew old and crotchety, he developed a full-gallop phobia of street musicians, particularly organ-grinders.[11] He said they interfered with his work. The historian B. V. Bowden wrote that Babbage's attempts to still the musicians made him the object of public scorn.

Jeering children followed him through the streets; drum and fife bands came miles out of their way to serenade him, and indignant citizens who had an hour or two to spare made a point of having a drink at some local hostelry, and then blowing bugles and other instruments under his windows at all hours of the day and night.

Yet he still tried to raise the money for a new computer. He applied again to the government for funds. "Science was weighed against gold by a new standard," he wrote later, "and it was

10. In the mid-1970s, the U.S. Defense Department contracted for a master computer program to permit all of its thousands of computers to "talk" to each other. It was named ADA.
11. The hatred was shared by Carlyle, who fled into a soundproof room when he heard them coming.

resolved to proceed no further. . . . I cannot but feel that whilst the public has already derived advantage from my labours, I have myself only experienced loss and neglect."

He attempted to get his occulting light for signaling and for lighthouses shown at the Exposition of 1851, but withdrew in a huff when the prize money was decreased. He put the light in a window on the top floor of his house, where it could be seen for blocks.

By 1862 Babbage, then seventy-one, had agreed to let the first Difference Engine go on display in South Kensington. Babbage would show up at the museum from time to time to explain how it worked to the visitors.

He finally sat down to write his autobiography, *Passages from the Life of a Philosopher,* a book filled with surprising detail, great wit, and bitterness. Someone who visited him in his last years wrote that the visit was one of the "sad memories of my life." Babbage took him through his workshop, showing him parts of machinery and plans. At each stop Babbage explained why he never finished what he had begun. Except for his book on operations research and his autobiography, Babbage never completed anything he had started. The visitor noted, "I took leave of the old man with a heavy heart."

M. V. Wilkes wrote that the general feeling one gets from reading Babbage's unpublished notes is one of stark loneliness. Except for his son Henry, Babbage did not seem to have anyone with whom to discuss his work. His other sons had moved to Australia, and he knew he would never see them again. "Ever since going through Babbage's notebooks, I have been haunted by the thought of the loneliness of his intellectual life during the period when, as he later tells us, he was working up to ten or eleven hours a day on the Analytical Engine," Wilkes remarked. "Perhaps he found that he could not get people to understand what he was aiming at and, after a while, decided to say little."

Babbage died during the night of October 18, 1871, attended by his son Henry. He could not die in peace; street musicians from all over London arrived on his street to harass him on his deathbed.[12] After his death his brain was removed for study. It

12. His obituary in the London *Times* reported that he lived to be almost eighty, "in spite of organ-grinding persecutions."

was not found to be remarkable, and is still preserved by the Royal College of Surgeons.

Babbage was forgotten when he died. Those who followed him on his path were not aware anyone had preceded them. It was only in the middle of the next century that Babbage, largely through the work of Ada, was rediscovered.

Babbage himself once said he would gladly die early if he could come back for three days 500 years later to see what the world would be like. If he had come back only 100 years later, he would have found the world filled with Difference Engines— and his ideas finally understood.

3. Hollerith

Chicken salad.

HERMAN HOLLERITH, *describing why he invented his mechanical calculator*

THE URGE TO COUNT HEADS is one of humanity's oldest impulses, and records of censuses are among our oldest intellectual artifacts. The census was not merely a political exercise; in order to tax a populace and predict revenues, a government needed to know how many people there were. That required a census.

The Babylonians led the way. There are records of a Babylonian census of taxpayers that go back to 3500 B.C. Babylonian censuses were frequent and complex, the records voluminous. Around 30,000 clay tablets have been found.

Some of the most famous ancient censuses were recorded in the Old Testament. No sooner did the children of Israel escape from Egypt than God ordered Moses to take a census to establish how many fighting men Israel could count on. Moses was ordered to count every male Israelite over the age of twenty. He found he had 603,550 men, a fairly substantial army.

Another biblical census is one that modern census takers wish had never happened. David was king in Israel in 1017 B.C., and he ordered a census. Many of the Israelites strongly resisted the counting, and David had to use the army. Nine months and twenty-two days later, the army reported the results: 1,300,000 warriors. According to the Bible, God was so angry at David's act that he gave the king the choice of three years of famine, defeat in battle, or three days of the plague. David opted for the plague, and 70,000 men died. Since then the notion that the Deity does not approve of censuses has passed down through the ages; even in our own time, census takers find pockets of religious resistance to the counting.

Yet the need to count heads persisted, for taxation purposes if no other. The most famous example of a taxation census was the one ordered in Roman Judea that led Mary and Joseph toward Jerusalem.

As censuses became more complex and as populations grew, the census takers came up against the technological limits of calculating and computing. Governments frequently ordered more information than just a head count; they also asked about profession, marital status, children, possessions, livestock. Each answer was a number, and all the numbers had to be counted.

Few nations have been as adept at taking the census as the United States. Since the Constitution went into effect, the United States has never missed a decennial census, leaving us 190 years of unbroken records of who we are and what we are like.

The need for such a national head count became apparent in 1774 when the First Continental Congress, meeting in Philadelphia, decided that the vote of each state in Congress should depend on population. Determining the population required a census. That idea, first propounded by Patrick Henry, failed—in part because organizing such a census was beyond the Congress's ability—so every state was given one vote instead.[1]

In 1787 the writers of the Constitution opted for two houses of Congress after a bitter debate over representation. One house

1. Historians believe that there were 2.5 million Americans, one-fifth of them black, at the time of the Revolution. America had passed the one-million mark around 1745. Philadelphia was the largest city with about 40,000 people (in fact, it was the largest English-speaking city apart from London). Boston was second. New York did not become the largest city until 1810.

was to be determined by relative population, and that made a census necessary. Article 1, Section 3, called for a census within three years of the meeting of the first Congress and for others every ten years thereafter.

The census taking began on August 2, 1790. Families, not individuals, were counted. The interviewing for the census took nine months and showed 3,893,637 Americans, excluding those in the territories. The results were controversial because it was widely believed that there were more than four million people in the United States. George Washington, for one, thought the count was off because many people refused to cooperate on religious grounds (shades of King David) and because many feared it would be used for taxation purposes. Historians now think the count was actually pretty close to the real number.

A pattern was set with this 1790 census: the census would ask for more than just the number of people. James Madison proposed that if the questionnaire was broad enough, the results would help Congress pass legislation. The questions could also serve as an internal check on the accuracy of the individual questionnaires. Congress agreed, and the first census contained six columns to be filled out by the census taker: free white males under sixteen, free white males above sixteen, white females, free blacks, slaves, and "the number of persons employed in the various arts and professions carried on in the United States." This last question was the first of many to draw a profile of the American.

The first census count took about a year. Clerks did it by hand.

Every ten years, the United States counted itself again. Each time, the population was much greater than the time before. Indeed, until the Civil War, the population always increased almost exactly 34.6 percent between each census. The Civil War was the turning point; growth never again matched the records set during the first half of the century.

By 1860 there were 31,440,000 Americans who needed to be counted. With the population growth came such a proliferation of questions that in 1850 Congress enacted a statutory limit of 100. It took longer to complete the count, required more people, and cost more money. The census had become a mammoth undertaking. There were six separate questionnaires counting things such as people engaged in agriculture or industry. There was even a form for tabulating vital statistics regarding everyone who had died the preceding year. It began to take so long to calculate the census that many observers envisioned the day when one census would become due before the last one was completed. What good would it do to have statistics that were ten years old?

The solution to this problem was to use some kind of mechanization. The first attempt came in the census of 1870, when machines invented by Col. Charles W. Seaton, chief clerk of the census, were used. The machine was sorely needed, because there were 40 million Americans to be counted. Seaton's device was a wooden machine in which paper was inserted over a series of rollers. The wooden box was fitted with slots exposing a small section of the paper. The operator entered figures from the census data onto the paper through the slots all across the paper. The operator would then turn a crank and another horizontal line would appear. When each form was finished, the paper was removed from the roll and consolidated with other forms. That's all there was to it, but it was an enormous aid in helping the census clerks keep their columns neat, and prevented considerable eyestrain.

Clearly, that was not going to get the Census Office out of its jam. It turned out, however, that Seaton had a young man working for him who would have the answer to the problem. He was Herman Hollerith, and he became, to a large extent, responsible for modern computing and data processing.

Hollerith was a practical, almost humorless, driven man, staunchly independent and showing little sense of romance or frivolity. He had few outside interests, virtually no hobby but work, no taste for fame or honors. He could take a trip to England and pass up the historical sites and the beautiful countryside to crawl under subway cars in order to see what kind of brakes they used. There are some similarities between Hollerith and Babbage, mostly in temperament. Both men suffered because of their stubbornness. There is an important difference, however: unlike

Babbage, Hollerith had a long list of useful innovations to his credit which earned him considerable amounts of money and which made a lasting impression on the world.

Hollerith probably learned his stubborn independence from his father, a freethinker who had fled Germany after participating in the revolution of 1848. The Holleriths moved to Buffalo, New York, where Herman was born. Herman's father died in an accident when Herman was seven.

The boy clearly had a mechanical talent, but apparently not much else. When only fifteen, Hollerith entered the Columbia School of Mines, an excellent school housed in a converted broom factory at Fourth Avenue and Fiftieth Street in Manhattan. This was before the days when engineering was taught as a theoretical science; Columbia emphasized practical experience. Nonetheless, Hollerith took a broad range of subjects, including chemistry and physics. During the summers, he went to Michigan to work in the mines.

In 1879, at the age of nineteen, Hollerith graduated from the school with a degree in mining engineering. He had a run of good luck. First, 1879 was the year before the United States was to take the tenth census. Second, one of his professors, William Trowbridge, was acting as a special agent in the census, in charge of a survey of power machinery used in manufacturing. Trowbridge offered Hollerith a job at $600 a year to go to Washington with him. Rather than go into the mines, Hollerith happily accepted.

Hollerith's job was not very demanding. He helped Trowbridge write a report on steam and water usage, which was promptly ignored. For a time Hollerith led the life of a dashing man-about-town, frequenting parties or the Potomac Boat Club. His only hobby was photography, but he had a serious aversion to having his own pictures taken. The few photos that exist of Hollerith in the early Washington years show a slim, awkwardly dapper young man with an enormous mustache, the very paragon of a late-Victorian bachelor.

One of Hollerith's acquaintances in the Census Office was Dr. John Shaw Billings, who was in charge of vital statistics. Billings was a physician who had served as the medical inspector for the Army of the Potomac during the Civil War, helped build the surgeon general's medical library, and organized the Johns Hopkins Hospital, in Baltimore. He taught hygiene and medical statistics at the University of Pennsylvania and was director of its hospital. After his retirement from Penn, in 1896, he organized the New York Public Library, which was constructed from his postcard sketch. When he first met Hollerith, he was responsible for the collection and tabulation of the data for the next census, an enumeration in which the data were clearly going to overwhelm the procedure.

Billings was also the father of a beautiful daughter. One summer night in 1881, Hollerith and Kate Sherman Billings had a date at the boat club. According to Hollerith's biographer Geoffrey D. Austrian, he tried mightily to impress the young woman by buying up every single door-prize lottery ticket but one. That one turned out to be the winning ticket. To make up for the loss, Hollerith squired her to the buffet, where he attacked the chicken salad. Kate was so impressed that she invited him home to dinner; her mother made a great chicken salad.[2]

It was while they were eating the chicken salad that Hollerith and Billings began a conversation that would determine Hollerith's future. There are several versions of the story, just as there are two versions of the conversation between Babbage and Herschel that led to the development of the Difference Engine. Hollerith provided one version several years later, and since it seems to conform with the facts, it is accepted here. Sometime during the course of the conversation at Billings's home, Billings described his problem. Hollerith wrote:

He said to me there ought to be a machine for doing the purely mechanical work of tabulating population and similar statistics. . . . his idea was something like a type distributing machine. He thought of using cards with the description of the individual shown by notches punched in the edge of the card. . . . After studying the problem I went back to Dr. Billings and said that I thought I could work out a solution for the problem and asked him if he would go in with me. The Doctor said he was not interested any further than to see some solution of the problem worked out.

2. Kate eventually married someone else.

Hollerith never failed to credit Billings with the idea. Billings never failed to credit Hollerith with the actual invention. In the history of the computer, as we shall see, that kind of agreement was quite rare.

In the fall of 1882, Hollerith was offered a job at the Massachusetts Institute of Technology teaching mechanical engineering. The superintendent of the census, Francis A. Walker, had left the Census Office to become president of MIT, and he encouraged Hollerith to take the job. Hollerith was apparently a good teacher. He also used some of his time at MIT to work on a census machine.

Hollerith, in a scientific paper published in the *School of Mines Quarterly* in 1889, suggested that "few, who have not come directly in contact with a census office can form any adequate idea of the labor involved" in taking a census. It was estimated that the census of 1890 would count around 62 million Americans, yet the method employed would be essentially the same one used since the Babylonians: "that of making tally-marks in small squares and then adding and counting such tally marks. . . . These methods were at the time described as 'barbarous.' " Hollerith pointed out that the increase in the cost of the census greatly exceeded the growth in the population. He likened taking a census to taking a photograph of "the social and economic conditions of a people," and concluded that the cost of this photograph had gotten out of hand.

Staying at MIT only one year, Hollerith moved back to Washington and went to work for a short time at the U.S. Patent Office, where he could learn as much as possible about patent law. He then left the Patent Office and set himself up in business as an "Expert and Solicitor of Patents." He knew the risks involved in what he wanted to do, but he could quote one of his mentors who said that "half the art of invention consists of knowing what needs to be invented." Hollerith would have the knack of knowing that all his life.

He built some working parts of a computing device and took them to Seaton in the Census Office, who thought the idea had merit. The census wanted some demonstrations. With that encouragement and with the backing of $2,500 from his brother-in-law, he took out his first patent on September 23, 1884, for "certain new and useful improvements in the Art of Compiling Statistics."

In order to record the information, Hollerith at first fiddled with the notion of punching holes in paper tape, a method similar to that used in the automatic telegraph of his time and in teleprinters years later. The first patent was for a machine in which a strip of paper would run over a roller. Pins in the roller would sense a hole in the tape and make a connection to be counted. He later concluded that this was too cumbersome, making access to the data much too difficult. The solution lay in something he remembered from a railroad trip to the mines of Michigan. "I was travelling in the West and I had a ticket with what I think was called a punch photograph . . . the conductor . . . punched out a description of the individual, as light hair, dark eyes, large nose, etc."

Hollerith adopted this punch photograph as a means of recording data for the census. The punch card had the information around the edges because the puncher could not reach the middle of the card. Later he would find a way to punch holes in a rectangular card; he had reinvented the punch card of Jacquard and Babbage.[3] Oddly, he never patented the card; he patented only the machinery that punched and counted the cards, believing they were more important. Later patents would cover a card-reading machine.[4]

Hollerith looked around for ways to prove that his new machine worked and to support himself. He went to the city of Baltimore and offered his services in organizing their health records. The records were a mess. There was no way to systematize records of that volume, and the idea of learning anything from them was preposterous. Hollerith used the punch card tabula-

3. Since his brother-in-law was in the silk-weaving business, Hollerith may have heard of Jacquard from him.
4. Hollerith took a little time out during this period to invent brakes for railroad cars. His electrically actuated brakes could stop an entire train of cars, a distinct improvement over George Westinghouse's brakes, which worked so slowly that the cars in the rear piled into the cars in the front. Westinghouse eventually adopted Hollerith's ideas and beat him out of the railroad-brake business. Many years later Hollerith would get his revenge on the railroads.

tor. It was brutal work. On any given day, he might punch 1,000 cards, a dozen holes in each. His future mother-in-law wrote, "He has done it all with a hand punch and his arm was aching and paining dreadfully. He really looked quite badly."

The results proved that the punch card concept worked. The cards were much easier to handle and could be used over and over. Moreover, they made it easier to get at particular information than was the case with paper tape. Punch cards had the added advantage of permitting tabulators to enter their data anywhere in the country and then to collect them in one central place for later computation. The cards also made possible presorting, so that the computation could be organized on a rational basis. Each card equaled one person, and each hole represented information about such matters as occupation, race, birthplace, and cause of death.

Hollerith devised a box with springs on its lid. If the punch card reader detected a card with certain characteristics, the lid would spring open and the card would fall in—a punch card sorter. He took out another patent, bearing the number 395,781, on June 8, 1887, for the first punch card calculator.

The Baltimore trial was so successful that the state of New Jersey and the city of New York asked Hollerith to perform his magic with their health records. In each case his machine worked perfectly, and Hollerith, who was now getting the attention of the newspapers, was ready to take on the federal government.

First, however, he had to attend to some personal business. Several years earlier Hollerith had been engaged to a lovely young woman named Flora Fergusson, but she died of typhoid.[5] At a party one evening Hollerith saw a woman who reminded him of Flora. Her name was Lucia Talcott, "Lu" to her friends. He wangled an introduction, fell in love, and went courting. He also decided to increase the odds in his favor by a furious campaign to win over her mother. The mother was wise enough to know that Hollerith was "fattening the cow to catch the calf." None-

5. This event turned Hollerith into something of a food fanatic. He blamed most ill health on poor diet and suggested that eating well was the cure for many of life's ailments. He took his own advice and became quite portly toward the end of his life.

theless, Mrs. Talcott was charmed and Lu was won over. It was a happy, three-way marriage, as the future mother-in-law attained a position of trust and counsel, impressive in that Hollerith was a stubbornly private and independent man. Their letters, in fact, became one of the best sources for biographers of Hollerith.

Hollerith's success with the health departments of New Jersey and New York City came to the attention of the vital-statistics branch of the surgeon general's office in the War Department. They needed help in keeping track of the health statistics of servicemen. The department was willing to rent Hollerith's machine for $1,000 a year, plus the cost of the punch cards, if Hollerith could prove he could do the job. Their statistics were different from any Hollerith had tried before because the amount of data was so huge it required aggregates. To keep the card from getting too large, Hollerith designed the card so that one hole would mean one thing and that this hole in combination with another would mean something entirely different. For example, a hole in the number-one position could stand for one piece of information; the same hole, combined with a nine would have an altogether different meaning. Think of a typewriter. Pressing the key for the number 1 means *1;* pressing the same key while pressing the shift key could mean a *!*. This produced complex numbers, requiring the accumulator to carry numbers from one counter to another.

To test this new machine, he went back to New York City and its health records. His device worked perfectly. This satisfied the War Department, and on December 9, 1888, Hollerith installed his machine.

He was becoming quite famous. He was invited to bring a calculating machine to the Paris Universal Exposition of 1889. He also demonstrated the machine in Germany and took out a German patent.

Back in the United States, a friend of Hollerith's, Robert P. Porter, had been named superintendent for the 1890 census. Porter firmly believed in Hollerith's machines and offered him Billings's old job in vital statistics. Hollerith turned the offer down, believing there was a conflict of interest: he wanted the contract for the computation.

Hollerith was not the only one who had a device designed to help win the census contract. Porter decided that the best way to choose a calculator was to conduct a contest. Hollerith's machine, which was grandly called the Hollerith Electric Tabulating System, was pitted against two other inventions. One used multicolored slips of paper; another used chips and colored cards; all were hard sorted. The test involved 10,491 people, the 1880 census for four districts in St. Louis.

Instead of a hand puncher, Hollerith used a "pantograph," a keyboard device for punching the holes, built for him by Pratt & Whitney in Connecticut. The card was placed under a metal plate containing awls. A handle fit over the plate, and the operator pushed down onto one of the awls, cutting a hole in the card.

Hollerith's system was the clear winner, finishing the St. Louis data in 72 hours, 27 minutes. The closest competitor was the "chip" method, which took 110 hours, 56 minutes. Putting the data onto Hollerith's cards took most of the time; once that was accomplished, the tabulating machine whizzed through the cards in a five and a half hours, several days faster than its competitor. The Census Office ordered fifty-six Hollerith machines—at a cost of $56,000 in annual rentals. There was every reason to think the office would need that many again.

Hollerith agreed to service the machines constantly, to keep spares handy, and to pay a penalty of $10 a day for each day a machine was not working. The Census Office anticipated around-the-clock shifts.

Hollerith was now in business. His first employee was Lu's brother Ned. He arranged for Western Electric to build his machines for the Census Office.

The machine consisted of the puncher and the tabulator. The latter included a hard-rubber plate to hold the cards. The plate had a series of holes or cups corresponding to the potential holes in the card. A thin nail was driven through the bottom of each cup, and the cup was half filled with mercury to form an electrical connection. Above the plate was the lid to the box, which contained spring-actuated points, also corresponding to the holes. A card would be placed on the plate; the lid would be closed.

Wherever the point found a hole, it would stick down into the mercury and closed the connection.

Above this device was the counter, a table with a vertical panel containing four rows of ten clocklike dials. Each electrical connection registered on the dial. Each dial had 100 marks and two hands, one for units, one for hundreds. Numbers could be carried from one dial to the other. The counts were collected by reading the dials. Someone called it a "statistical piano." It combined safeguards against internal errors, as long as the punch card operators did not make a mistake.

The world was impressed. Newspapers proclaimed a new age. The Franklin Institute in Philadelphia awarded Hollerith its Elliot Cresson Medal for revolutionizing statistics. He received an honorary degree from his old school, which published his article on the tabulator and accepted it as his dissertation.

Hollerith's machines were hoisted up the side of the census building, on Ninth Street in Washington, and hammered and wired into place. Clerks, many of them young women, went to work punching the cards and feeding them into the tabulators. Hollerith had devised a card counter to provide quick and dirty totals.[6] His machines were designed mainly for the complicated tabulation of the demographic questions.

The work was not fun for the young women, many of whom, driven to near madness by the monotony of their work, walked out. One employee, quoted by Austrian, remembered:

Mechanics were there frequently . . . to get the ailing machines back in operation. The trouble was usually that somebody had extracted the mercury . . . from one of the little cups with an eye-dropper and squirted it into a spittoon, just to get some un-needed rest.

One young woman collected 16,071 families, about 80,000 people. In a single day the census tabulators recorded 1,342,318 families, or 6,711,590 people. Some time later, at a party that Hollerith threw for the census administrators, he said:

Consider a stack of schedules of thin paper higher than the Washington Monument. . . . Imagine the work required in turning over such a pile

6. This worked so well that the Census Bureau was able to give a preliminary total count six weeks after the complete data were delivered to Washington.

of schedules page by page, and recording the number of persons reported in each schedule. This is what was done in one day by the population division of the Census Office.

One variable alone required the punching of a billion holes.

Despite what seemed to be the obvious success of Hollerith's machines, the Census Office was criticized in some quarters for using them. The 1890 census cost $11.5 million, about twice as much as the preceding census. Porter suggested that the machines saved the government about $5 million in labor costs. He added that the machines also made the tabulating far more comprehensive than that of any earlier census had been.

There is also no doubt that the use of the machines altered the content of the census—the questions were determined by the means of processing, not the other way around. Nonetheless, the census of 1890 marked a turning point: for the first time a large practical statistical problem was handled by machines. They enabled demographers to reach far more complex, interesting, and important conclusions from the data because Hollerith's machines permitted them to cross-tabulate questions. More than that, however, the census represented the beginning of modern statistical analysis, the kind that would have been impossible before Hollerith's machines. It also ushered in modern data processing, and, as we shall see, its effects are still very much with us today. The census also provided a test of the technology that Hollerith would soon take into the world of commerce, radically altering how Americans went about their business. And, as some social historians have pointed out, the census involved the first large-scale employment of women as office workers. Their awesome performance helped put to rest the notion that women were incapable of functioning in a complex office situation. Hollerith opened the door for the modern working woman.

The usefulness of Hollerith's machines was not lost on census managers elsewhere; even before the U.S. census was complete, Hollerith received queries from overseas. One of the first contracts he signed was with Austria, but the Austrians wasted no time in abrogating Hollerith's Austrian patent, and for several years he had to compete against his own invention, manufactured with the connivance of the Austrian government in Vienna. Nonetheless, Hollerith completed the Austrian census and then took his machines to Canada and Norway.

He opened a shop along the Chesapeake and Potomac Canal. The sign on the wall announced "The Tabulating Machine Company," although there was, as yet, no such company. The shop assembled and put the finishing touches on the Hollerith machine. Parts and sections came from suppliers all over the East. Hollerith sent representatives to several large eastern and midwestern cities to act as his sales representatives

Hollerith was a stern though fair employer, loyal to his employees, but capable of going to great lengths to get a fair day's work from them. Geoffrey Austrian relates that Hollerith once grew upset that some of his workers spent too much time on the toilet reading instead of working. Hollerith rigged a set of nails in the toilet seat, filed them down so they would not be felt, and then ran wires from the nails to a dynamo in his office. He watched the malingerers through a peephole. If he saw someone sitting and reading, he turned a crank—and a shot of electricity spoiled the reverie. It was probably effective.

Hollerith went to Europe to set up subsidiaries. He had become part of a worldwide community of census people. His machines were now considered indispensable for anyone wishing to carry out a modern census. But Hollerith was smart enough to know that his machines were good for other things besides tabulating a census, and he recognized that the success of his company, and its financial future, depended on his getting noncensus business. In 1893–94 the country was in the throes of a deep depression, and Hollerith was running out of money. He turned to the railroads.

His machine had gone through several changes by this time. Whereas the census generally asked questions that could be answered yes or no, business dealt with numbers and things. He now had tabulators, used in the census of American agriculture, that could carry numbers and integrate totals. They were electric, but weights on cables and pulleys actually operated the machines. He had to convince the railroads that they needed adaptations of these machines.

The railroads had grown into enterprises of gigantic proportions. They had thousands of freight cars and engines, offices and stations, employees and customers. Yet all the paperwork—and tons of it were produced every day—was sorted by hand. The railroad managers had virtually no idea where their cars were at any given time, and could not tell for days or weeks how many passengers they had carried last Wednesday or what bills were in arrears today. The task of keeping track of four million waybills a year by hand was mind boggling. The railroad managers, however, were a conservative lot, and, after all, they had always done things that way. After teaching himself as much as he could about railroad accounting, Hollerith was convinced he had a better way.

First he had to make some changes in his system. The greatest change was in the punch card. Hollerith devised a new card, exactly the size of the current dollar bill (6⅝ by 3¼ inches), which had vertical columns across the width of the card. The card contained 960 positions at which holes could be punched. Unlike the census cards, which the operator could not read, his cards contained the numbers that corresponded to the possible holes. He also printed lines up and down the cards delineating fields, groups of columns that all signified the same variable. The first two columns could signify a city, the next five could contain the data for the occupation, and so on. This use of fields made the cards easier to punch, made it possible for people to excerpt from the cards by simply looking at them, and made it easier for the machine to find one field and compare it with another. The accumulator might go directly to the field for a particular city, then seek the field for blacksmiths, and then tabulate the number of blacksmiths in that city. The punch card has not been changed to this day; it is still called the Hollerith card.

His first attempt to get railroad business, the small Richmond & Danville Railroad, failed—the managers wouldn't take the risk. Hollerith turned to the two eastern giants, the New York Central and the Pennsylvania. He offered to run his machines in the railroads' offices to prove they could handle the work load. The New York Central was the first to agree, and Hollerith installed several of the newest models of his machines. The experiment did not go well. While Hollerith was in Europe trying to get the czarist regime in Russia to use his machines for its planned colossal census, the Central management threw Hollerith's machines out after three months.

Although he was, by this time, desperate for income, he was not one to take defeat lightly. He redesigned his railroad tabulator, getting rid of the counters and replacing them with electric adding machines. Each adding machine was associated with a field on the punch card. Every time the press on the tabulator was pushed down, the adding machines gave a new total. Magnets were used instead of mercury cups. When the machine sensed a hole in the card, a magnet under the hole activated a swinging arm that connected to an adding wheel. Blocks of figures could be counted simultaneously.

Hollerith talked the Central into conducting a new test, entirely at his expense. He would run the machines for one year free of charge. At the end of the year, he would take his machines out; or, the railroad could at any time decide to place an order. The railroad agreed to the experiment.

Hollerith had also received inquiries from other companies, including the Pennslyvania Railroad, but he did not have the capital to produce the machines. He laid off most of his workers and had to borrow money from his mother-in-law to pay his life insurance premiums. He even sold his horse.

Salvation came from a Boston organization called the Library Bureau. This group, formed by the American Library Association, provided supplies and know-how to libraries. The deal it struck with Hollerith provided him the capital to build his machines. The bureau would also pay Hollerith royalties, and would market, operate, and service Hollerith machines for customers, who were often not libraries. Essentially, the agreement created data-processing services, similar to the ones common today. The bureau immediately set up a one-year trial at the Travelers' Insurance Company. That relieved some of the financial pressure. So did a contract with the French government for census machines.

It did not take a full year for the New York Central to recognize that it needed the Hollerith machine. On August 20, the

Central agreed to rent the machines for one year at $5,000 a month. Hollerith agreed to supply and service the machines and, through the Library Bureau, to supply the peripheral machines for handling the cards. The railroad would buy the punch cards from Hollerith. He wrote to his mother-in-law:

> I have no hesitation now in saying that I believe the methods of railway accounting will be revolutionized in the next five years. Here I am doing the very thing I said I never liked to do ... what I say, however, is simply intended to show you that perhaps your confidence in me has not been misplaced and perhaps, after all, I will come out on top. I think I have won.

Not yet. Although the Central was convinced, the other railroads were not interested. It would be a few more years before he got his revenge on the railroad establishment for rejecting his brake.

On December 15, 1896, he finally signed a contract to supply machines for the Russian census. He sold the machines for $1,700 each instead of adhering to his usual practice of renting them out. They were the largest machines he had built yet, eighty counters and thirty relays. The parts were made at Hollerith's plant and then shipped to Russia for assembly. The total contract came to $67,571.30.[7]

Hollerith had been saved from financial disaster, but he was not out of financial trouble. His family had grown (he and Lu would have six children), and he had moved out of his mother-in-law's house and into a Victorian house in the Maryland suburb of Garrett Park. He was thirty-six. He decided it was time to formalize his business, and on December 3, 1896, he incorporated in the state of New Jersey under the name The Tabulating Machine Company, essentially the world's first computer company.

A number of his friends and acquaintances took stock and formed the board of directors, including George Mead Bond of Pratt & Whitney; Ferdinand W. Roebling, the Trenton, New Jersey, steel maker;[8] Henry C. Adams, a friend from the Census

7. The Russians reported a total population of 129,211,113.
8. He was the brother of Washington Roebling, who built the Brooklyn Bridge, which their father, John A. Roebling, had designed.

Office; and Prof. George F. Swain, who had been with Hollerith at the Census Office and at MIT. The most important was Harry Bates Thayer, head of Western Electric's New York facility and Hollerith's chief subcontractor. It was an exemplary group of men, who served Hollerith well. For some it turned out to be the best investment they would ever make.

Roebling was elected president of Tabulating Machine. Hollerith was the majority stockholder. Within six months after the organizational meeting, the company had paid off all its debts and issued a 4 percent dividend. The new company also terminated its contract with the Library Bureau. Tabulating Machine was on its own.

Nonetheless, as Austrian has written, Hollerith seemed to sense that times had changed. He became a bit crankier and even more ill-tempered than usual, turning on some of his older employees or writing blistering letters to a railroad one of whose trains had arrived a minute early. It is possible that this was a reaction to his having lost some of the independence he had savored all these years.

Hollerith prepared for the next census, in 1900. The new head of the census, William R. Merriam, had no trouble deciding that the office was not going back to the bad old days of hand tabulation. Since he could not give the contract for machines outright to Hollerith, he went through the charade of another competition, again against the old chip method. Hollerith wiped out the competitor. Merriam ordered fifty machines at $1,000 a machine per year, the same terms as those in the 1890 census. Hollerith contracted with the Woonsocket, Rhode Island, firm of Taft-Peirce to build the machines. An engineer there, Eugene Amzi Ford, modified the keypunch machine with a typewriter keyboard, a design that lasted for decades. Hollerith also produced a more complex machine, which he had designed for the complicated agricultural census.

Hollerith made some further modifications. He added an automatic card feeder to the tabulator. The cards were stacked in a chute with a weight on top and were pushed one at a time into the counter. He also added automatic sorters.

Eventually, Hollerith's company provided 311 tabulating

machines, 20 sorters, and 1,021 punchers. One hundred and
twenty million cards were used. Hollerith received $428,239 in
fees. The machines worked well. The amount of information
collected and tabulated exceeded anything attempted before.[9]

Tabulating Machine bought out Taft-Peirce, to secure its own
manufacturing facility. But the company still had not completely
probed the commercial market. One test of how the tabulating
equipment might work was set up at Taft-Peirce itself to keep
track of the accounts. A second contract was arranged with
Pennsylvania Steel Company, in Philadelphia, because the firm's
auditor, Gershom Smith, believed in the technology. Another
customer, who approached Hollerith on his own, was Marshall
Field, the department store tycoon in Chicago, who wanted to
use the tabulators for auditing, inventory, and sales analysis—
the first use by a retailer of automatic auditing.

Hollerith modified the way he went about his business, again
setting precedents for practices still with us today. In order to be
fair, he concluded, large users of his machinery ought to pay
more than those whose need was not as great. The best measure
of this was the number of punch cards used. As part of his contract, he required that all cards be purchased from his company.
Because his new machines were much faster than the old ones
(one automatic sorter handled 140,448 cards in a six-and-a-half-
hour day), this was a considerable matter. In fact, Hollerith
thought he might not have to charge for the machines at all—
the punch card business would provide the profit. He moved a
press into the Washington building and began making his own
punch cards.

Others also reached this conclusion. George Eastman found
that the money in photography was not in the camera but in the
film, so the cameras were cheap and the film turned the profit.
King Gillette came to the same conclusion with razors: the money
was not in the razors but in the blades. Computer companies in
the future would follow this pattern. Indeed, for years, much of
IBM's profit came not from its machines but from its punch cards.

Hollerith was scrupulously honest. Repairs on his machines

9. The census showed there were 75,994,575 Americans on June 1, 1900.

were completely free for the first six months and provided at cost thereafter. He was even reluctant to raise the prices he charged his old customers, on grounds that this would break his word.

More customers dribbled in, including Yale & Towne Manufacturing, in New Haven. It was at about this time that Hollerith got his revenge on railroad barons. In 1902, the Interstate Commerce Commission ordered the railroads to provide far more statistics than they had in the past. The railroads were angry; this would increase their paperwork load beyond their imagination. The testifiers before the ICC were furious—except for the man from the New York Central. No problem, he assured the commissioners with a smile; we can get you the figures. The other railroads were beside themselves. It was perfectly clear that the actuaries at the Central knew more about their own business than they did about theirs, a very dangerous situation for a competitor. The explanation, of course, was that the Central was using Hollerith machines and had its business under control. This touched off bedlam in the industry, and Hollerith soon found he had far more business than he could handle.

There was more census work from around the world, but trouble was now brewing with Hollerith's best customer, the U.S. Census Bureau. It had been made a permanent agency in the Department of Commerce and Labor, and a new superintendant had been installed, Simon Newton Dexter North, a New York journalist. North signed a contract with Hollerith for more machines but was dissatisfied with the state of affairs. Tabulating Machine was the only supplier of the kind of equipment the Census Bureau needed, and as such could fairly well determine the price and conditions. North believed that Hollerith was overcharging, that the vaunted saving of $5 million in the past census was illusory.

North's charges came at a time when the issue of "trusts" was prominent in the public's eye. The country was being strangled, many believed, by huge monopolies. Distrust of the big-business man was rampant, and the government was trying to enforce antitrust legislation. Hollerith ran a monopoly. The fact that his monopoly had been honestly won and was being honestly maintained seemed beside the point. North won considerable public and newspaper support for his objections to the Hollerith contracts.

This touched off a bitter personal war between two extremely stubborn men that lasted for years. The situation was made infinitely worse because Hollerith became obsessed. Almost as if the ghost of Charles Babbage were loose, Hollerith now took on the government.

The battle was fought over the 1910 census. William Merriam, the former head of the census, was now president of Tabulating Machine. The practice of having a former government official go to work for a government contractor was fairly new then. It is, alas, far more common now. This arrangement further strained relations between the company and the bureau. North held an ace in his hand; he knew that in 1906 Hollerith's first patent, the one for the hand-operated tabulator, would reach its seventeenth birthday and be void. The census was now using Hollerith's automatic machines, still covered by patent, but North saw a chance to break Hollerith.

He submitted a proposal to the company which contained prices considerably below what Hollerith was going to charge. He also hinted that the 1910 census might use other equipment. Hollerith was depressed. His depression deepened when his board voted to negotiate a new agreement with North. He threatened to emigrate to Germany. His friend Thayer tried to calm him down. In a gentle letter, his friend suggested that Hollerith was being blinded by anger and that his friends had his best interests at heart, as indeed they had. "Which is the truer friendship," Thayer wrote, "to back you up in your quarrel at an expense to you of the Census Office business or to back the Governor [Merriam] up in trying to save something out of it for you?"

Merriam signed an interim agreement with North. North, in the meantime, decided to play his ace. He obtained $40,000 from Congress to set up a research arm to develop census equipment. North was smart enough to know he really wanted the business. Both men, in their own way, were trying to save the contract on acceptable terms. Their nature failed them; neither man could reach terms that would enable him to save face.

On July 1, 1905, North threw out the rented Hollerith machines. By this time Hollerith was producing machines greatly streamlined in design and faster than the 1900 census machines. His commercial business was booming, and almost every major company wanted his machines. Once installed, they quickly became indispensable. Even the stock-market panic in 1907 failed to cut business—indeed, Hollerith was having great difficulty supplying machines for all the customers who needed them. Yet Hollerith wanted that census contract.

North tried to make good his promise. He put together a team, including lawyers, to see whether they could construct tabulators that got around Hollerith's remaining patents. The basis would be the hand-operated machines. The team also included several of Hollerith's former employees, some of whom genuinely disliked Hollerith. In essence, the government was now in the position of trying to skirt around patents that the government itself, under constitutional mandate, had issued, and of financing Hollerith's competition. The political war erupted in full fury, and Hollerith pulled every political IOU he had, even taking the issue to the president's office. Hollerith wanted to choke off funds for North's research project. He failed.

Thayer and the others were not terribly upset: they were convinced that nothing North's people could come up with could do the job and that sooner or later the Census Bureau would have to use Hollerith machines. But the bureau's engineers had made progress. They had a semiautomatic machine, much slower than Hollerith's, but better than any alternative. They also attached a printer to the tabulator, a vital addition that Hollerith, curiously, never considered. At this point North introduced a mysterious engineer named James Powers, whose name was odd for a Russian.

Almost nothing is known about Powers, except that he was born in Russia. He worked for several electrical firms in the New York area before he joined the Census Bureau, and was clearly a very good engineer and inventor. North put him in charge of the machine-shop operation. Powers immediately invented a nearly foolproof puncher that resembled a giant electric typewriter. It was better than Hollerith's old punchers and perhaps than his new ones as well. The effect was to force Hollerith to modify his own machines. He was, for the first time, responding to competition.

North moved Powers's shop to New York City. The work coming out of the shop gave North confidence he might actually pull off his coup—run his own machines instead of Hollerith's. Hollerith went to his lawyers to see about patent infringement. Unfortunately the law did not provide for an inventor to sue the government for infringement. The next step, Hollerith saw, was to change the law.

Again the political infighting was fierce. Congress actually passed the law, but President Roosevelt issued a pocket veto. The law provided for the court of claims to adjudicate the matter, and the Justice Department doubted that this would work. Hollerith furiously wrote to Roosevelt, who passed the letter on to his commerce secretary, who, of course, defended North. North proceeded to build the new Powers machines.

But in 1909, with the census a year away, a new commerce secretary came into office, and he was not sure North was doing the right thing. Hollerith, ever the letter writer, did his best to undermine the relationship. Hollerith wanted North's head. Hollerith got it on May 26 and threw a party to celebrate. The celebration was premature. North's successor, Edward Dana Durand, issued a contract with Sloan & Chase, of Newark, New Jersey, for 300 Powers punches and 100 semiautomatic tabulators. Even within the bureau this was controversial. The Powers tabulators were only about a third as fast as Hollerith's latest model. Durand also announced that the bureau would modify some of Hollerith's old agricultural census machines, which the bureau owned for the 1910 census.

Altering Hollerith machines to change their legal identity was a wholly different matter in law. Hollerith threatened to sue for damages. Durand, apparently a reasonable man, met with Hollerith's lawyer to try and settle the matter. He provided the lawyer with details on the modifications made on the agricultural machines. The lawyer sent the details to the leading patent attorney in the country, who said the modifications did indeed violate Hollerith's patents. Durand, however, did not agree. The board of Tabulating Machine authorized a lawsuit.

The case of *Tabulating Machine* vs. *Durand* would oddly portend another lawsuit at another time and place concerning the invention of computers. As in the later case, the trial was before a judge sitting without a jury. And, as in the later case, the decision left many of those involved feeling that the judge's decision flew in the face of the facts. After hearing census people say Hollerith's work in the 1900 census was not very good and after hearing his machines defended by users all over the country, the judge ruled that the government had the right to use the machines, that Hollerith did not have them patented when he sold them to the government, and that the alterations of the machines, which were generally confined to the feed mechanism, did not violate Hollerith's later patents.

Tabulating Machine appealed and won, a month later in the circuit court of appeals, but by this time it was too late.[10] The Census Bureau was keyed up for the 1910 counting. The Powers machines were delivered late and did not work very well. Neither did the census. The slow tabulation prevented the bureau from cross-tabulating many of the results and proved that Hollerith had been right—that he had the only machines that could do the job.

Powers resigned from the bureau and went into business for himself, eventually giving Hollerith and his immediate successors considerable competition. In some ways Powers's machines were better than those of Tabulating Machine. His could automatically print results, used an electrical punch instead of Hollerith's hand punch, and had a more convenient sorter. Powers also rented his machines for less. His firm subsequently became part of Remington Rand and, later still, of Sperry Rand. They will be heard from later.

At the time of the 1910 census, Hollerith was in his fifties and suffered from a bad heart. His doctors ordered him to take it easy. At this point an extraordinary man named Charles Ranlett Flint entered Hollerith's life. He would make Hollerith a millionaire and have a profound influence on the development of American business.

A native of Maine, Flint was a small man with muttonchop

10. The U.S. Supreme Court eventually ruled in favor of Durand, overthrowing the circuit court's decision.

whiskers and a surplus of nervous energy. He flew airplanes at a time when that was a decidedly risky thing to do. He was a founder of the American Automobile Association and was an avid outdoorsman and adventurer. "It has been said, perhaps too frequently," he once wrote, "that a rolling stone gathers no moss. But I have never heard anyone speak about the fun the rolling stone has a-rolling."

Flint's early specialty was international trade (he once supplied the guns for both sides of a war in Latin America), but he quickly found a new purpose in life. He believed in consolidating companies that had business in common and in producing a larger, more powerful, more efficient company from that consolidation. In an age in which trusts were anathema, Flint created new trusts. This wasn't just a job, it was a philosophical imperative. Flint was an operator.

His first attempt at consolidation involved a company called U.S. Lighting, whose owner wanted to merge with Edison and Westinghouse. Edison and Westinghouse were not interested. Undaunted, he tried again. He had a number of crude-rubber companies as his customers in Latin America. He drew up a plan for their merger which was accepted by the collective stockholders. The result was U.S. Rubber. He engineered other consolidations, including American Chicle (Chiclets).

In 1900 he merged a group of time-clock companies into the International Time Recording Company, of Binghamton, New York. The new firm dominated the industry within ten years. In 1901 he formed the Computing Scale Company, of Dayton, Ohio. This new company was not doing well by 1911. To save Computing Scale, he wanted to merge it with some other companies. Flint went to see Ferdinand Roebling.

Flint seemed to know all there was to know about Tabulating Machine. He had even gone up to Grand Central Station to examine the Hollerith machines there. Somehow Flint and Hollerith got together. Hollerith was interested. The reasons are not unclear: Tabulating Machine was still short of capital, Hollerith's main patents would soon run out, Powers's company was providing real competition, and Hollerith's doctors had ordered him to work less. More important, perhaps, Tabulating Machine was no longer his own company. The enterprise had grown too large to be controlled entirely by him. The days when he and Thayer had done everything but build the machines themselves were over. Perhaps Hollerith was simply tired. He agreed to Flint's terms. Flint raised the money and paid $450 for each share of Tabulating Machine Company stock. Hollerith received $1,210,500 for his shares and instantly became a millionaire. Several of his stockholders also took shares in Flint's new enterprise.

Flint had what he wanted. He took his three companies, threw in a fourth, the Bundy Manufacturing Company, of Endicott, New York, and formed the Computing-Tabulating-Recording Company, better known as CTR.

Hollerith promptly "retired" to the Maryland shore, where he built a huge farm for his large family. He still provided consulting services for the new company and once even toyed with the idea of starting another company on his own with some new ideas. But his creative years were over. Hollerith had transformed American business with his machines, given businessmen the tools they needed to perform statistical research, and set dozens of precedents that still prevail in business today. His impact on the course of American history was enormous.

His biographer Geoffrey Austrian found a letter Hollerith wrote to his wife that makes it clear that, unlike some who would follow in his footsteps, he really knew what he was doing to the world.

This machine or the principle will be potent factors in Statistical Science long after I am gone. Whether I or someone else will do it, this system is bound to be developed in many ways. It will take many years and perhaps it will be something for the . . . boys . . . to be able to say their daddy originated it. . . . This may appear like conceit and vanity on my part but you will understand how I say it, and I have no idea of ever talking like this to anyone else.

On May 1, 1914, CTR hired a young salesman from the National Cash Register Company named Thomas Watson to act as general manager. Watson soon took control of CTR, and under his leadership the Tabulating Machine division quickly overtook the other divisions as a profit center for the new company. Watson was careful to treat Hollerith with respect and frequently asked his counsel. If Hollerith had an idea for a new machine, Watson ordered his engineers to work on it. Several new and useful machines resulted. Yet Hollerith cooled to the young man, probably because Watson symbolized the end of Hollerith's creative era. It saddened him that many of his longtime employees had transferred their loyalty to the new regime. There is no evidence that Watson was responsible for the break between him and Hollerith.

Hollerith could still hold a grudge. A former employee, Daniel Pickrell, met Hollerith on a Washington street in 1920. Hollerith remembered him and asked what he was doing then. Pickrell, with embarrassment, confessed he was working for Powers. "He didn't even stop to say good-bye," Pickrell reported. "The next thing I heard, the cane hit the ground and away he went. It was the last time I ever saw him."

Hollerith died on November 17, 1929.

By that time, however, his old company had changed dramatically. Even the name was no longer the same. In February 1924 Watson had changed the name of CTR to International Business Machines, or IBM.

4. Dinosaurs and Flip-Flops

I built the first electronic digital computer and the prototype was finished up in October or November of 1939.

JOHN VINCENT ATANASOFF

He lies like a rug.

J. PRESPER ECKERT

HERMAN HOLLERITH was hardly the only one to grasp the need for mechanical calculators. Scientists still hungered for help, and it was obvious to many of them that modern businesses required more mechanical means of keeping some control over the paperwork and statistics that kept them running. Whole industries, including that of life insurance, used numbers as the coinage of their commerce.

The first patent for a desk-top calculator, called an arithmometer, was issued by the U.S. Patent Office in 1857, but the machine did not work. In 1876 an obscure inventor by the name of George Barnard Grant displayed a gear-operated difference engine at the Philadelphia Centennial Fair. No desk-top affair this, it weighed a ton, was five feet high and eight feet long, and had 15,000 moving parts. Grant's machine was given to the University of Pennsylvania, and a duplicate was sent to the Provident Mutual Life Insurance Company, of Philaladelphia, which used it for twenty years to figure actuarial tables.

Other inventors kept working on desk-top devices to help with bookkeeping. Dorr E. Felt began work on a key-driven calculator on Thanksgiving Day, 1884, using a macaroni box, meat skewers, metal staples, and rubber bands. He received a patent three years later for the machine, which he called the Comptometer. Models of his machine had a virtual monopoly on the desk-top calculator market for about fifteen years, being used extensively at the U.S. Treasury and the New York Weather Bureau.

The problem with Felt's comptometer was that it did not record the results of its calculations. William S. Burroughs solved that problem. Burroughs, born in 1855, spent considerable time as a boy working in an Auburn, New York, bank. He was appalled at the inaccuracies built into the hand accounting system. When he moved to St. Louis because of ill health, he went to work in a machine shop. He put together a working model of a printing adding machine, patented it in 1888, and then convinced a group of local businessmen to put up $100,000 to support a company to manufacture his machines. Things went very slowly. By 1891, when Hollerith was mechanizing the census, Burroughs had produced exactly fifty machines. Not only were there too few of them but Burroughs did not think the machines met his standards. He opened his office window and, one by one, hurled all fifty machines to the pavement two floors below. In the next year, he patented an improved model, which printed each number and a grand total. By 1895 he had sold only 284 of the machines.

Burrough's health did him in just before his business took off; he died of tuberculosis in 1898. His company was soon building and selling 5,000 machines a year, and by 1913 it dominated the manufacture of office equipment. The Burroughs Corporation is still in business, deeply involved in computers.

Frank Stephen Baldwin, as mentioned earlier, designed a mechanical calculating machine in 1872 and patented it a year later. He set up shop in Philadelphia and went into business with Jay Randolph Monroe, a former auditor with Western Electric. Monroe produced Baldwin-designed machines begining in 1911; unfortunately for Baldwin, they became known the world over as Monroe calculators.

Essentially, the Monroe-Baldwin merger began the calculating-machine industry. Monroe's company is still in business; in various forms, so are the companies of Friden and of Marchant, who also produced mechanical calculators. These machines, along with the punch card equipment produced by Hollerith's and Powers's companies, ran modern business until the invention of the electronic computer.

All this was well and good for the businessman; the machines were quite adequate for handling large amounts of data that needed to be treated the same way, for what is now called data processing. They were not very good computers; they certainly did not do the kinds of things scientists needed to have done.

Nonetheless, a number of scientists made innovative uses of office machines. Astronomers were the first to take advantage of the technology. In 1926 L. J. Comrie, of the British Nautical Almanac Office, used a Burroughs adding machine and the method of calculating differences to compute and print astronomical tables. He then went to work adopting the Hollerith punch card machine to determine the positions of the moon, an enormously complicated problem. He worked out the moon's position for every twelve hours from the years 1935 to 2000 by punching 20 million holes in half a million Hollerith cards. This took seven months.

But scientists knew that those machines would not solve their computational problems. Something entirely new was needed.

The first serious attempt at designing a computer for scientists was made in 1930 by the engineer Vannevar Bush. Bush was an extraordinary man; he was both a scientist and a politician. For many years he was at the center of the scientific establishment in the United States, one of the most powerful scientists in the world. In the words of the *New York Times,* Bush "marshalled American technology for World War II and ushered in the atomic age."

In 1940 Bush met with Franklin Delano Roosevelt and suggested that the scientific community in the United States be organized for the coming war in Europe. With Roosevelt's blessing he created the National Defense Research Committee to enlist the "support of the scientific and educational institutions and organize the scientists and engineers throughout the country." Instead of building federal laboratories, he farmed out most of his work to universities. He acted as the buffer between the scientists and the government and military, a frequently difficult job.

Bush later ran the Office of Scientific Research and Development, one section of which, under James Conant, of Harvard, worked on the possibility of harnessing nuclear fission for the war effort. That undertaking later became the Manhattan Project. Before the war was over, probably two-thirds of all the physicists in the United States worked for Bush. It was Bush who had to explain to Harry Truman how the atomic bomb worked and who recommended its use against the Japanese. When the war ended, he wrote a long exposition on the role government should play in scientific research; the result of his efforts was the formation of the National Science Foundation, the single largest contributor of funds for basic scientific research in the free world.

It was in his prewar role as an engineer that Bush contributed most directly to the development of the scientific computer. In the 1920s, when he was at MIT, he was interested in producing machines that solved specific problems confronting electrical engineers, such as how to keep track of electrical current in power grids. In 1927, he and two colleagues designed an analog machine that could solve simple equations and were useful in solving "problems in connection with electrical circuits." The machine was based on the same principle used in measuring electricity in a home meter. That machine, called a product integraph, was built by one of Bush's students as a master's thesis. Another of his students, Harold Locke Hazen, determined that a variant of that machine could solve certain kinds of differential equations, the basic equations of calculus.[1] He wrote a penciled note to Bush suggesting how to alter the machine.

Bush thought the time was "peculiarly favorable" for the development of a large machine that could help with many kinds of computations. Engineering, he wrote in the *Journal of the Franklin Institute,* had changed in recent years and many engineers were

baffled by the mathematics thus presented and requiring solution. Mathematical physicists are continually being hampered by the complexity rather than the profundity of the equations they employ; and here also even a numerical solution or two would often be a relief.

Not any one machine, nor even any one program of development can meet these needs. It was a long hard road from the adding machines of Pascal to the perforated card accounting machines of the present day. There must be much labor and many struggles before the full ideal of Leibniz can be consummated.

He was wrong in thinking that one machine couldn't meet all the needs, but his comments, which hark back to the motives of Babbage, again show the pull of necessity on the invention of computing devices.[2]

In 1927 Bush and Hazen coauthored a paper suggesting the nature of the bigger machine. They built it in 1930 and described it in another paper a year later. The machine used a number of engineering developments made by others, particularly a device called a torque amplifier designed in 1927 by C. W. Niemann, of the Bethlehem Steel Company. Bush's device came to be called a differential analyzer,[3] a name used for an earlier device invented by Lord Kelvin. For the decade between 1930 and 1940, differential analyzers, Herman Goldstine wrote, were the "best computing instruments available" to scientists.

Essentially, the differential analyzer was a collection of shafts, gears, and wires. As an analog computer, it measured movement

1. A typical differential equation that could be solved by Bush's machine had one variable, e.g., $x^2 + x = y$.
2. It is not known whether Bush was acquainted with Babbage's work, although he did make a reference to Babbage in his 1936 lecture on his differential analyzer.
3. Despite its name, it did not use the method of differences relied upon by Charles Babbage. It used a method mathematicians call integration.

and distances and, like the slide rule, performed computations with these measurements. The original Bush differential analyzer had six integrators, devices that handled the accumulation of numbers, the arithmetic control of the machine. They consisted of glass disks on movable tables. One set of measurements determined the movement of the table, another determined the rotation of the disk, and a metal wheel on the glass disk measured still a third variable by its distance from the disk. All of this was controlled by Niemann's torque amplifiers, which the mathematician Arthur Burks described as operating something like power steering on an automobile: they permitted the wheels and shafts running the differential analyzer to move easily without impermissible slippage. Since the physical movement of things in an analog computer is what does the computing, things must move precisely.

All of this was run by a collection of shafts and straps connected to servomotors through the torque amplifiers. The differential analyzer was purely mechanical; electricity was used only for powering the amplifiers, the shafts, and the printers.

Bush eventually produced several modifications to the original design. One was a clever improvement of the method used for driving the shaft that produced the printer results. Two polarized disks were mounted on the ends of the shaft and connected to a photoelectric cell. A light was shone down the shaft. If the two polaroid disks were aligned, the light registered on the cell; if they were in any other position, the cell recorded nothing.

While it was the best anyone had done so far, it was a sluggish, cumbersome, cranky gadget that frequently took two or three days to be set up for a problem. Each shaft and wheel had to be set very precisely for each problem. The number 1 would require a shaft and wheel in one position; a 9 would require another position. The x-axis would mean one combination, the y-axis another. The machine was terribly inefficient unless it was used to produce many solutions to a single set of equations. If the problem was long enough, requiring a run of days or weeks, the set-up time was considered acceptable. The longer the machine ran, the more likely it was that something would slip out of place, forcing the operators to stop the run and carefully fix the machine.

Bush recognized this shortcoming, and beginning in 1935 he began designing a second model of the differential analyzer. In this new version, some of the physical procedures were replaced or enhanced with electrical ones. Here the position of one shaft was reported to another shaft through electrical connections and a central switchboard. The switchboard was set, or programmed, using instructions from paper punch tape. The gear boxes were shifted electromagnetically with great precision. This process, too, was programmed by paper tape.

The new machine was much faster than the old one with eighteen integrators and room for twelve more. It was also more accurate, "making an error of one part per 25,000." Bush wrote:

The advantages of the new machine for handling short problems have clearly been demonstrated. In one actual case a fresh problem was brought to the machine in the morning and eight solutions were furnished during the day. Within all this time all preparatory work was done, including preparation of the assembly diagram and connection sheets, calculation of gear ratios and scale factors, and tape punching. . . . For average problems the machine is ready to run within about fifteen minutes after the tapes are available.

This incredible contraption weighed 100 tons and included 2,000 vacuum tubes, several thousand relays, 150 motors, and about 200 miles of wires.[4]

Despite its shortcomings, it was obvious to the scientific community that the differential analyzer was a valuable tool in certain instances. Several laboratories asked for plans, and duplicates of the differential analyzer were set up at the U.S. Army's Ballistics Research Laboratory at the Aberdeen Proving Ground, in Maryland, and at the Moore School of Electrical Engineering, at the University of Pennsylvania.[5]

The connection between Aberdeen and the Moore School

4. The differential analyzer had an unintended effect on research at MIT. Engineers there were diverted to analog computers, which kept them from performing research on digital machines, something that did not happen at the University of Pennsylvania, for reasons that will become clear later.
5. Another differential analyzer was built, with the aid of MIT plans, by Douglas R. Hartree at the University of Manchester, in England.

was providential. The reason for the tie had to do with ballistics.

No more complex—and to some, fascinating—problems confront the mathematician than those of ballistics, which deal with what happens to a shell from the moment it leaves the muzzle to the time it strikes its target.

There are two approaches to the problems: the mathematical and the practical. The mathematical approach goes back to Isaac Newton, who was fascinated by the influence of gravity and air resistance on the flight of projectiles. His legendary falling apple was just such a projectile. So are the balls Galileo dropped from the Leaning Tower of Pisa. Countless mathematicians have worked on the equations since Newton.[6]

The complications are enormous. For instance, consider the function of drag (air resistance). A number of variables must be taken into account when one figures drag. During World War I, the Germans designed a naval artillery piece that sent a projectile twice as far as the firing tables indicated it could. The problem was that the tables were based on the assumption that the air through which the projectile flew was of uniform density. In fact, that was not so. The projectile went so high that the shell spent a considerable part of its flight in air only half as dense as that at ground level. The German ordnance people used this knowledge to invent "Big Bertha," the huge and very accurate cannon that they fired at Paris.

At the practical level, armies had to produce firing tables so that their gunners could aim the cannons. During World War I, the U.S. Army had two units producing firing tables. One, under Forest Ray Moulton, was in Washington at the ballistics branch of the Office of the Chief of Ordnance. The other, under the eminent mathematician Oswald Veblen, was at Sandy Hook, New Jersey, and was later moved to Aberdeen. Their job was to test-fire the weapons and to produce firing tables for them.

"In principle, they knew how to make the tables, [but] you can't make the tables until you have the equipment," Goldstine explained years later. "The reason for it is that you have to have

6. In his *Principia* Newton wrote, "In mediums void of all tenacity, the resistances made to bodies are as the square of the velocity."

a separate table for every gun, projectile, fuse combination. If you change the fuse, or you change the shell, you change the firing table, because there is a fundamental physical constant called the ballistic coefficient which is associated with that projectile-fuse combination.

"You can only get that coefficient by actual physical experiment, and so those physical experiments were done at Aberdeen by firing . . . shells."

The tables had to consider such things as the hardness of the ground under the canon, atmospheric pressure, and even, to some extent, the Coriolus effect, the effect on objects moving on a rotating planet. For all these reasons the ordnance experts at Aberdeen asked Bush for a differential analyzer.

The request from the Moore School was simpler to understand. The Moore School was generally considered to rank second only to MIT as the leading engineering school in the nation. Its scientists and engineers had the same reasons for wanting a differential analyzer as did those at MIT.

In order to get funds to build the differential analyzer, the Moore School sought out the Civil Works Administration, a Depression-era agency. The CWA agreed to fund a differential analyzer if it was sponsored by another government agency. Harold Pender, the dean of the Moore School, got in touch with the people at the ballistics lab at Aberdeen, who agreed to act as sponsor if Pender, in turn, agreed that in case of a national emergency Aberdeen could take over the machine. Pender also agreed to help Aberdeen build its copy.

The agreement was of great importance. First, it provided for a differential analyzer in the Moore School, which gave the engineers there a feel for computing. Second, it gave the University of Pennsylvania its first real experience with government research grants, rare in those days when liberal-arts faculties dominated universities.

What the Moore School people built was much larger than Bush's MIT machine. No rivalry was then involved; MIT engineers traveled to Philadelphia to help the Moore School engineers build their differential analyzer. The Moore School plans were sent on to Aberdeen so that the machine could be built.[7] The Moore School differential analyzer was completed in 1935. The engineer placed in charge of the construction and operation was Cornelius Weygandt.

"It worked on the principle of the winch," Weygandt recalled. "It was very ingenious but very tricky and hard to adjust. It was very sensitive to humidity; the bands would slip when it got damp. . . . In the first stage [the bands] were fish line. We got it from a fish store. The second [stage] was a steel band covered with a webbing material which was impregnated with the same stuff they use for brake lining in automobiles. We had to make these things up. We got the steel bands from one place and the webbing from another. We threaded the webbing on the bands and sent it out to some firm in Philadelphia which impregnated it with the brake compound."

A one-quarter-horsepower engine was sufficient to drive the Moore School differential analyzer. The engineers had the advantage of being able to learn from MIT's mistakes, so that they could make the machine much larger and more reliable. It took two years to build, and it was placed in the basement of the Moore School building in the old boiler room. The university allowed outside scientists, as well as Moore School engineers, time on the machine. Like the MIT machine, it became a resource for the scientific and engineering community.

The differential analyzer was not the only attempt at scientific computing during years before World War II, because the need for assistance was too great and the differential analyzer was quite limited in its functions.

One firm that sorely needed computing ability was the telephone company. Scientists and engineers at the Bell Telephone Laboratories, the American Telephone & Telegraph's splendid research facility in New Jersey, worked on digital devices, machines that counted digits, not movement or placement.

When someone dials a normal rotary telephone, a number is transmitted to the switching devices, which had become automated since 1903. It was determined that the decimal system

7. Moreover, about half a dozen other differential analyzers were built in Great Britain, Germany, and the Soviet Union during the 1930s.

took too much time and effort, so the Bell System developed machines that converted each digit to a four-pulse code. Considering even that wasteful, the Bell scientists began studying binary systems—counting systems made up of only two numbers, usually a 1 and a 0.

The use of binary numbers is, of course, crucial to the story of computers. The usefulness of such a system was already appreciated by Leibniz, but it reached real scientific respectability with the work of George Boole, a self-taught English mathematician of the nineteenth century. In 1854 Boole proposed making use of two digits for a new form of algebra and logic.

In Boolean algebra, 1 stood for things, anything being studied, while the 0 stood for nothing, or the absence of the thing being studied. There are, additionally, two functions in Boolean algebra, the plus and the multiplication sign, the dot. As Goldstine has explained, if x stands for black things and y stands for cows, then $x \cdot y$ or xy stands for black cows; xy is something that has the properties of both x and y. The plus sign stands for the addition of two things that normally do not modify each other. For instance, if x stands for men and y stands for women, then $x + y$ equals men and women. If z stands for Americans then $z(x + y)$ equals American men and women. All this would be expressed in equations making use of just the 1 and 0. It is not necessary to go more deeply into the subject; it is fairly easy to see how a system of logic was reduced to mathematical symbols.

To Bell Labs scientists such as George R. Stibitz, Boolean algebra, with both its logic and its binary system, represented a rational path to follow in designing circuitry for automatic switching machines and, Stibitz noted, for doing computation. Engineers had already developed a relay called a flip-flop, which could count either the presence or the absence of a current. The relay was a metal bar attached to a spring, triggered by a magnet when electricity passed through it. This relay seemed well suited for both tasks. The relays were connected to each other, so that if two relays were closed by an electric current, a third relay (representing the sum) closed to keep the answer. If the relays for 3 and 2 were closed, the relay denoting 5 closed.

Stibitz's computer converted decimal numbers to binary dig-

its and then reconverted them at the other end, producing decimal answers. He called his first machine the Complex Number
Computer. He built it in 1937, mostly on his kitchen table. A
Bell engineer, Samuel B. Williams, added push buttons to the
device to make it simpler to operate, and in October 1939 it was
finished and sent to Bell Labs' New York City office.

Stibitz felt the device was important enough to be shown off.
He arranged for a demonstration at a meeting of the American
Mathematical Association at Dartmouth College, in New Hamp-
shire, on September 11, 1940. Using a teleprinter, he had mathematicians at the meeting pose problems to the computer back
in New York City. Answers came flying back on the telephone-
line hookup within one minute, in what was the first example of
remote computing. The mathematicans were awed. Stibitz built
a number of other machines during World War II, all based on
mechanical relays.

The idea of electromechanical computers occurred also to a
Harvard graduate student named Howard H. Aiken. Aiken was
a professor at the University of Miami and owned his own company, but he went to Harvard for his Ph.D. In 1937 he set down
some thoughts on what the ideal computer ought to be. He said
it would have the ability to handle negative as well as positive
numbers, to utilize most mathematical functions, to operate
automatically, and to carry out calculations in the normal mathematical sequence. He proposed to modify standard IBM punch
card technology for just such a computer. Essentially, he proposed a marriage between the ideas of Babbage and Hollerith,
for his machine was an electromechanical Analytical Engine with
IBM card handling.

Aiken took his idea to one of his professors, T. H. Brown,
who took him to the astronomer Wallace Eckert,[8] at the Watson
Computing Bureau, at Columbia University, which was established by Thomas Watson, Sr. An alliance was formed between
Aiken, Harvard, and IBM's Clair D. Lake to build Aiken's
machine. Work began in 1939.

The machine was called the IBM Automatic Sequence Con-

8. He was no relation to J. Presper Eckert, who will appear in the next chapter.

trolled Calculator (ASCC), or the Mark I. It contained seventy-two counters for storing numbers, each holding twenty-three digits plus a function sign. It received instructions by punch tape, and data by punch cards. Each instruction consisted of twenty-four binary digits. There were sixty registers controlled by manual switches. Each wheel was on a rotating shaft connected by a clutch so that it could be set at a predetermined position. Electrical contacts were used to sense the number on the wheel. Clutches then transferred the number to a second wheel as needed by the calculation. Three units were used for multiplication, twelve for division, and three for logarithms, exponentials, and trigonometric functions. The ASCC could add or subtract two numbers of twenty-three digits in three-tenths of a second, multiply them in four seconds, and divide them in ten, a little faster than the speed Babbage had estimated. Output was either by punch card or by teleprinter. Aiken also used relays, and someone remarked that when the ASCC was working full tilt it sounded like "a room of ladies knitting." The ASCC was not elegant; it had more than 750,000 parts.

Aiken's machine, finished in 1944, was the first automatic computer. Very fast for its time, it could handle six months' worth of calculations in one day, Aiken said. Charles Babbage would have been proud. Aiken himself admitted that "if Babbage had lived 75 years later, I would have been out of a job."

Like the differential analyzer and Stibitz's computer, his machine was a very clever device, but all electromechanical computers were essentially dinosaurs and dead ends. A number of scientists and engineers were already working on the idea of using electronics—an idea that would trigger a revolution.

In Ames, Iowa, a mathematician and physicist named John Vincent Atanasoff was thinking about electronics as well. Atanasoff is one of the most controversial people in the history of the computer; his role is obscured by time, by conflict, by clashing egos. It is difficult to place him in the proper perspective. Simply put, Atanasoff either is or is not the inventor of the first electronic digital special-purpose computer.

Atanasoff was born in 1904, the son of a Bulgarian immigrant, Ivan, known as John. Ivan was an engineer and worked in a phosphate mine in Florida. Atanasoff retains the soft Florida accent.

According to Atanasoff, he began tinkering with his father's slide rule at the age of nine. "I went to work on the slide rule—vigorously—I don't know why. I'd study the slide rule and then go out and play baseball and come back and study the slide rule. And boy, could I read! From the very beginning, could I read!"

His mother helped him with his mathematics, and the rest he later claimed to have taught himself. "She didn't know logarithms, so I got that out of the book. I studied physics. I studied chemistry. Nineteen-thirteen, and I was less than ten."[9]

"By the time I was in high school, I decided to become a theoretical physicist. I was absolutely sure. . . . I studied physics and I studied chemistry. I could see a place there, and that's what I wanted to be."

Atanasoff went to the University of Florida, earning a degree in electrical engineering and a graduate assistantship at Iowa State College (now Iowa State University) for $800 a year. In 1929 he got a master's degree in mathematics, with a minor in physics. He went to the University of Wisconsin for his Ph.D. in physics, after which he returned to Ames with a joint appointment in mathematics and physics. "I didn't know any electronics, so I studied electronics," he said.

"I have been an agnostic since the age of six. If I were a good Methodist, I would say that divine guidance led me on. As I look back over it, I could see the bits commence to come together," he said. He began using vacuum tubes to build radios, he remembered, and started thinking about using current punch card technology for scientific work. He concluded that "the future lay with digital computers. It was nonsense to build an analog [computer]."[10] He said that at one time he went to Washington to confer with Bush about his ideas but that Bush had nothing to say.

9. In 1982, when I interviewed Atanasoff in his home, his mother, aged 101, was still alive and in reasonably good health.
10. Atanasoff claims to have invented the word *analog* as it pertains to computers.

Atanasoff's goal was to build a machine that could solve partial differential equations digitally and electronically. "I needed a computer, and I needed a computer very, very badly," he recalled.

"I was wondering how I could go, how it can work. I tried and tried and tried to find anything that would do the job, that would be adequate for the job. I had graduate students working on the field using Monroe calculators. . . . I investigated every possible machine. I investigated everything. By that time I found out that it had to [use] a base 2."

One winter afternoon in 1938, Atanasoff said, he found he was stumped. "I was so nervous I couldn't sit still. I went out and got my car and did something I did in those days. . . . I started to drive." He drove the 189 miles from Ames across the Mississippi River into Illinois, then stopped in a bar and had a bourbon and soda. "That moment I knew that my mind was better than it had ever been. I had just one thing to think about, and that was computers."

He drove back to Ames, he said, with a clearer idea for an electronic computer.

"One kind of memory I wanted to use was a magnetic memory, but then I decided not to use a magnetic memory, because I knew the level would be too low and I couldn't afford the vacuum tubes; money was very scarce. I was, at that time, making $2,300 for ten months' work. . . .

"My additions and subtractions, and consequently multiplications and divisions, were to be done by a box, and inside that box it had vacuum tubes; that's all I knew about the inner workings at that time."

By this time Atanasoff had acquired a brilliant young graduate student named Clifford Berry. He and Berry went to work on a computing machine in the spring of 1939 and had a prototype working that fall, he said. "It worked. Boy, it worked!"

Atanasoff had built a small device that did arithmetic electronically. He was probably the first person in the world to have done that. But what he designed was not yet a computer, and his goals were somewhat limited. At least at that stage, Atanasoff thought only of a machine that solved particular kinds of differential equations. His prototype was a complex device that did simple arithmetic. Even he admitted later, "People would come to see us, and they couldn't understand how so much apparatus [was needed] to do simple additions and subtraction. I knew it was something new." He said it did just what he had intended it to do. He and Berry decided it was time to convert the prototype into a large working computer.

Atanasoff's design was ingenious. He used electrical capacitors, which can store an electrical charge,[11] to store numbers mounted on two Bakelite drums eight inches in diameter and eleven inches long. Each drum could store thirty binary numbers of fifty binary digits (bits) each on a band of contacts. The numbers could be read off as the drums rotated. There were thirty add-subtract units, also electronic.

Input was on base-10 punch cards, five numbers per card. Each number consisted of fifteen digits and a sign. A keyboard was available as an alternative. The arithmetic was done after the numbers had been converted to binary numbers. Operation was manual: an operator pushed a button indicating where numbers were to go, placed a card in the holder, and closed the contact. Rows of brushes read the card. To store intermediate results, Atanasoff devised a system in which electric sparks charred cards at appropriate places. Since the charred, or carbonized, areas had less electrical resistance, it was possible to read the card by applying electricity to the card.

The difficulty in putting this into historical perspective arises because Atanasoff and Berry never actually produced a complete working computer. They abandoned the project for war work before it was finished.

Arthur Burks has said that Atanasoff "had succeeded in designing and building an electronic computer whose computing system worked," only the binary card punching system failed. Hence Burks has called Atanasoff "the inventor of the first electronic computer." But Isaac Auerbach, who "discovered" Atanasoff three decades later and is responsible for bringing him to public attention, said that "Atanasoff built pieces. They talked

11. Sometimes called Leyden jars.

about components of the computer. He built a memory drum, he built arithmetic units. He never built a computer. . . . it was never assembled into a computer." Goldstine has written that Atanasoff as machine "never saw the light of day as a serious tool for computation since it was somewhat premature in its engineering conception and limited in its logical one."

The word *inventor* seems to be the key. Auerbach's company studied Atanasoff's plans in the late 1960s and concluded that the design would probably have produced an electronic special-purpose machine. History is replete with inventors whose innovations brought them to the edge of discovery and proud feats but who narrowly missed succeeding. The evidence indicates that Atanasoff fits into this category and that the Atanasoff-Berry computer was a clever near-miss.

All of this is only the beginning of the controversy surrounding the work of Atanasoff.

In December 1940 Atanasoff traveled to Philadelphia to the annual meeting of the American Association for the Advancement of Science, held at Bennett Hall, on the campus of the University of Pennsylvania. He found himself in the audience of a talk by a physicist from Ursinus College, Collegeville, Pennsylvania, a small school about forty miles outside of Philadelphia. The speaker was named John Mauchly, and he was discussing the potential use of analog computing machines in working out problems in meteorology.

John William Mauchly was a second-generation scientist, part of that gentleman class which ran American science in the first half of the twentieth century. His father was a physicist. Although Mauchly was born in Cincinnati in 1907, his father went to work for the Carnegie Institution of Washington as head of the Department of Terrestrial Magnetism, and Mauchly grew up in Washington's Maryland suburbs. He, like apparently everyone else in this story, was a precocious child, forever sticking his fingers into things, taking things apart, exploring.

He claimed to have had his first experience with electricity at the age of five when he fashioned a flashlight with a dry cell, a bulb, and a socket in order to explore a dark attic with a friend.

The friend's mother feared that this unholy gadget would start a fire, so she took the flashlight from him and gave him a candle. In grade school, he earned money installing electric doorbells for neighbors. He loved to read in bed. He rigged a trigger on the stairs so that when his mother walked up to make sure he was sleeping, his reading light was automatically turned off. When she went back downstairs, the light came on again.

Mauchly enrolled in the engineering school at Johns Hopkins University, in Baltimore, but switched to physics when engineering bored him. He received his Ph.D. in physics in 1932, stayed a year as a research associate, and then went looking for a job.

"When I got my first job out of school, . . . everybody thought I was damn lucky . . . because there was a depression," he said years later. "The job was at Ursinus. All I was supposed to do was teach physics, but it's always a good idea for people to keep their interests in research and scholarship and all that, no matter what you're doing for a living."

The problem was that his research required complicated and expensive equipment, which was available to him at Hopkins but which Ursinus could not afford and saw no reason to obtain.

"The . . . thing I had been doing at Hopkins was compute for finding the energies which are characteristic of molecules and tell you how they work. So I decided I would do some computation on energy levels, and that the crying need to my mind was [to do] one computation to end all computation on this particular problem," he said. "There had been some theoretical work done that enabled you to do that computation, and I started to do some of it at Hopkins when I got this job at Ursinus. So I bought myself an old [Marchant] adding machine, which was cheap because a bank had failed in Philadelphia, and for seventy-five bucks I got what would have otherwise been a $1,000 machine."

He found that a professor at Penn and a scientist at the Arthur D. Little company had already computed some of the equations using either the differential analyzer or IBM punch card equipment. He had been outclassed, so he changed the goal of his research to meteorology.

"What I started to do was to put some statistics together which would enable weather predictions to be improved. I strongly believed, and I still believe, that it's possible by statistical analysis to do a lot to improve weather predictions."

Essentially, Mauchly believed that the cycles of the sun played a large part in terrestrial weather. The seed of the idea came from his father's work at Carnegie and from the cosmic-ray research done by a friend of his father at the Bartol Foundation of the Franklin Institute, at nearby Swarthmore College. He collected all the data he could and put graduate students to work on them using office adding machines. The students were paid fifty cents an hour by the National Youth Administration. "The students were math students who preferred that to raking leaves," he said.

"Apparently there was a recurrence relationship, a quasi-persistence, to be very fancy about it, in the weather, particularly in rainfall, precipitation, that tended to be every thirteen or fourteen days. ... There were other people who had already, with proper scientific recognition, proved that the sun rotates in twenty-nine-day [cycles]. Half periods of solar rotation would likely turn up in sunspots and magnetism and other effects from the sun, so I thought this was a pretty good indication that the sunspots or some other agent on the sun could influence the weather." He acknowledged that most meteorologists considered this a crackpot notion.[12]

To make any sense out of these data and to support his point, he needed a computer. He had no money. Ursinus had a budget for teaching, not for research. "No way could I stretch the truth," he said; he could only buy vacuum tubes for teaching purposes. "Some of these things could be used experimentally to try out a few ... methods of what we called counting circuits."

"In fact binary counters and vacuum tubes were already known to me; they existed in cosmic-ray labs [like his father's]; they existed over there in Bartol at Swarthmore. So I thought, see, if they could count at something like a million per second with

12. Many of them still do; the possibility of solar influence on weather remains a topic of considerable debate in the meteorological community, and Mauchly experimented with the idea until his death.

vacuum tubes; why it's sort of silly to use these punch card machines, which can only do maybe a hundred cards a minute and don't seem to do much at that. I went, for instance, in 1939, to the world's fair in New York, and I spent several days up there looking at machines which Remington Rand and IBM had on exhibit. The only thing that they could do very impressively was—Rand had a multiplying device which could multiply six digits by six digits—decimal digits these are—and punch the results back on a punch card at a rate of something like a hundred a minute. IBM took five or six seconds to do multiplication.

"I was interested in all these things; how could I multiply faster? One clue to faster, certainly, is use electrons. When I looked around to see what [there] was I could do cheaply, why I sort of got put off into gas tubes because you didn't have to supply much power to them."

He began building electronic counting devices, positive that this was how computing would have to be done. Because he had little money, he used neon tubes. RCA had demonstrated that these kinds of tubes worked, and they were cheaper than vacuum tubes although much slower, emitting about 200 pulses a second. They could be triggered by very weak radio signals and could be connected to relays. He went out and bought as many of these 0A46 tubes as he could afford. He also "borrowed" some from students' radios that had been brought to his shop to be fixed. His idea originally was to take an ordinary desk calculator and replace the mechanical parts with electronics. It would be a decimal machine because it was easier for his students to handle decimal numbers; converting to binary was convenient for the machine, not the user.

He built several small devices. One was called his railroad signal.[13] The tubes were put in wooden blocks and were set up as "flip-flops." If a signal was sent into the circuits, one side of the device lit; if the current was interrupted, the other side lit—a binary counter. He then built a cryptographic device that he tried to peddle to the War Department, but it was rejected because it was not portable. It used base 3.

13. Most of these devices are at Mauchly's house in Ambler, Pennsylvania. His work is also remembered by his former students.

"I tried to make a circuit which would be part of a computer which would store the numbers and advance on counts . . . except this was on the cheap." He designed one device that came close: "a board with five tubes [with a sixth socket for a spare] and the tubes would interact with each other. . . . When one tube went on, it would turn off the others and so on, but connected around a ring of five [so that I] could count up to five. Combining them with a binary counter, which I could do cheaply . . . then I would have a decimal system, a counting system, not for peanuts, but for something on the order of $1 for each of these tubes, maybe $10 for the whole thing." He also bought an oscilloscope in order to watch what happened to the voltage, and a 6L76 glass tube in order to form pulses and test the counter.

"I could count with these glass-tube counters at least 500 times a second; it began to be a little doubtful as to whether they would be able to work reliably at higher rates, and that really didn't concern me too much then."

There exist at least two letters to friends in which he described what he really wanted: an electronic computer.

. . . We are now considering construction of an electrical computing machine to obtain sums of squares and cross-products as rapidly as the number can be punched into the machine. The machine would perform its operations in about 1/200 second, using vacuum tube relays, and yielding mathmatically [*sic*] exact, not approximate, results. . . . With conventional tubes it would be rather bulky, but special tubes could be designed to make it very compact.

Since none of this solved his weather-prediction problem, he built an analog device called a harmonic analyzer, which was perfect for measuring changes in data. He actually built several, using tubes in little boxes.[14]

He was still frustrated, in part because he did not understand electronics. He signed up for a course at Penn, hoping it would teach him what he needed to know, but was disappointed. A second try at Penn also failed, when the course was canceled

14. His work on electronic circuits at Ursinus was ignored by the court in the subsequent patent case because the lawyers thought it unimportant. In fact, it is vital to an understanding of what happened next and what Atanasoff's true role was.

because of insufficient enrollment. The only advantage Mauchly received from his visits to Philadelphia was that he met Irven Travis, a professor at the Moore School who was also interested in computing. Travis wanted to build an electronic differential analyzer.

Mauchly was increasingly frustrated at his lack of research money at Ursinus and was then looking for a way to get out. He received a few feelers from industry, and a friend, Carl Chambers, tried to convince him to make the jump. Mauchly even considered a teaching job at a Hazleton, Pennsylvania, high school. But he wanted to remain in academe and started working as a consultant to make some extra money. He had heard about another course at the Moore School, and now applied.

Mauchly was at this stage when he gave his paper on weather statistics to the American Association for the Advancement of Science. He was at the physics section because he was convinced the meteorologists would not take data from the harmonic analyzer seriously. No matter what he showed, unless he could explain the mechanism for solar influence on weather, he would be ignored.

When the speech was over, a man from the back of the room came up to Mauchly, introduced himself as John Atanasoff, and said that he too was interested in computing—that he was, in fact, building a computer using vacuum tubes at Iowa State. He told Mauchly he could do it for $2 a digit. Mauchly was paying $10.

(From this moment on in the history of the computer, there is very little with which everyone will agree; there exist at least two versions of almost everything.)

Atanasoff invited Mauchly to visit him at Ames. According to Atanasoff, Mauchly discussed only his work using analog computers, that is, the harmonic analyzer. He said nothing about digital computing or his work on digital counters, Atanasoff later maintained.

"I think he lies when he says he built a digital computer before that," Atanasoff stated. "It was an artificial construct after the time. That's what I think. That's what I believe." In fact, Mauchly never claimed he had built an electronic computer before that time; he claimed, with significant supporting evidence, he had built digital counters with vacuum tubes and had rejected any notion of an analog machine to solve the problems he needed to solve.

Why Mauchly kept his digital work secret from Atanasoff is a mystery—if that is, in fact, what he did. In a letter to a friend, dated December 1940 (i.e., before the trip to Iowa), he wrote:

> For your own private information, I expect to have, in a year or so, when I can get the stuff and put it together, an electronic computing machine, which will have the answer as fast as the buttons can be depressed. The secret lies in "scaling circuits," of course. Keep this dark, since I haven't the equipment this year to carry it out and I would like to "be the first."

Perhaps he did not want Atanasoff to know what he was working on. But there is no reason why he should have wanted to keep a secret at that stage.

Whatever else Mauchly said, he accepted the invitation to Ames. A trip to Collegeville by Atanasoff never materialized, and a meeting in Washington later in the year failed. Several letters mention Atanasoff's computer. In one letter, Atanasoff tells Mauchly he was doing some national-defense work and had received a visit from Samuel Caldwell, of MIT, one of the designers of Bush's new differential analyzer. He wrote that he now believed he could convert his new computer (the Atanasoff-Berry Computer, or ABC) into an integraph, an electronic digital machine that did the same thing as the differential analyzer. He said it would be just as fast as Bush's machine and much more accurate.

A physics meeting took place at the University of Iowa in June, and Mauchly found two friends who needed transportation to the Midwest and were prepared to share the gas costs. He packed the passengers and his young son, James, into his car and drove to Iowa, arriving there on June 14, 1941. He and his son stayed at Atanasoff's house. Again, Atanasoff later insisted, Mauchly said nothing about digital computing.

"If he had done such things, he would have told me about them at the time," Atanasoff held. "He was out there as my friend.

He almost would have to, wouldn't he? We were talking about computers."

Berry put together a demonstration using some of the pieces of ABC to perform simple arithmetic functions. According to Atanasoff, Mauchly "expressed joy at the results." That is not how Mauchly described what he saw.

"I found that although he used vacuum tubes—and he did do it relatively cheaply—why he lost the advantage of vacuum tubes because he wasn't doing it fast," Mauchly said years later. "There are trade-offs which you've got to take into account, that if you're going to do this thing electronically, why you might as well have the advantage of the vacuum tubes . . . and for the same money you might produce 10, 20, 100 times as much." The machine was also manual, and that slowed down its operation.

Mauchly said, moreover, Atanasoff had told him he and Berry had not been able to make flip-flops work reliably, something Mauchly had done at Ursinus.

Atanasoff said Mauchly was fascinated. Mauchly said he saw immediately he had wasted his time. Atanasoff showed him a written description of the machine, but Mauchly said he did not bother to read it, since he could put any questions he wanted directly to Atanasoff.

Mauchly's trip was cut short when his wife called to inform him he had been accepted at the Moore School, as a student in the course on defense electronics. He gladly left Ames and drove north.

Mauchly turned down the high-school job at Hazleton and visited the American Optical Company plant in Southbridge, Massachusetts, for a job interview. He wrote to Atanasoff:

On the way back east a lot of ideas came barging into my consciousness, but I haven't had time to sift them or organize them. They were on the subject of computing devices, of course. If any of them look promising, you may hear more later.

Mauchly did not know it at the time, but the trip to Iowa may very well have been one of the worst mistakes of his life.

5. Eckert and Mauchly

Simon, give Goldstine the money!
OSWALD VEBLEN

FEW CITIES IN AMERICA have been molded by the work and genius of one man as much as Philadelphia has been influenced by Benjamin Franklin. This consummate American, who came to Philadelphia from his native Boston as a young man, left his mark on much of what is old and valuable about his adopted city. From the fire department and the insurance plaques on the eighteenth-century houses to the splendid library and America's first (and still operating) hospital, many of Philadelphia's finest institutions were founded by Franklin. His exploits continue to be taught in the city's schools with reverence. His grave, in a Chestnut Street cemetery, accessible to passersby, collects thousands of pennies on the grave marker for local charities. Philadelphia remains very much his city.

One exploit and one institution in Philadelphia are pertinent to our story. In 1740 Franklin founded the Charity School of Philadelphia, and nine years later, in his "Proposals Relating to the Education of Youth in Pennsylvania," he urged that the students of the school be taught carefully what was really important in the world.

> As to their Studies, it would be very well if they could be taught every Thing that is useful, and every Thing that is ornamental: But Art is long, and their Time is short. It is therefore propos'd that they learn those Things that are likely to be most useful and most ornamental, Regard being had to the several Professions for which they are intended.

In 1752 Franklin and a young assistant walked outside during a thunderstorm near the school he had founded. Franklin attached a key to the thread of a kite and launched the kite toward a blackening cloud. A bolt of lightning hit the kite, traveled down the thread, and caused a spark to jump from the key. The experiment demonstrated two things: first, that Franklin was not always as bright as he thought he was (that he was not instantly fried was a matter of pure luck), and, second, that lightning and electricity were one and the same, a discovery which led immediately to his invention of the lightning rod and which was a first step toward taming electricity.

The institution that began as the Charity School of Philadelphia became the University of Pennsylvania, which grew into one of the most respected universities in America. One of its schools is dedicated to applying electricity to human uses. In 1922 Alfred Fitler Moore, the third-generation proprietor of a company that produced insulated electric wire,[1] died and left in his will the request that a school for the "proper education and instruction of young people in the science of electrical engineering and its cognate branches" be formed in honor of his parents. Given the bequest, the University of Pennsylvania organized the Moore School of Electrical Engineering in 1923. The Moore School operates as an independent organization within the university.

By the end of the 1930s, the University of Pennsylvania had long since established its outstanding reputation as a liberal-arts, Ivy League university, but the Moore School, like most engi-

---

1. The company provided the wire for Samuel Morse's experiments with telegraphy and transmitted the famous "What hath God wrought" message.

neering schools, lived deep in the shadow of MIT and the California Institute of Technology. The Moore School was respected, but it lacked the prestige of MIT, especially within the scientific community. To a great extent, this lack of prestige, and the institutional inertia that sometimes goes with it, provided the Moore School with a considerable advantage in what was to happen there in the early 1940s.

As far as John Mauchly knew as he drove east from Iowa in June of 1941, he was going to attend a summer defense-training course. "The government, in its wisdom, decided that with war breaking out all over in Europe, it was just a matter of time before we got into it," Mauchly said years later. "You couldn't call it 'war training'; you have to call it 'defense training.' Fifty or sixty graduates in math, physics, and whatever had their tuition paid in a course given at the Moore School to work them into electronic engineers."

Downstairs at the Moore School's red-brick-and-marble building on Walnut and Thirty-third, Mauchly found that Cornelius Weygandt and his staff were nursing the differential analyzer. In 1940, when President Roosevelt declared a national emergency, Aberdeen exercised its rights under the contract with the Moore School. Weygandt was working on a problem for a researcher at Harvard when two people showed up—a man with a bad limp, and a woman. They announced that they had come to take over the differential analyzer. The man carried a foot-operated calculating machine. The two also brought a diagram drawn from the Aberdeen machine. Weygandt was ordered to set up the Moore School analyzer exactly the way the diagram and its complete instructions dictated. Weygandt took a look at the directions and protested.

"I knew that our machine had left-handed screws on the output tables . . . because then it made [a] plot in the conventional way. Aberdeen had a right-handed screw, so all their plots were backwards," Weygandt remembered. He offered to set up his machine with altered gears to reverse the shafts, but the man from Aberdeen, a civil servant to the end, told him, "No, I can't do that. My orders are to put it on exactly according to this diagram."

"I said, 'All right, but it won't work.' So we put it on, and of course it didn't work. The Aberdeen people went back to Maryland and had their orders changed." And the differential analyzer went to war.

The Ballistics Research Laboratory at Aberdeen, under Cols. Leslie Simon and Paul Gillon, both of whom held master's degrees from MIT, also instituted a program to speed up long ballistics tabulation. They began looking for young women with math training who could be taught how to compute the equations manually. Half of the program was to be at Aberdeen, the other half at Philadelphia. Philadelphia was considered a prime source of these women because it had the highest concentration of colleges and universities in America. Women were sought because the able-bodied and able-minded men were all about to be drafted. The Moore School, an all-male domain until then, began to turn coeducational.

Research at the Moore School was directed by John Grist Brainerd, known informally by his middle name. Under him, the university was beginning to get into the business of government research contracts, but only hesitantly and somewhat reluctantly. In 1940 the Moore School received a navy contract to help design airborne minesweepers (aircraft would dangle wires containing direct current in the water as they flew over the ocean, hoping to detonate mines—but it didn't work). By and large, however, the University of Pennsylvania and the Moore School had not been interested in getting into the kind of big-time research that made MIT famous. Now it was getting a close look at government contracts. More important to what followed, Brainerd was getting intimate with Simon and Gillon and the Aberdeen establishment.

When Mauchly arrived for the defense course, he found that there were only two Ph.D.'s in the class—he and a logician-mathematician from Michigan, Arthur Burks. He also found that the experiments required for the course were the same ones he had ordered up from his students at Ursinus. He was in great danger of wasting his time until he met the laboratory instructor, a twenty-two-year-old graduate student named J. Presper Eckert, Jr.

The two men, twelve years apart in age, were not much alike, but they were made for each other.

Eckert was the son of a prominent family of real-estate developers and builders in the Philadelphia area. His uncle was the contractor for the Reading Terminal, a huge building in Center City[2] which houses the terminal for commuter trains from the suburbs on the top floors, and a large farmer's market, with produce mainly from Amish farms, on the street level. Eckert's father built in southern New Jersey. Eckert himself, as is true of many in the story of the computer, appears to have been a born engineer.

"I was an only child. My family traveled a lot," Eckert said. "By the time I was twelve, I had traveled about 100,000 miles— without airplanes. I had been to every state of the union.

"When I was twelve years old, I saw a little boat in Luna Park in Paris. They had a thing where you could turn a wheel and steer a little boat around the pond controlled by a magnet underneath. I came home with Erector-set parts and balsa wood and glass and pieces of old trains and motors and odds and ends, and I built one. . . . It had cables and switches and wires. I put it in a hobby fair . . . and won first prize. In fact the prize was a rowing machine, which is still sitting there in our basement.

"When I was eight or nine years old, I built a crystal set on top of a lead pencil. I took the eraser out and put a crystal on top of it, and wound the coil around the pencil. I built radios by the time I was twelve that had two tubes in them. When I was fourteen, I built the amplifiers. By the time I was in high school, I built a hi-fi at Penn Charter[3] . . . for the music department. By the time I was graduated from . . . school, I was building sound systems for cemeteries." He built a sound system for Laurel Hill cemetery, because the proprietors did not like mourners in the chapel to hear the roar of the crematorium next door. Eckert put speakers in the stone of the building, and the music drowned out, or at least distracted, patrons from the cremations. Outdoor

2. Philadelphians never refer to the downtown area as "downtown." The downtown area is called Center City. "Downtown," to a native, is South Philadelphia, the ethnic, mainly Italian section that houses the great Italian Market and the sports stadiums.
3. An excellent and expensive private school in the city.

systems played chimes to make it sound as if a cathedral were nearby.

Eckert's mother doted on him. She persuaded his father not to let him go to MIT, because she did not want him to leave home. The elder Eckert made up the excuse that he did not have enough money. When the son found out about the lie, he was "sore as hell," and "the net effect of making me mad was that my grades went to pieces the first year [at Penn], and then they slowly recovered." He learned his stubbornness, which would be a major characteristic throughout his life, from his father.

"My father, as a young man, down in Cape May [New Jersey] had 100 men working for him, 40 skilled workmen. He carried the money for these 100 people in his belt. He had a couple of knives thrown at him. So he gets out a small pistol, a show pistol, nickel-plated, and you use for stunts. He got all of his men together in front of this old boarded-up hotel . . . which they had rehabilitated. (The hotel had probably been a fancy bordello back in the turn of the century. It had a forty-foot mahogany bar in it.) He said, 'My hobby is target shooting, tricks with guns. I thought you'd be amused to see me demonstrate my hobby. . . .' He put the bottles and cans on the fence and shot them from his hip. He got some guy to throw some cans, and he shot the cans with his pistol. After this he just carried this gun in a leather holster for the several years he was down there and never had any trouble."

The young Eckert was drawn to electrical engineering, and Philadelphia was the center of the American electrical business in the years before World War II. The Radio Corporation of America (RCA) was across the Delaware River in Camden, New Jersey. The Columbia Broadcasting System (CBS) was founded at radio station WCAU. Philco, which built 40 percent of the radios for America, was located at Ninth Street and Tioga Avenue. Atwater Kent was located in the city, and the slightly mad genius Philo T. Farnsworth had a laboratory on Greene Street, within a mile of the Eckert residence. Farnsworth was an inventor of television and ran the first television station in the country.

"I had a television set," Eckert said. "Just before the war broke out, RCA built some experimental ones. I hooked up one of those for sixty bucks and got it to work. We had the only stations in the country here. Farnsworth had a station up in Chestnut Hill. We would listen to television, and they would announce that they had run out of shows. We would call them up, and they would say, 'If you got some guys who could put on a play or a spelling bee, come on over.' Some of our friends would come over to my house and watch, and some of us would go over to the station to put on a show for the other guys to watch. I had the background of seeing a lot of things beginning to happen in this area."

He was clearly the brightest graduate student at the Moore School, and he spent his summers consulting for industrial firms and using electronic measurement devices. He and Mauchly quickly became friends. Mauchly had been trying to interest members of the Moore School faculty in electronic computing. He could see the trouble the Moore School was having coping with the work load. It was not that Mauchly was eager to build an electronic computer but that he wanted to use one. Mauchly found little enthusiasm. Eckert, on the other hand, simply said he could see no reason that electronic computing could not be feasible. Mauchly had his first attentive ear. The men would meet in the early hours of the morning, either in their rooms, with Eckert characteristically squatting on a table top, or over coffee or sundaes at Linton's, an all-night restaurant on Market Street, near the Penn campus.

"We would sit around the lab table, dangling our legs, spending the hours talking about what we were interested in. Funny, I don't remember what Eckert was interested in," Mauchly said years later, in an interview with Esther Carr. "But there was no doubt that he had a patent already, and that was very impressive, a patent in television, a method of scanning television tubes by defraction of sound waves. . . . He was twelve years younger than I.

"I get asked quite often, was he one of my students? Sometimes I answered, 'No, I was his student.'

"I wanted to know what could be done about building computers with electronic vacuum tubes as the main elements to get some speed, and as I talked to Eckert about this, as I certainly

did then, I was considerably cheered up because he thought this
was a very sensible idea. Why not do things like this? It didn't
seem to him to be beyond possibility at all. He didn't say he knew
the answer; it's just that in the kinds of [consulting] work that
he'd been doing, he had to attend all kinds of design problems
including reliability. He had to measure a smoke-measuring device
for somebody's smokestack. He had to make it so that under the
conditions of being wherever it had to be . . . that it gave reliable
readings. He understood this just as an engineer should take it;
this was a question of what are you trying to accomplish, and
what are you trying to do it with, and take account of the pecu-
liarities of the things we are going to use, such as vacuum tubes.

"I was convinced by Eckert that he had the right approach to
this, the right attitude toward design, that when he said, 'I don't
see why we can't do it," that he was seriously saying one ought
to try."

"He and I had a lot of fun doing this," Mauchly said about
his conversations with Eckert. "The most important thing about
it as far as I was concerned was that, first, he understood what I
was talking about and, second, that he saw no bars to the feasibility of what I was talking about. He didn't raise the 'bogey,'
which a lot of people did: 'Oh, vacuum tubes are so unreliable.
You'd never get anything to work long enough to be useful.' "

The differential analyzer was the first serious attempt at
computing at the Moore School, but the faculty was not totally
uninterested. One professor, Irven Travis, tinkered for several
years with the idea of computing. Travis tried to offer a few
courses in computing technology in the night school, but there
were not enough takers. In 1938 General Electric asked him to
look into the possibility of building a computer by stringing
together ("ganging" was the term used) a group of conventional
desk calculators with magnets and wires. That turned out to be
a bad idea, because such a device would be totally unreliable,
and Travis never pursued it. The Moore School engineers and
the army would have to make do with the differential analyzer.

Meanwhile, the world was quickly slipping toward war. Travis,
a navy reservist, was pulled into active duty, leaving an open

teaching position and an empty office. On August 6, 1941, Mauchly wrote to the dean, Harold Pender, requesting a job.

I ask that I be considered for appointment to the teaching staff of the Moore School. For the last eight years, I have been head of the Department of Physics at Ursinus College. My rank has always been Associate Professor. . . . Although I look forward to promotion to full professorship in the next few years, it seems to me that my opportunities for ultimate advancement will be better elsewhere.

Mauchly wanted the job desperately. He did not wish to go back to Ursinus, with its nonexistent research budget (and his salary of $2,000 as department chairman); he thought he might be able to get funds for his research at Penn, and he probably wanted to continue his relationship with Eckert. Pender hired Mauchly and also added Arthur Burks, the only Ph.D.'s he had free at the school.

Burks, a graduate of DePauw University, in Indiana, had a doctorate from the University of Michigan in philosophy, having specialized in symbolic logic and the philosophy of science. Finding little demand for philosophers in the late 1930s (America was being flooded with them from Europe), he had signed up for the defense course to "do electrical engineering during the war and find some useful role that way."

At the Ballistics Research Laboratory at Aberdeen, the mathematician Oswald Veblen, of the Institute for Advanced Study, in Princeton, had created a first-rank scientific staff from universities all over America in mathematics, physics, astrophysics, astronomy, and physical chemistry. One mathematician was Herman Goldstine, a Ph.D. from the University of Chicago. Goldstine had studied under Gilbert A. Bliss, and taught several of Bliss's courses, including one in exterior ballistics. Bliss had developed the mathematics to determine the effects of small perturbations on the flight of a shell, generally from his work at Aberdeen during World War I. He worked for Veblen at Aberdeen.

Goldstine left Chicago for the University of Michigan, and

when the war broke out and it was clear he had to join the military, Bliss contacted Veblen, who pulled sufficient strings to get Goldstine transferred to Aberdeen. Goldstine was given the rank of first lieutenant and placed under Gillon, who was in charge of ballistic computation.

As business was growing at the Moore School, Gillon told Goldstine to go to Philadelphia and take charge of the operation there.

On September 1 of that year [1942] Gillon and I went to inspect the small activity at the Moore School. We found things in a not very good state. This stemmed from three causes: first, this project, like many other other new ones, suffered from growing pains; second, the faculty chosen by the University to teach mathematics consisted of several quite elderly professors emeriti who were no longer up to the strain of teaching day-long courses; and third, the cadre of trained people sent up from Aberdeen to run the differential analyzer and to do the other things needed to prepare firing and bombing tables was in need of leadership.

By the end of the month, the twenty-nine-year-old Goldstine and his wife, Adele, also a mathematician, moved to Philadelphia to take charge.

"The station at Philadelphia had two main objectives," he said later. "It had the differential analyzer, and it had a very large group of girls who ran desk computers—Fridens, Marchants, Monroes. The reason for this was that Aberdeen was halfway between Baltimore and Philadelphia, and it's a little hick town and not many people were willing to go to Aberdeen to live. So it was decided that a good place to hire people to work would be Philadelphia, because they could draw on Bryn Mawr, Haverford, the University of Pennsylvania, Temple, Drexel, the whole bit." Almost 200 young women were there.

One of the first hired was the twenty-two-year-old Kathleen McNulty, a graduate with a math major from Chestnut Hill College, a small Catholic women's school. "In those days not many women majored in math. There were something like ninety-two in my class, and there were three math majors," she remembered. "I always had an interest in statistics, and I thought, well, I might work in an insurance company or something. I just didn't know. I just knew I loved math; that was the only thing I was really good at. It was one of those subjects you don't have to study. No matter what the problem is, you just sit down and work it out like a puzzle."

A week after graduation McNulty answered an ad in a local newspaper. She and a friend, Fran Bilas, went to an office on North Broad Street and were told Aberdeen was hiring mathematicians. The job was at Penn. When Bilas and McNulty got there, fifteen people had just arrived from Aberdeen. Neither of them knew a thing about computing trajectories. They were handed a book written by a man named Scarborough which had a chapter on computing using a method of integration.

"Fran and I read the book, and we still didn't know what to do," she remembered. It was so complicated. . . . Then they showed us these great big sheets of paper on which they were doing these computations. You would have x and then x^2 and then the first derivative of x and the second derivative of x and so on, and they showed us how to do it. . . .

"I never heard of numerical integration. We had never done anything like that. Numerical integration is where you take, in this particular case, . . . the path of a bullet from the time it leaves the muzzle of the gun until it reaches the ground. It is a very complex equation; it has about fifteen multiplications and a square root and I don't know what else. You have to find out where the bullet is every 10th of a second from the time it leaves the muzzle of the gun, and you have to take into account all the things that are going to affect the path of the bullet. The very first things that affect the path of the bullet [are] the speed at which it shoots out of the gun [the muzzle velocity], the angle at which it is shot out of the gun, and the size. That's all incorporated in a function which they give you—a [ballistic] coefficient.

"As the bullet travels through the air, before it reaches its highest point, it is constantly being pressed down by gravity. It is also being acted upon by air pressure, even by the temperature. As the bullet reached a certain muzzle velocity—usually a declining muzzle velocity, because a typical muzzle velocity would be 2,800 feet per second—when it got down to the point of 1,100 fps, the speed of sound, then it wobbled terribly. . . . So, instead of computing now at a 10th of a second, you might have broken this down to 100th of a second to very carefully calculate this path as it went through there. Then what you had to do, when you finished the whole calculation, you interpolated the values to find out what was the very highest point and where it hit the ground.

"Every four lines we had to check our computations by something called Simpson's rule to prove that we were performing the functions correctly. All of it was done using numbers so that you kept constantly finding differences and correcting back."

After a few weeks of doing this by hand, Bilas and McNulty were offered a chance to run tables on Weygandt's differential analyzer. By hand, each trajectory took five days; on the analyzer, it took an hour. The Aberdeen people were "very fussy," Weygandt said, and unusually demanding. He thought they were not using the machine efficiently.

"The differential analyzer was fine if you wanted to work 1 percent accuracy; then you didn't have to be too fussy. It was fast and could do decent work," Weygandt said. "But they wanted $\frac{1}{10}$ percent and by being very, very fussy you could get a $\frac{1}{10}$ accuracy. . . . Every morning we had to run a test run, and the test run had been done on hand computers to more significant numbers than we had. We had a printer that printed out. It had little wheels and hammers that hit them like a typewriter; the wheels had numbers on them, just like a counter wheel, and there were little hammers driven by air that hit the thing and printed it. So we had about six quantities we printed out; every one of those had to agree with the test run within $\frac{1}{10}$ percent each morning before we could proceed. Sometimes we would have to make six or eight test runs.

"They didn't need that kind of accuracy; they thought they did. That was the way they operated. We got them to relax later and use it more efficiently."

The analyzer was also used to plot the bombing and gunnery tables for bombers. The latter was complicated because the crew had to avoid what was called the "suicide angle." If a gunner fired his weapon above the aircraft, there was always the danger the plane would fly through the trajectory of the shell as it was coming down. The guns were so designed that if they were aimed at the "suicide angle," they would not fire. Weygandt had no trouble convincing ordnance to accept 1 percent accuracy on those guns.

The analyzer was operated on two shifts during the day; a third shift, generally for maintenance, came at night.

Eckert was called in to help speed up the machine. He, Weygandt, a student, and some other technicians replaced some of the winchlike mechanical amplifiers with photoelectric cells—an idea they had borrowed from GE. They also added servomotors taken from spare aircraft gun turrets, and vacuum tubes to sense the photocells. Photocells were used, too, to follow plotted curves, something that had been done manually.

"We ended up with a couple of hundred radio tubes hooked onto the machine," Eckert said later, "and probably about two dozen motors, and a bunch of what are called amplifying generators, which are motors, and a bunch of electromechanical or electronic paraphernalia. We did this fairly rapidly, I mean over months, not years. . . . With the war on, we worked on the damn thing night and day. . . . The net result of this was that we got the old mechanical analog machine about ten times faster, [and] about ten times more accurate at the same time. We also realized that if we wanted to get another ten to one in both areas, we would end up with a machine that we probably couldn't build. . . . We realized that on analog machines we were running into trouble.

"To get an overall accuracy of $\frac{1}{10}$ of a percent, we had to make the integrators accurate to $\frac{1}{100}$ of a percent because of the way they interact; and to do that we were already machining the wheels in the integrators to better than $\frac{1}{10}$ of $\frac{1}{1000}$ of an inch. We were getting close to the practical limits of the machine in a practical sense, not a theoretical sense. You could machine higher, but next week it [the machine] would be out."

The basement room containing the analyzer was air conditioned and filtered to remove dust from the air. Nonetheless, the Moore School people had gone as far as they could go with mechanical analog machines.

And still the need for faster computation was growing all the time. Goldstine was under pressure. His liaison with the university was Brainerd, whom Goldstine described as an "honest, kindly, and well-meaning gentleman." He and Brainerd got along well, an advantage for all. Second under Brainerd was Carl C. Chambers, who was responsible for the analyzer and the training programs. Goldstine persuaded the Moore School to let the professors emeriti go back into retirement. His wife, Adele, Mauchly's wife, Mary, and Mildred Kramer, the wife of a Sumerian scholar at Penn's University Museum, were assigned to be on the teaching staff for the women "computers." The ranks of the students were augmented by the first members of the Women's Army Corps (WACs).

Even this able group couldn't handle the work load. Goldstine thought that a good rule for figuring out how long it would take to compute a series of equations was to estimate just the time needed for multiplication and to multiply that by a factor of 2.57. This meant if it took one hour to do the multiplication in a problem, it would take three hours to do the computation, including adding, subtracting, multiplying, dividing, writing down the answers, checking, and so on.

Goldstine said it would take five minutes for a human to multiply two ten-digit numbers without mechanical assistance. A desk calculator cut this time down to ten to fifteen seconds, a twenty- or thirtyfold speedup. But the person had to write down the figures, doubling the length of time it took. The Aiken machine at Harvard took three seconds to multiply those numbers. The improved version cut that time to 0.4 seconds. The Bell Labs machines took one second (about one-fifth as long as it took a human with a calculator), and it could do two calculations simultaneously.

But, Goldstine explained, it required 750 multiplications to calculate a single trajectory, taking ten to twenty minutes for the differential analyzer to do just the multiplication, and twelve hours for a human with a calculator.

A typical firing table for one gun contained 2,000 to 4,000 individual trajectories! It required thirty days for the analyzer, if it was working properly, to finish one such table, and no gun could be put out in the field until the artillerymen were provided with just such a table. Goldstine wrote:

These estimates reveal a situation that was unsupportable both because the volume of work was too large and, perhaps more importantly, because the work had to be done very promptly to avoid delays in putting weapons into the hands of the troops in the field. For these reasons Gillon and I were constantly on the lookout for better—quicker and more accurate—ways to expedite table calculation.

This was precisely what Mauchly and Eckert were talking about. Their conversations continued throughout this period. They had so far managed to get no one else in the Moore School interested in what they were talking about, because there was a strong feeling that electronics were not reliable. The weakness, almost everyone felt, was with vacuum tubes.

The vacuum tube goes back to Thomas Edison and is the result of almost the only piece of real scientific work Edison ever performed. Edison was not a scientist but an engineer and technician. He had a low regard for pure science, particularly mathematics.

"Oh, these mathematicians make me tired!" he once said. "When you ask them to work out a sum they take a piece of paper, cover it with rows of *a*'s, *b*'s and *x*'s and *y*'s . . . scatter a mess of flyspecks over them, and then give you an answer that's all wrong." Nonetheless, Edison discovered something now called the Edison effect. When he stuck a plate of metal into one of his light bulbs, he was able to detect an electric current flowing through the vacuum from the filament to the metal plate when the bulb was turned on. Edison did not have a good idea of what to do with this discovery, but an Englishman, John Ambrose Fleming, did.

Fleming found that the metal plate could not only pick up measurable electricity but also detect radio waves and convert them to electricity. This was a two-element tube, a diode. The Fleming diode was not useful, because the signal could not be amplified. This problem was solved by an American, Lee De

Forest, who added a third element to the Fleming tube—a control grid composed of either a crooked metal wire or a metal plate full of holes. This addition made the tube more sensitive. De Forest did not realize at the time that the grid also amplified the signal.

De Forest patented his tube, the triode (which he called an audion), in 1907 and promptly set himself up in business. Setting a pattern that would be followed by that of many other inventors in our story, the business quickly collapsed. De Forest proceeded to leave New York and take a job with Federal Telegraph, in Palo Alto, California.[4] While employed by Federal Telegraph, he also worked in his own lab, on Emerson Street, and there he and his technicians discovered the amplifying characteristics of his tube. De Forest attached some of the tubes to one of Edison's mechanical phonographs, ran out of the house, and found he could hear the amplified sound two blocks away. He could even pick up the footsteps of a fly walking on a piece of paper.[5]

The patent for the triode was immediately acquired by the American Telephone & Telegraph Company (AT&T), which needed the tube for a repeater so that telephone conversations could carry over long distances. The tube was also the linchpin of wireless communication, and De Forest, who was not a modest man, called himself the "Father of Radio," an epithet whose accuracy is debatable.

World War I, which some historians consider to be the first war in which science played a significant role, produced an explosion of research. One of the first devices to make use of the vacuum tube was a crude sonar developed to detect submarines in the English Channel. By World War II, electronics, symbol-

---

4. Palo Alto sits on what is now the northern end of "Silicon Valley," America's computer and electronics center. Federal was one of the first electronics firms in the area. The city is the home of Stanford University, where Frederick Terman ran the engineering school and founded the electronics empire that spread from Palo Alto south to San Jose.

5. Edwin Armstrong of Columbia University, working with a De Forest tube, discovered amplification at about the same time. Armstrong sold his patent to Westinghouse. The patent fight between Armstrong and De Forest lasted for nineteen years, with De Forest winding up the victor.

ized by the vacuum tube, was reaching primacy.

Vacuum tubes were a boon to the modern world, but their limitations were well known. Tubes were mortal, they burned out. Sooner or later they needed replacement. The more tubes in a device, the more often something burned out and had to be replaced. Tubes were also difficult to produce with any consistency. Eckert said that if he bought a box of tubes from RCA or any other reputable manufacturer, the tubes in the box would vary in quality. Mauchly was met with skepticism principally because it was widely, and not unfairly, believed that a very large machine with vacuum tubes could not be made reliable.

Eckert, however, thought everyone was wrong. He could think of at least one precedent for large tube-operated electronic devices, although an unlikely one—theater organs. Eckert was an expert on theater organs.

According to Eckert, the first electric organ was produced in 1898 by a man named Thaddeus Cahill. Cahill was so delighted with his instrument that he hooked it into the telephone lines of his neighbors so that they could hear it too. Unfortunately, the music bled into the phone lines of all the people around him, some of whom did not appreciate his glee, and the phone company ordered him off the line.

By the late 1930s, Hammond was building a machine, the Novachord, that contained seventy-two notes, with two tubes for each note. One tube served as a frequency divider, actually producing the tone; the other tube modulated the size of the signal. The Hammond was also filled with ninety-one small tubes that acted as miniature generators. The generator tubes never seemed to wear out.

The secret was that the tubes in the organ were never run with full current or voltages. Eckert found that RCA had been using vacuum tubes in machines designed to detect very weak signals. The tubes were run at 10 to 20 percent below the conventional power, and seemed to last forever.

The variation in the tubes proved to be tolerable. "If you know the distribution," Mauchly said, "if you know the variations of how different they are, you can design a circuit such that it will do what you want. It'll count. And you can design circuits that will also 'switch'—they'll select which of two routes the next part of the calculation is going to make."

Eckert told all this to Mauchly. "He gave me considerable encouragement," Mauchly said. "If it hadn't been for J. Presper Eckert, I don't know what would have happened next."

Mauchly put his ideas in a memo entitled "The Use of High-Speed Vacuum Tube Devices for Calculating," in which he wrote:

There are many sorts of mathematical problems which require the calculation by formulas which can readily be put in the form of iterative equations. Purely mechanical calculating devices can be devised to expedite the work. However, a great gain in the speed of the calculation can be obtained if the devices which are used employ electronic means for the performance of the calculation, because the speed of such devices can be made very much higher than that of any mechanical device. It is the purpose of this discussion to consider the speed of the calculation and the advantages which may be obtained by the use of electronic circuits which are interconnected in such a way as to perform a number of multiplications, additions, subtractions or divisions in sequence, and which can therefore be used for the solution of difference equations. Since a sufficiently approximate solution of many differential equations can be had simply by solving an associated difference equation, it is to be expected that one of the chief fields of usefulness for an electronic computer would be found in the solution of differential equations. . . .

In five typewritten pages, he went on to compare what he was proposing with the differential analyzer in both speed and accuracy, including the ability to find malfunctions and correct them. He proposed a machine with twenty or thirty devices that functioned like electronic desk calculators. It would be a decade device, which meant it would not use binary digits, at least as far as the operators were concerned. He estimated that the machine would be able to perform 1,000 multiplications per second, and to perform complete trajectories in a minute or two.

What happened next still rankles the participants thirty years later: the memo got lost. It disappeared. Mauchly said he gave a copy to Brainerd and dispatched other copies to everyone in the Moore School. All the copies seemed to have disappeared. Years later the original was found in Brainerd's files with an approving notation. The best guess is that Mauchly gave Brainerd a copy of the memo and asked him to duplicate it and pass it around the Moore School. Either Brainerd misplaced it or his secretary did, for no one, apparently, received any copies of the memo.[6] From August of 1942, when it was written, until the end of March of the next year, Mauchly's memo was missing.

There was plenty of work to do. Brainerd had obtained a contract from the signal corps to do an analysis of the pattern of a parabolic radar dish, to see whether the standard dish could be improved by a change of its geometry, perhaps "taking bites out of it."

"This required an awful lot of tedious point-to-point integration of vector equations over the surface," Mauchly said. "I got a lot of experience there. It took a lot of time. And wonder of wonders, when I said, 'Well, we'll just have to have some computing machines around here to do this; this can't be done on a differential analyzer. What have you got?' " the answer was one adding machine without an automatic multiplying button.

At the same time, Burks and Eckert were on the roof of the Moore School experimenting with a radar dish. The people in the building had to make computations based on measurements made on the roof. No calculating machines were to be had, since the office-machine companies had stopped producing their normal machines and were instead turning out war matériel. To get machines, one needed official priority. Mauchly found that the machines he had been offered at Ursinus—the ones he could not afford—now could not be obtained at any price, even with the government behind him.

He went scouting for machines. First, he contacted Ursinus to see what had happened to the Monroe he had squeezed out of his budget while he was there. "I found that there were all kinds of reasons now that the college just had to have a Monroe desk calculator with an automatic multiplication feature. It never occurred to them that they had to have that while I was there. Once I had sold them the idea that they ought to be able to allow a little budget for that, why it suddenly developed that every-

6. Brainerd later denied that he lost the memo, but there is no other logical explanation for the fact that it disappeared for about six months and no one else had a copy.

body needed this for averaging grades and all kinds of important work." After Mauchly wrote to an assistant to Ursinus's
president, the machine was lent for the duration.

The second source was the Wharton School, Penn's famed
business school. Wharton had dozens of machines in its statistical laboratories, and Mauchly was able to obtain them during
school holidays. He rounded up about a dozen students from
the Moore School to push the buttons, and they finally finished
the signal-corps project. What had been calculated in the building matched what was observed on the roof. Then Mauchly had
to return the calculators to Wharton.

The ballistics situation was intolerable. The Allies had invaded
North Africa, and the gunners found that their firing tables were
off. The ground in North Africa was softer than the ground in
Maryland, and the guns were recoiling in unpredictable ways.
Ordnance would have listened to any reasonable suggestion for
speeding up the ballistics.

One morning in March 1943, Goldstine was down in the dif-
ferential-analyzer room. Joe Chapline, a former Ursinus student
hired at Mauchly's suggestion to help maintain the analyzer, was
laying out some cable. Goldstine mentioned the enormous backlog of ballistics tables. Chapline suggested he go upstairs to see
Mauchly, who had a scheme to speed up the computation a
thousandfold. Goldstine went upstairs.

Mauchly told him what he wanted to build and what Eckert
had said about its feasibility. Goldstine was intrigued. He asked
Mauchly to put all this in a memo. Mauchly said he already had,
and told him to go see Brainerd. Brainerd couldn't find the
August memo. Furious, Mauchly got his secretary, also a former
Ursinus student, to reconstruct the memo from her notes. She
produced what turned out to be a remarkable facsimile. Goldstine was convinced.

"Yes, it occurred to me that it would work; it was the only
real solution to the problem," he said many years later. "We really
were at the end of our rope as far as hiring people is concerned.
And even hiring people simply didn't do it; there was just too
much work. There was practically an infinite backlog. In some

sense money was cheap at that period, and it was evidently the right way to go." There were some doubts in his mind, he recalled, "but it was worth a try." He told Mauchly that if ordnance was capable of giving General Motors $1 million to build a prototype tank and then discard the tank if it did not suit their needs, "why not spend equal or similar amounts of money on trying out an electronic computer?"

Brainerd asked Eckert and Mauchly for more details. The two worked "on a twenty-four-hour basis" for several days and came up with a proposal that contained more details. "We tried to set down a little more clearly how we would do this," Eckert said. They finally gave their proposal to Brainerd. He presented it to Colonel Simon, T. H. Johnson, and Oswald Veblen. Veblen tilted back in his chair as Goldstine outlined what the Moore School proposed to do. When he had heard enough, he crashed his chair forward, stood up, and said, "Simon, give Goldstine the money!" and left the room.

It was Eckert's twenty-fourth birthday.

Other meetings followed. Finally, the big presentation of the Moore School proposal was scheduled for April 9. Goldstine rounded up Eckert and Mauchly in his car and drove out to Paoli, the last town on Philadelphia's Main Line, to pick up Brainerd. They waited while Brainerd finished his breakfast. The final proposal had not been completed; Eckert and Mauchly had been up all night and had not had time to eat. When Brainerd was ready, they rode to Aberdeen, continuing to work in the car. On arriving at the ballistics laboratory, Goldstine and Brainerd went in to meet the officers in charge, while Mauchly and Eckert worked in a side room with a secretary.

"And so we worked and we worked and we worked, and the meeting went on somewhere," Mauchly told Esther Carr. "After a while we got hungry, but nevertheless we still thought we could do best by continuing to work on this report, get more typed pages ready."

Going without meals was not an easy matter for Mauchly. He suffered from a genetic disease called hereditary hemorrhagic telangiectasia, which produced bloody noses and purple lesions on his face, fingers, and toes. He was usually bleeding internally. Unless he received regular doses of nutrients, particularly iron, he was uncomfortable.[7]

After the presentation, Brainerd was asked to leave the room. Shortly Veblen walked out and saw Brainerd standing there.

"You look like the cat that swallowed the canary," he told Brainerd. Brainerd took that to mean the contract was settled. Eckert and Mauchly were informed that this was true. The army had authorized the construction of the world's first electronic all-purpose computer.

Since Goldstine was to remain behind, Mauchly, Eckert, and Brainerd went to the station to take a northbound train to Philadelphia. They spotted a luncheonette at the station, and Eckert and Mauchly decided it was time to eat. Although he had eaten lunch at the officer's club, Brainerd decided to join them. He ordered a soup and a sandwich; the other two ordered just sandwiches. The waitress brought the soup, and assumed that Brainerd's companions would want to wait for their sandwiches until Brainerd was done. Naturally, the train came as Brainerd finished his soup, and the other two went hungry again.

Thirty years later Mauchly also was still bitter about the missed meals.

7. Mauchly eventually died of the disease. Three of his five children have it.

6. ENIAC

*There's no reason technically why this job couldn't have been
done ten years sooner.*

J. PRESPER ECKERT

IF NECESSITY is the mother of invention, then war can be said to
be the grandmother. The gathering clouds of war presented scientists and engineers with new demands, and the Americans were
not alone in recognizing the necessity for high-speed computing.

In Britain, in the mid-1930s, a large number of electrical
engineers seemed to "disappear." Mathematicians and physicists
soon followed. Britain was gathering its resources. Many of these
experts quietly found their way to Bletchley Park, a huge Victorian estate in Buckinghamshire, near London. Bletchley Park
was one of Britain's most closely held secrets.[1] The house was
the headquarters of the Post Office Research Station for the

1. Much of what happened at Bletchley Park is still hidden under Britain's Official Secrets Act. Besides being a bane to historians, this act keeps Britain's press
one of the least free in the Western world.

Government Code and Cipher School.

Cipher is the game mathematicians love to play most. They consider creating and breaking codes great sport and intellectual exercise, and almost every mathematician has indulged in it. By the outbreak of World War II, codes and code-making machines had reached a level of complexity that made it possible to create a code almost impossible to break. Such a code is good to have; being able to break one is even better. The goal of the people at Bletchley Park was to break the German military code. They employed a secret weapon—an extraordinary young mathematician, Alan Turing.

Even in a story filled with genius and idiosyncrasy, Turing stands out. Born in England to a family of Indian colonial civil servants, he studied mathematics at Cambridge but did not do as well as he might have, because he was easily bored, and tests particularly bored him. He spent two years doing graduate work at Princeton with the eminent mathematician John von Neumann, who tried to recruit him for the university. Turing was a large, strong man with an upper-class stammer and a laugh that many of his friends conceded was as pleasurable as a fingernail on a blackboard. His hay fever was so bad that he sometimes bicycled around Buckinghamshire wearing a gas mask.

Anecdotes about his eccentricities are plentiful. His mother wrote that at one time Turing had trouble with his bicycle: the chain would fall off periodically. He studied the matter and concluded that it happened after a certain number of revolutions. As he bicycled, he began to count the revolutions, got off the bike, and secured the chain before it could fall off. When he got tired of counting, he rigged a mechanical counter to keep track of the revolutions. It never occurred to him to take the bicycle into a shop, where a repairman could have fixed it in a few minutes.

He liked long-distance running, chess, and rumpled clothing. He was a homosexual. Some of those who admired him most found it hard to like him.

Age is a critical factor in mathematics. It has been said that mathematicians frequently peak in their late teens, physicists in their early twenties. Why this may be so is a matter for endless debate, but Turing, like many mathematicians, did his best work early, shortly after leaving Cambridge. He published a paper in the *Proceedings of the London Mathematical Society* in which he concluded that certain kinds of mathematical problems could not be solved by automatic computing machines. Since there were no such things as automatic computing machines at the time, Turing, an admirer of Babbage, described one. His imaginary machine was fed by paper tape, which was divided into squares. The machine could read one square, or write one square on tape, at a time. His universal machine could solve any problem presented to it in binary digits (bits). He did not expand on how this computing was accomplished; it was not important to his paper. All that was required for the computing was to convert the problem into the proper algorithm.[2]

A large part of what modern computer programmers do with their machines originated withTuring's paper. His work also inspired what happened at Bletchley Park: the ULTRA project.

In 1938 a young Polish engineer named Richard Lewinski, perhaps the least-known hero of the war, offered his services to the British embassy. Lewinski had worked in a factory in eastern Germany assembling what he thought was a secret signaling device. He was able to memorize details of the instrument, and after he was fired from the factory (for being Jewish), he contacted a British intelligence officer and offered to sell what he knew about the machine. Col. Stewart Menzies, of the British intelligence service, sought expert opinion and enlisted Dilwyn Knox, a cryptographer, and Turing, just back from Princeton, to go to Warsaw and interrogate Lewinski.

Knox and Turing were impressed; Lewinski and his wife were smuggled out of Warsaw with fake diplomatic passports and hidden in an apartment in Paris by French intelligence agents. With the help of a carpenter, Lewinski, who had a remarkable memory, was able to reconstruct the machine he had seen in

2. Turing's point in the paper was that certain kinds of mathematical and logical problems could not be converted to algorithms and hence could not be programmed into a computer—had one existed at the time.

Germany. He built an oversized version of ENIGMA, the device used by the German armed forces to encode and decode messages to the troops in the field.

ENIGMA used two electric typewriters. A message in plain text was typed on one machine. The message was encoded according to a "key," and the coded version came out on the other typewriter. The key could be varied for every message, the possible combinations of codes numbering about a trillion. The Germans used machines three times the size of ENIGMA, variously called Fish or *Geheimschreiber,* which encoded and decoded the most secret communications. But first the British had to tackle ENIGMA.

Having a copy of ENIGMA did not mean that the British could decode messages automatically—the Germans changed the key three times a day—but it did mean that the Bletchley Park people had an idea how the codes were created. The code breakers devised several electromechanical machines to scour through intercepted ENIGMA messages and to keep crunching the letters until the machines found something that made sense. Turing and other mathematicians developed methods that enabled the machines to reduce the possibilities to a reasonable level. Once the machines found the key, it was easy to decode the message.

F. W. Winterbotham, who passed on ENIGMA messages to Winston Churchill, described the ENIGMA machine as looking like a "bronze-coloured column surmounted by a larger circular bronze-coloured face, like some Eastern Goddess who was destined to become the oracle of Bletchley, at least when she felt like it." In 1940 the Luftwaffe began sending test messages, around its network. The signals were picked up, and the "oracle" decoded them.

Decoding the *Geheimschreiber* was a different matter. Wheras ENIGMA had three rotors containing the potential keys, the *Geheimschreiber* had ten. Mere mechanics and mathematical inspiration would not suffice. Turing and others, particularly T. H. Flowers and M. H. A. Newman, began building an electronic decoder in January 1943. By December of that year, the machine called COLOSSUS was in service.

By any standards COLOSSUS was a working electronic computer, perhaps the world's first. The machine was limited because it was designed for a particular function and was virtually useless for anything else. COLOSSUS computed with 1,800 vacuum tubes, which the British call thermionic valves. Information was fed into the machine on paper tape at the astonishing rate of 5,000 characters a second—so fast that the steel pins were grooved by the flying paper. The tubes counted, compared, and performed rudimentary arithmetic. There was no internal memory, but the operators apparently could adjust the function of the machine according to how close it seemed to be to making sense out of the coded messages.

A year later an even bigger COLOSSUS, the Mark II, was in business at Bletchley.

The existence of the ULTRA project was so valuable a secret that when ULTRA overheard the plans to bomb Coventry, Churchill ordered that there be no civil defense preparation. He was ready to sacrifice the lives of the people of Coventry rather than tip off the Germans that the British had broken their code.

John Mauchly could not have known it, but COLOSSUS proved his point: vacuum tubes could be used for high-speed data processing.

Across the Channel, the Germans, too, were feeling the need for computation. Konrad Zuse was experimenting with electro-mechanical computers. Zuse, an engineer and a student of Babbage, toyed with using vacuum tubes as switching devices but felt more secure with mechanical relays. He worked with Gerhard Overhoff, the chief engineer at the Henschel Flugzeugwerke, in Berlin, which tested drone rockets. Overhoff was convinced of the need for mathematical computation to help in the testing, and in 1941, when Zuse told him about a relay machine he had built in his parents' living room in Berlin, Overhoff was fascinated. The two formed a team.

Zuse built a second machine (called the Z3—for there were earlier prototypes) with the help of the German Research Institute for Aerodynamics. In 1943 the German air ministry ordered a general-purpose machine from Zuse (the Z4) and later added an order for two special-purpose research machines. The Z4 used old movie film instead of paper tape. Zuse and Overhoff went into business in a firm called Zuse Apparatebau, but all their machines were bombed out in 1944. Zuse claimed that a patent he took out on his machine, which apparently was a small, useful general-purpose electromechanical computer, predated any other computer invention or patent.

The British computer expert Christopher Evans has written, "It has frequently been said the Britain's secret code-cracking computer . . . ensured victory for the Allies. Might not the possession of a fully operational machine in German hands at an early stage of the war have had the reverse effect?" If the Germans had known what Zuse's machine could do and if Zuse had used vacuum tubes, the answer might have been yes.

The Moore School contingent knew none of the above. They were busy with their own project and with the politics of science. Having convinced the officials at Aberdeen that it was worth the effort to try to build an electronic computer did not solve matters for Eckert, Mauchly, Brainerd, and Goldstine. There were too many skeptics around, some of them in the highest government scientific agencies, some at the University of Pennsylvania.

Opposition at Aberdeen consisted of mathematicians who thought that a faster machine was not necessary—that the new differential analyzers would suffice—and engineers who simply said that an electronic computer would not work, because of potential tube failure.

Another obstacle was Vannevar Bush's National Defense Research Committee (NDRC), created in 1940 to mobilize America's scientific community. In the spring of 1943, NDRC passed judgment on the computer scheme. The fact that no one officially asked for its opinion did not matter. The army informed NDRC of the project because NDRC knew something about the subject, having funded several electronic calculating projects in 1941 and 1942. The committee also had access to funds that could have helped out the Moore School project. As the historian Nancy Stern has pointed out, the committee was also prestigious enough that it could have made life much easier for the Moore School researchers if it had lent its support. It did nothing of the sort.

If one were to design a committee least likely to support the notion of electronic computers, one might create NDRC. Bush, as we have seen, was the developer of the analog differential analyzer. His devotion to analog machines was intense. The committee also included Samuel Caldwell and Harold Hazen, of MIT, the home of the differential analyzer. So devoted were they to the technology that MIT was hopelessly committed to analog machines and was not in the race for digital computing until years later. Another member of the committee was George Stibitz, who had built electromechanical machines for the Bell Labs. His lack of enthusiasm for the Moore School project was notable. The problem was not lack of monay; Stibitz recalled years later that all he had to do to get NDRC funds for his Bell Labs work was ask for it.

The problem was, rather, a very conservative group of people whose experience lay largely with a competing technology, and a competing mind-set. They represented the scientific elite of America, what some call the "Cambridge syndrome," and the idea of something important coming from the banks of the Schuylkill River instead of the Charles was too much for them. The Moore School researchers were, moreover, too young (Brainerd was the oldest, thirty-nine), and most were engineers without Ph.D.'s.

The attitude of the committee ranged from indifference to outright hostility, and Simon and Gillon bore the brunt of the antipathy. The committee became aware of the project on April 14, 1943, when Brainerd gave a written proposal to Johnson at Aberdeen. Brainerd referred to the machine as a "diff. analyzer," perhaps to make it more palatable to people like Hazen and Caldwell. What the Moore School was proposing was certainly not a differential analyzer; Brainerd was thus simply being cute. "This was in part a matter of salesmanship," he said, "because the people with whom we were dealing were accustomed to differential analyzers. So we gave the thing a name that tied it more closely with something with which they were familiar. . . . We hoped by this method to encounter less sales resistance."

That didn't work. Johnson passed the letter on to Hazen. Hazen was unimpressed. He wrote in his diary:

Regarding a proposed electronic differential analyzer, TJ [Johnson] described in general terms a proposal, which as far as he knew, originated with Brainerd at the Moore School of the University of Pennsylvania. . . . TJ indicated that the Aberdeen group thought this might be an interesting project for NDRC. There was a brief discussion on the technical phases of the subject in which it was agreed by TJ and HLH [Hazen] that the techniques proposed were sadly outdated and that NCR [National Cash Register] or the RCA development under the Division 7 contract just terminated should most certainly be taken into account if such a device were to be undertaken. . . . HLH talked over the phone with SHC [Caldwell] who rightly emphasized the emergence of considerable new differential analyzer capacity in that the new differential analyzer at MIT is now actually doing ballistic solutions in shakedown operations.

Hazen then suggested that if such a technology was feasible, RCA or NCR ought to handle it. He also doubted that such a project would be finished before the war ended. He then added, "How's for some bright ideas as to how to get Moore School profitably occupied."

Caldwell seconded the motions. In a letter to Hazen a few months later, he reminded Hazen that "as far back as 1939, we realized that we could build a machine for electronic computation. But, although it was possible to build such a machine and possible to make it work, we did not consider it practical." Caldwell said that vacuum tubes were too unreliable. "Another thing which caused us to discard the idea of building a complete machine immediately was the very large number of small parts required. Col. Gillon speaks of the machine containing thousands of tubes." He also added that he and Hazen ought to keep on the subject because the Moore School plan entailed stepping onto their territory.[3]

Stern wrote that the MIT people were particularly upset because they were working on a new analog device, called the Rockefeller Analyzer.

"MIT was into building a better analog machine," Eckert said. "They built, not a faster, but a more easily programmed version of the kind of thing that I had worked on [at the Moore School],

3. Stern, from University of Pennsylvania Archives.

in which all the signals could be hooked together in relays instead of a paper tape. The machine was bigger, more complex; it wasn't any more accurate or faster. Ours took anywhere from a day to two or three days to set up with screwdrivers and hammers and wrenches and so on. Their machine you could set up in a matter of minutes by means of paper tape."[4]

The Moore School's computer contract with the army also meant that Penn had to drop its share of the rooftop radar project, on which they worked with MIT. Earlier, MIT had tried to recruit the Moore School team for the radar work in Cambridge.

"We got the contract in April of 1943," Brainerd said. "And in March or so we got a delegation from the radiation laboratory [at MIT]. They wanted the whole group of us to move up there and join them. They were pretty insistent that they had very important wartime work going on. I talked to a professor at MIT, and he was pretty disgusted with me because we wouldn't take them up on it. He didn't think anyone should stand in his way." Brainerd said the reason they would not be recruited was that they were betting on the computer project, although that is probably just hindsight. Finally, as Stern has pointed out, Hazen was obviously upset because the Moore School had already built a bigger analyzer than the MIT machine.

Stibitz agreed with all the adverse comments, claiming that the Moore School project would do nothing his Bell Labs people were not already working on. "I am very sure that the development time for the electronic equipment will be four to six times as long as that for relay equipment," he concluded.

The comments of the NDRC were passed on to Gillon, who refused to give in. He pointed out that the Moore School project differed from anything proposed elsewhere, that it would be much faster, and that the army's funding of it did not mean that the army would not fund other projects.

But the opposition did not stop with diary and letter writing. Some members of NDRC actively sought to interfere with the Philadelphia project. In one instance Stibitz refused to give RCA permission to pass some documents to the Moore School. Gillon

4. Interview with the author.

finally stepped in and told the NDRC to mind its own business. He told Goldstine he hoped that this would "kill their impertinent interference once and for all."[5]

What the opposition eventually did was to fire up the Penn researchers. If there had been no competition with MIT before, there was now.

"They were the rich guys up there who did everything the hard way, as far as we were concerned," Eckert said. The competition was stepped up also by the fact that Pender, the dean of the school, was an MIT man. Unfortunately Pender was part of the other problem, the skepticism within the university. Brainerd bore the brunt of this opposition.

On one level, Pender supported his crew. "The university wasn't accustomed to handling contracts," Brainerd explained. "Even by the spring of 1943, Dean Pender and I had to get together and build up a very strong argument and get the approval of the then administrative vice-president. He happened to be a professor of English who thought we shouldn't do such things at a university. . . . We got around that one."

On another level, Pender was one of the early skeptics.[6] He was afraid an electronic computer would not work. (If no one else had built one, he reasoned, why should we think we can?) He worried about what would happen to the university, to the Moore School, and, not incidentally, to himself if the engineers failed. He bluntly told Brainerd that if the scheme did not work, Brainerd would need a new job.

The official contract went through on May 17, 1943,[7] with an estimated expenditure of $61,700 for the first six months. It was signed on June 5, Brainerd being listed as project supervisor, Eckert as chief engineer, Mauchly as principal consultant, and Goldstine as technical liaison.

Just before work began, on May 31, there was a meeting between Gillon, Johnson, the astronomer L. E. Cunningham, who

5. Stern, from University of Pennsylvania Archives.
6. Pender later became a convert but would play a role in destroying the university's head start, as we shall see.
7. Fixed Price Development and Research Contract No. W-670-ORD-4926, between the United States of America and the Trustees of the University of Pennsylvania.

be operated at more than a certain percent of its rated capacity, no resistor could be operated at more than a certain percent of its capacity, and so on for every kind of element. And he made standard circuits, and everybody had to conform to these circuits; whatever unit they designed had to be built out of little components made up of circuits that he had designed. And this was, I think, one of the real reasons why this was a success, because of the rigidity of the standards he imposed.

"It wasn't so that every time you got a new designer come in to build something that you got a whole new set of problems. Everybody had to conform to those standards . . . and it was very uniform for the entire machine," Goldstine added. "So, in a sense, everybody understood every piece of the apparatus pretty early because it all broke down into the same units."

Eckert felt that it was imperative that everyone on the project knew that every part would meet the same standards, that a tube built in one room would be expected to react to a known gadget being built in another room, and that there be no surprises. This conformity applied even to the electric current. Eckert designed a circuit that shaped the electrical pulse into the tubes so that the signal that went into them was uniform. The tolerance was set reasonably, but Eckert insisted that the circuitry be able to respond to a signal that fell within that tolerance, and then made sure that the signals themselves conformed. The tubes knew what to expect.

"[He set] these rules in advance," Mauchly said, "that this was the way it was going to be, and no matter whether there's one engineer designing this circuit or twelve engineers using it, all of us as a team [can] count on that fact—that pulses that some other part of the machine send to my circuit will be within these limits, and I don't have to design for anything except pulses of that size, shape, and so forth. And that's how my part of the machine would be tested."

Testing was a problem because no devices capable of meeting Eckert's standards existed. The project engineers were ordered to invent some.

One such order went to a Moore School undergraduate named

Herman Lukoff, assigned to the PX project during a vacation
period. Without being informed at the time what the test equipment was being used for, Lukoff was told by Eckert:

The Moore School expected to get some super-super electronic development project, and that there was no test equipment in existence that
was fast enough or good enough to use in developing the super-super.
Our job that summer was to design the necessary equipment. Pres went
on to explain [that] the various modules required, for example, an oscilloscope that could be externally triggered and would display pulses up
to 1 MHz [one million pulses a second] rate. Clearly, there were no
commercial oscilloscopes available within an order of magnitude of that
performance.

Lukoff's job was to design a signal generator that could vary
its frequency. It would be one of three test modules that could
be rolled around on wheeled carts as they constructed ENIAC.

Pres gave me several good leads on how to go about the design. He
would stop around my workbench once or twice a day to see how I was
progressing. I found him to be as smart as a whip and lucid in his expla-
nations. He had a tremendous knack for being able to reduce things to
a practical level, using simple engineering principles. Pres wasn't one to
get lost in a myriad of equations. I developed a deep respect and great
admiration for him. He knew what he was doing and I had a lot to learn
from him.

Lukoff had such a good time that he volunteered for PX when
he graduated. Eckert could finally tell him about ENIAC.

The ENIAC project had taken over a converted storeroom
on the first floor of the Moore School, on the southwest corner
of the building. Downstairs, work on the ballistics table continued. Weygandt still chugged out data on the differential analyzer. All around the building, young women sat in rows of desks
with desk calculators, turning out ballistics tables. It was a heady,
busy atmosphere. Mostly it was work; there was little time for
humor. The only member of the staff who seemed to provide
any entertainment was Shaw, an unlikely source of amusement.

Shaw began life with one strike against him: he was an albino.
During the time he was doing graduate work in mathematics at

Princeton, he acquired a second: a rare spinal disease that left his legs partially paralyzed. He hobbled about with a cane. Yet Shaw had a grand sense of humor and loved practical jokes. His favorite was placing the little neon tubes used for the counters along a 110-volt power strip that encircled the lab. Turning on the power produced a flash of purple lightning and a crack of thunder.

Because of his very poor eyesight, he had to work with his face just a few inches from anything he was handling. His engineering board was usually in total chaos, with wires going in every direction, most of them carrying hundreds of volts.

"We kept worrying about the possibility of Bob's blowing off his nose or damaging his eyes," Lukoff said. Shaw did not. Because he was a fine engineer with a phenomenal memory, his penchant for explosive humor was tolerated.

The work area bustled. Each engineer had his own work table, and the tables circled the room. The hardware was being assembled in the center of the room. Technicians scrambled about with miles of wires, soldering irons, clips, and tape.

Supplies inundated the Moore School, particularly vacuum tubes. The first estimates were that 5,000 tubes would be needed, but as work progressed 17,000 to 18,000 seemed a more likely figure. Many of the tubes did not meet Eckert's standards and were rejected. Transformers ordered from a widely respected company were found to fail the standards. They were sent to a small local company to be fixed.

"In the beginning, I was in charge of everything," Goldstine said. Finally, when the work load got too great, he called an assistant in from Aberdeen and put him in charge of the analyzer and the desk calculators, while he devoted his full time to ENIAC. Chedaker managed the actual construction of the machine under Eckert.

Eckert later remembered the whole thing as having been fun, but it did not always look like it at the time.

"The use of the word *fun* in connection with Pres Eckert is a kind of misnomer," Goldstine said. "It was his whole life. It was morning, noon, and night. You would be more likely to use the word *fun* in connection with Mauchly than with Eckert. Eckert is just an extraordinarily skilled ... tremendously hard-driven engineer."

Mauchly and Eckert conceived of constructing the machine from modules; each module would have a separate role and would act in association with the other modules. ENIAC eventually comprised thirty separate units.

The heart of the machine, where the actual computation took place, was the accumulator, which also stored the numbers. Each accumulator could hold a ten-digit number and cooperated with other accumulators to perform arithmetic functions. The accumulators consisted of flip-flops and counters. ENIAC had no other memory that could be altered as the computer ran, what is now called a read-write memory. A separate storage device could hold as many as 300 numbers, but the operators could not alter those numbers during a computation.[10]

The accumulators worked in a manner analogous to those of the electromechanical computers of the past, in which a wheel containing numbers turned in response to an electrical signal. In ENIAC, the ring counters replaced the wheels; neon vacuum tubes fashioned in a ring responded to each other. When the last tube in the ring registered, the next signal went back to the first tube, and on around in a circle. The circle behaved just the way a numbered wheel did.

Each ten-digit number sent into ENIAC was accompanied by a plus or a minus sign. There were ten ring counters in ten stages and two counters for the signs. They were all connected by "carry" circuits, so that when one ring hit 10, the 1 carried over to the next ring. Each number consisted of a train of electrical pulses rushing at the speed of 100,000 cycles per second. The sign counters were set up so that no pulse equaled a positive number, and a 9 meant a negative one.

A number received in an accumulator was added to the numbers already there. Subtraction was handled through the complement of the number, a throwback to Pascal's idea. Each accumulator had 500 tubes. Burks was in charge of the multiplication and the square roots.

---

10. In modern computer jargon, this is known as a read-only memory, a ROM.

At the suggestions of Cunningham, the engineers built function tables, in which the answers to the questions were already set up—mathematicians call this "table look-up." Here lay the read-only memory. Instead of actually computing a square root, the engineers could preprogram a function table containing all the square roots within a given field. When the machine was asked for one of those square roots, it could simply look up the answer instead of doing the computation. For technical reasons, it was decided to do the square-root computation, but the function tables contained things such as sines and cosines, the trigonometry of ballistics.[11]

The function tables, however, provided ENIAC with the ability to perform almost any task and proved to the engineers that the machine they were building was a general-purpose machine, unlike those being developed anywhere else they knew about. ENIAC was designed this way for two reasons: first, because no one knew the right algorithm for computing the ballistics tables (the method used by the women in the building was too complicated), and, second, because the goal was not only to compute the trajectories but also to print charts the artillerymen could take into the field, a task much more difficult than just computing and one requiring considerable versatility.

"It was [Aberdeen's] requirement from the very start that the machine that we would build was not just a machine to calculate firing tables, although that was the crying need at that moment; but that after the war was over they would have a tool useful in all kinds of scientific research," Mauchly said.

"At first they decided they only needed two function tables; a little later they decided they needed three. There were other decisions like that, where the amount of equipment we were going to build got upped later after we started off with the design," Mauchly added.

The number of accumulators, in fact, jumped from ten to twenty. Each was assigned a particular job. Six were to handle just the multiplication. One held the multiplier, a second the

11. Function tables were invented independently by J. A. Rajchman, of RCA, and Perry O. Crawford, Jr., of MIT, but it was RCA that provided the idea for the ENIAC researchers. The tables operate by a system of electrical resistance.

multiplicand. Two others stored the product, since the result of multiplying two ten-digit numbers was a twenty-digit number. The other two did the work.

The numbers were fed to ENIAC through IBM card readers via something called a constant transmitter, at a speed of 125 cards per minute. The card reader and puncher were obtained from Thomas Watson, Sr., at IBM, at the request of Gillon. Watson was told in general terms what the equipment was for. Bell Labs and AT&T's Western Electric subsidiary provided the constant transmitter. Bell's Oliver E. Buckley was also informed about the ENIAC project. Output was at the rate of 100 IBM cards per minute.

The Moore School engineers devised two kinds of circuits, numerical and programming. This separation made ENIAC a programmable computer, which was part of its versatility. The numerical circuits carried electric charges representing numbers; the programming circuits carried changes that ordered the numerical circuits to perform certain functions.

The various units of ENIAC "talked" to each other in bursts of electric charges of approximately fifty volts, each lasting 2.5 milliseconds. Thick coaxial cables with large plugs carried the messages. The plugs connected to big trays, each eight feet long, nine inches wide, and one and a half inches deep. The trays were divided into "digit trays" and "program trays," depending on their purpose.

Each number consisted of that number of electric pulses, that is, a 6 consisted of six pulses. In this way, the machine was decimal, not binary. Moreover, the numbers could be transmitted along the cables in parallel;[12] the eleven cables could carry the ten-digit number and the plus or minus sign.

"Nearly every panel . . . had its own control circuits in them," Eckert said, "so that a very complex function, like adding two

12. This is called parallel architecture. Almost every computer built since ENIAC has employed serial architecture, which means the numbers must line up behind each other and are transmitted one at a time. Think of the difference between one large pipe (the serial machine) or several small pipes (the parallel machine). Serial machines are easier to design but inherently slower. Given the speed of modern electronics, that did not matter until very recently. The newer, superfast computers such as the CRAY have reverted to Mauchly's parallel architecture.

Charles Babbage, photograph, 1860
(IBM Archives)

Babbage's Difference Engine *(IBM Archives)*

Herman Hollerith *(IBM Archives)*

Hollerith's Tabulator and Sorter Box, 1890 *(IBM Archives)*

Thomas Watson, Sr. *(IBM Archives)*

ENIAC, 1945 *(University of Pennsylvania)*

J. Presper Eckert and Walter Cronkite, election night, 1952
(Sperry Univac)

UNIVAC I, 1952 *(Sperry Univac)*

IBM 701, 1952 *(IBM Archives)*

John Mauchly (left) and J. Presper Eckert, later years *(Sperry Univac)*

numbers or subtracting, would happen by sending a sync pulse to that system to tell it to do it. This was received in any one of eight or ten circuits, and then, when that function was finished, it would give out a pulse and send it somewhere else in the machine.

"This was done because we were afraid to bring that many lead wires all over the place in those early days and get the signals crossed off into each other and confused. And it was done for a very simpleminded reason in addition to that: we didn't know, when we started the machine, how many additional panels the army was going to come along and add."

Without a real internal memory, the circuits had to be "hard-wired," meaning the machine had to be physically set and programmed by using switches and dials on the face of the machine and by rearranging the cables, trays, and function units.

ENIAC was a fixed-decimal machine, which meant the operator had to set the decimal place. This involved adjusting a plug into a terminal; each place signified a decimal place. With a ten-digit limit, rounding off became a problem. If you kept using rounded-off numbers, sooner or later the error in the calculation became significant. Brainerd drafted a professor from the math department to help work this out.

Burks worked on the accumulators, the multipliers, the function tables, and the master programmer. Shaw completed the function tables, the master programmer, and the constant transmitter. Sharpless was responsible for the cycling unit and the multiplier.

By the end of a year, ENIAC was ready for a test. Eckert decided that the concept would be proven if two accumulators could collect data, talk to each other, and follow orders. Engineers tested each accumulator. Finally, in May of 1944, the accumulators proved the point. Pender wrote to Goldstine, then ill in the Hospital of the University of Pennsylvania:

The actual operation of two accumulator units of the ENIAC has been a source of satisfaction to all of us. Some of the details have been described to you over the telephone. I thought I would take this opportunity to say that the results of the tests have been gratifying not only in a general way but also in very specific manners. For example, the actual operation has indicated that the numerous different types of subsidiary units which go into an accumulator have been properly designed. No major mistake has turned up.

Pender went on to say that the machine was already solving second-order differential equations for a sine wave, and was doing it so fast "that it is impossible to follow the results on indicating lights."

On the whole I believe there is reason for moderate optimism. This is, of course, a research and development project, and there is always the possibility that an unforseen problem will develop which may range from serious to impossible. However, up to the present time we have met no insuperable difficulties, and see nothing in the future which should be more difficult than has already been overcome in the past.

With that somewhat reluctant endorsement, Pender signaled that even he might be convinced that ENIAC would work. Others were less sanguine. Goldstine called it a "watershed" and said that from that day on "it was clear . . . that the machine would be finished successfully."

"There's a difference between confidence and certainty," Burks said. "The running of those two accumulators reliably, for hours on end, was a definite proof that the concept would work."

Eckert and Mauchly had trouble containing themselves. They hurried down to the differential analyzer room and invited McNulty and Elizabeth Snyder upstairs to see their computer.

"They said, 'Watch this,' and Pres or John put the number 5 in. They pushed this little button—they had this hand-held wire coming from the machine with a button on the end of it—flipped the 5" McNulty recalled. The number went to the accumulator, and three dials flipped, signifying 5,000. "There," one told the women, "you've multiplied 5 by 1,000!"

McNulty and Snyder were amazed—that it took so much equipment to multiply 5 by 1,000.

"The biggest device that anybody had built previously had 100 [or] 200 tubes in it . . . probably the electric organ. . . . We built something that was in order of magnitude [greater] electronically and gotten it to work," Eckert said. "It worked well enough that in my mind . . . another factor of twenty was in the cards. So I knew it was going to work. From then on we were building and adding panels and testing stuff."

The dozen engineers and the project's technicians put the machine together in bits and pieces. Soldered joints sometimes needed to be redone. At least once Mauchly had to lie on his back to fix a connection in one of the function tables that had come loose because the floor was uneven.

The machine consumed 174 kilowatts. Essentially, the Moore School had its own power supply.[13] The university received its power from a Philadelphia Electric Company power station across the Schuylkill. Thirteen thousand volts crossed the river on a very high tension line. The Moore School had its own transformers in a concrete room in the main building. There were three 50-kilowatt induction regulators.

The finished ENIAC consisted of forty separate panels, containing 17,468 vacuum tubes (using sixteen different types), approximately 1,500 relays, 70,000 resistors, 10,000 capacitors, and 6,000 switches. The panels were bunched in thirty separate groups, each having a specific function. To keep the panels cool, the machine was air-conditioned by means of forced outside air. ENIAC took up 1,800 square feet, was 100 feet long, 10 feet high, and 3 feet deep, and weighed thirty tons.

ENIAC could perform a multiplication in 2.8 milliseconds, divide in 24 milliseconds, add in 0.2 milliseconds. It could calculate a trajectory in 30 seconds.

It was clearly the most complex, sophisticated machine yet built. ENIAC was the world's first general-purpose electronic computer; as we shall see, it launched the computer age.

The birth of that age was not without its human problems. The Moore School team was not an entirely happy group. For one thing, Eckert and Mauchly (particularly Mauchly) did not get along with Brainerd.

"Eckert and Mauchly's relations to Brainerd were always very complicated," Goldstine said. "They were frustrated because they

---

13. An enduring legend has it that every time ENIAC was turned on, lights dimmed all over West Philadelphia. Not true. The Moore School's power was isolated from the power supplied to the rest of the campus and the surrounding area.

thought that Brainerd didn't pay as much attention to the project as he should. On the other hand, if he had spent more time doing what they thought he should be doing—namely, parading around downstairs supervising them—then there would have been such a fight as to be unimaginable about his interfering. So it was a no-win proposition for Brainerd, and I think he handled it very well by giving Eckert a great deal of freedom."

Mauchly was still unforgiving about the missing memo. Also, Mauchly's changing role as work progressed altered Brainerd's opinion of his value to the project. Mauchly, a sensitive man, felt this deeply. When the project began, Mauchly was a crucial figure; ENIAC was formed in general terms in his mind, and there can be little doubt it would not have been built without him. But as work progressed, as Eckert and the engineers actually built the machine, his active role diminished.

At one stage Mauchly's salary was cut by a third when one of his courses ended. "Bad enough," he wrote in his diary, "but the implications were that I wasn't worth very much to the project which I had originated."

Two incidents aggravated the problem. In February 1945 Warren Weaver, chief of the applied mathematics panel of the Office of Scientific Research and Development, the main government research and development agency,[14] asked Brainerd for a report on electronic computing. Brainerd waited for about nine months while he was trying to obtain clearance from Aberdeen. The clearance came in September; the report was due in November.

Eckert and Mauchly did not know of the report until Brainerd was almost finished with it. They then protested vehemently. Because of the security problem, they could not publish papers to establish their priority to the invention. They were afraid that the Brainerd report, which would be widely circulated, would make it appear that Brainerd was the inventor of ENIAC. They did not think that Brainerd would do this deliberately (and there is no reason to believe he had anything like that in mind), but they wanted to make sure it did not happen

14. The agency was the predecessor of the National Science Foundation, another Bush creation.

accidentally. For reasons we will take up later, they were beginning to think of patents. The issue was resolved when Eckert, Mauchly, and Goldstine were added as coauthors.

In October 1945 a conference on calculating machines was scheduled at MIT. Again, for security reasons, no one was permitted to publish papers, but those in attendance could meet with others in the field to talk about what they were doing. Going to such a meeting was important, the first real chance the Moore School people had to tell their peers about ENIAC, which would not be revealed to the public for some time.

Mauchly was not invited. He protested to Reid Warren, then in direct charge of ENIAC. Warren wrote to Brainerd:

John Mauchly is highly incensed in his mild and polite way, that he has not been asked to go to the MIT conference. My own feeling is that he and Eckert are on equal footing. The Dean is noncommittal; he thinks you have strong feelings against John's going. I think Caldwell [at MIT] can be persuaded to let four of us into the meeting.

Mauchly was finally invited.

Brainerd later summed up his opinion this way: "Well, speaking frankly, I felt that Eckert was an extremely good man and that John was not . . . he was much more of a sounding board."

Brainerd's opinion of Mauchly's contributions was not his alone; others involved in the project thought that Mauchly's work on the project, which he had initiated, was not significant. Mauchly was quick with ideas, but relied on Eckert to carry them through. Eckert told Mauchly that part of the problem was that Mauchly's work was less tangible than his. He later said that Mauchly "inspired people" and that he would have been reluctant to go on to further development without Mauchly's help.

At the core of this dispute was something far more serious, a disagreement that would tear the team apart.

By the fall of 1944, victory in the war seemed assured. Eckert and Mauchly began thinking of what to do next. Both believed that computers had considerable commercial value.

The army, at the same time, was concerned because no patents had been taken out on the Moore School work. This came to a head when it appeared that Samuel Williams at Bell Labs was about to take out a patent for an electronic calculating machine that, although no competitor to ENIAC, would muddy the patent waters. Simon feared that a patent awarded to Bell could drag both the government and the University of Pennsylvania into court and make Penn liable in case of a patent-infringement award. Aberdeen urged Eckert and Mauchly to start thinking about taking out a patent.

New at this kind of thing, the university had no formal policy, a naïveté that would prove costly. Pender, no stranger to the world of commerce, was initially sympathetic. (He had even founded his own firm, the International Resistance Company.) He worked out a compromise: since the government had put up the money and would be assigned the patents, the government, in turn, would grant the university the right to license any other university or nonprofit organization, and Eckert and Mauchly would hold the commercial rights. Between them they had agreed to go fifty-fifty.

As a result, on September 27, 1944, Eckert sent a letter to the other Moore School engineers, advising them that he and Mauchly intended to take out a patent and asking them to notify him of any contributions they felt they had made that were patentable. Kite Sharpless was the only one who suggested he, Sharpless, had originated such an idea, but he never pursued the matter. Nancy Stern has written that the other engineers were either content to let Eckert and Mauchly claim sole invention or did not see how such a patent would be of any real value.[15]

Brainerd was outraged. He testified later that when he heard of the letter he called Eckert to his office and "demanded" an explanation. He said he told Eckert he considered the letter an act of disloyalty to the Moore School. He felt the invention was

15. Some scientists later changed their minds. Eckert thinks that this happened only when they became aware of the commercial possibilities. Among those who did alter their opinion was Arthur Burks, who later claimed that he, Shaw, and Sharpless were also co-inventors of ENIAC. "Nobody ever explained to us what were the criteria for having an idea," he said, "and I had been led to believe that the patents belonged to Eckert and Mauchly." His claim was denied in court, and he has since spent considerable time fighting the notion that Eckert and Mauchly were the sole inventors of the computer.

a team effort, not the work of one or two members of the team. He said the letter "led to a cleavage in our group." Later he told Pender he would have nothing to do with the question of patents.

Brainerd considered the effort to gain a patent a violation of academic ethics. He was so incensed that he resigned from the ENIAC project (although not from computer research), and Warren took it over.

Eckert claimed that he wrote the letter only because Brainerd had been asked to apply for a patent and had failed to do so. Eckert had retained a patent attorney, George A. Smith, and Smith was demanding to know whose name should be on the patent.

Goldstine tended to favor Brainerd's point of view but admitted that the university did nothing about filing for patents.

"It's a very complicated story," he said. "The Moore School signed in its contracts with the government, it had agreed that it would furnish the government with material so that the government could take out patents [in the name of the inventors]. I believe the government in those days was willing to take out patents, keeping for the government a royalty-free license and giving the university the rights to the patents. The Moore School had done nothing about the patents. . . . I don't think it was important to the university at that point. I suppose most universities would have acted in exactly the same way. I don't think they were very conscious of [patents]; I think it was a new concept to them."

Goldstine said he felt the university was procrastinating and just assumed that sooner or later someone would "get the engineers to write up stuff in their notebooks and turn it over to the government."

"We were told at the beginning of our contract at the Moore School," Mauchly maintained, "that we would have the patent rights to exploit any of these [inventions]. . . ."

"This provided really the explosive matter which blew up the whole business eventually," Goldstine said. Indeed it would. As we shall see, Pender's compromise did not hold.

Meanwhile, work at the Moore School progressed. Unlike

Charles Babbage, Eckert knew when to freeze the design of his computer. Except for adding accumulators at the army's request, the engineers were involved in finishing ENIAC as it was then designed. They were already behind schedule, and it was growing increasingly clear that ENIAC would not be ready in time to have any effect on the war. The Moore School people also knew that ENIAC was primitive, that it had several basic flaws which would limit its use. They wanted to incorporate what they knew in a second machine.

The principal flaw was ENIAC's inability to hold easily altered instructions in its memory. Every time the machine needed reprogramming, operators had to run around the room turning dials, throwing switches, replugging cables, and rolling function tables about. Producing a stored memory entailed considerable complications, and the Moore School engineers decided that, for the sake of expediency, they would not try to build one for ENIAC. They explained to the army in a progress report, dated December 31, 1943:

no attempt has been made to make provision for setting up a problem automatically. This is for the sake of simplicity and because it is anticipated that the ENIAC will be used primarily for problems of a type in which one set-up will be used many times before another problem is placed on the machine.

"It was realized that this whole method of programming was a clumsy method, and archaic in relation to the high speed vacuum tubes," Burks said. It did not matter with firing tables, which permitted the same program to run for weeks, but it did matter with general computation.

The problem had been discussed several times in engineering meetings during the autumn of 1943 and through the winter of 1944. Harry Huskey, who joined the Moore School from Ohio State early in the year, reported having had at least one discussion with Eckert after he first arrived, in which Eckert indicated the problem to him. Eckert had several ideas for solving the problem, and on January 29, 1944,[16] he wrote down one of them

16. The date, as we shall see, is important.

in a memo, in which he described a "speedier, simpler machine," containing a shaft that carried several disks. One such disk

could generate such pulse or electric signals as were required in time to control and initiate the operations required in the calculations. This is similar to the tone generating mechanism used in some electric organs and offers a permanent way of storing the basic signals required. . . . If multiple shaft systems are used a great increase in the available facilities for allowing automatic programming of the facilities and processes involved may be made since longer scales are provided. This greatly extends the usefulness and attractiveness of such a machine. This programming may be of the temporary type set up on alloy discs or the permanent type on etched discs.

The engineers were also unhappy with the limited storage capacity of ENIAC, and thought a new machine could be built with a significant increase in memory.

Goldstine suggested to Simon in August 1944 that a "new R & D contract be entered into with the Moore School to permit that institution to continue research and development with the objective of building ultimately a new ENIAC of improved design." The new machine would be called the Electronic Discrete Variable Automatic Computer, or EDVAC. In the next month, Brainerd contributed a memo to Gillon pointing out the deficiencies in ENIAC.

In October 1944 army ordnance granted a $105,600 contract for the development of the new machine, to which every computer built since owes its parentage.

Eckert and Mauchly could not know, however, that they had already lost control of their invention. That had happened on a railroad platform in Aberdeen, in the summer of 1944.

7. Von Neumann

Only a man born in Budapest can enter a revolving door
behind you and come out in front.
JOHN VON NEUMANN

THE PHYSICISTS AT LOS ALAMOS long embraced a theory that
had nothing to do with nuclear weapons. According to this theory, all Hungarians are Martians.

Consider: Martians left their home planet centuries ago and
settled in central Europe. They hid their extraterrestrial origins
out of fear their neighbors would try to destroy them. Only three
characteristics gave them away. First, a wanderlust—the irre-
pressible gypsy. Second, their language—Hungarian is related
to no other language on earth except Finnish. Third, their ability to produce people who knew far more than mortal earthlings
should know—they brought forth in this century a group of men
of extraordinary genius, who dominated physics and mathematics far more than could be expected for a country as small as
Hungary.

They were all products of the middle class of Budapest, all

possessing enormous intellect. They all knew each other; many of them even went to the same high school, Budapest Lutheran.[1] They included Edward Teller, Leo Szilard, Eugene Wigner, Dennis Gabor, and Oskar Jászi.

The most unearthly genius of them all was John von Neumann, a mathematician who frequently crossed the line into physics in a manner unheard of in his time, and often ventured beyond science into metaphysics.

Von Neumann was born on December 28, 1903, in the golden sunset of Habsburg Budapest. His father, Max, was a Jewish banker, whom the Habsburgs elevated to nobility and whom they permitted to add to the family name Neumann the Hungarian honorific "Margattai." Neumann germanized the honorific to "von," as he legally could, and the family became von Neumann (always pronounced in the German fashion—fon-NOY-mahn).

Hungarian society at the turn of the century was mainly feudal, a conglomerate of Magyars ("true" Hungarians) and an assortment of ethnic groups such as Croats, Rumanians, Serbs, and Slovaks. Few of the latter spoke Hungarian. Relatively few Jews lived in Hungary at the time; most of those who did had immigrated from other parts of the Austro-Hungarian Empire and Russia. Upwardly mobile, however, they had migrated to Budapest in large enough numbers that at the turn of the century they constituted half the population of the city. Not a few, like Max von Neumann, were bankers, allied by mutual necessity to the hereditary nobility. They were mainly bilingual, speaking Hungarian when necessary, German when given the choice.

János von Neumann (who immediately acquired the nickname Jancsi, the equivalent of Johnny, pronounced Yon-shee) was the oldest of three sons. The family was a loving one; von Neumann's mother was a charming, intelligent, warm woman, with whom von Neumann always remained close.

In 1914 von Neumann was enrolled in the Lutheran gymnasium for boys. Almost immediately, his teacher Ladislas Ratz could tell the elder von Neumann that the ten-year-old boy was a mathematical prodigy, and recommended special education.

1. This is surprising because many of them were Jewish. It was the best school in Budapest, and the most tolerant, apparently.

With the father's permission,[2] the boy was introduced to J. Kuerschak, a leading mathematician at the university, who arranged for a young colleague, Michael Fekete, to tutor von Neumann at home. Von Neumann's reputation as a prodigy was spread throughout the intellectual community of Hungary before von Neumann could confront adolescence. He was always special. One of his childhood friends, the physicist Eugene Wigner,[3] remembered walks with von Neumann:

We often took walks and he told me about mathematics and about set theory and this and that. It was amazing. And he loved to talk about mathematics—he went on and on and I drank it in. He was inexhaustible on such occasions in telling me about set theory, number theory, and other mathematical subjects. It was really wonderful. He never thought of going home. . . . He was phenomenal. . . .

In school and among his colleagues, Jancsi was somewhat retiring. He participated in the pranks of the class, but a bit halfheartedly, just enough to avoid unpopularity. He had a few close friends and was respected by all—intellectual strength was recognized and approved of by the student body, if not always envied.

Throughout his life, in fact, intimacy in relationships seemed a threat to his intellect, and though von Neumann grew into the most charming of men, he was frequently described as "cold" and "aloof."

Before he even graduated from high school, von Neumann published an original mathematical paper.

The Budapest of the period was a gay, exciting, wonderful city, the city of Franz Lehár and the operettas. The actress Illona Massey held court in the same apartment building in which the von Neumanns lived. Theaters and nightclubs abounded. Budapest was a fine place in which to be young.

The peace and security were shattered by World War I. On the wrong side of the war, Hungary lost two-thirds of its territory and population, and the Magyars lost domination over the

2. Von Neumann and his father could joke together in classical Greek from the time von Neumann was six years old.
3. Wigner won the Nobel Prize in physics, in 1963, as a U.S. citizen. Dennis Gabor, also a part of the "Hungarian phenomenon," won the Nobel Prize in physics, as a British citizen, in 1971. Nobel made no provisions for a prize in mathematics.

other ethnic groups. Refugees poured into Budapest. Political debates were carried on everywhere, and rioting and violence were not uncommon. The government was taken over by liberal republicans, and then by Béla Kun and the Communists. Kun expropriated the banks, and the von Neumann family was forced to flee to Vienna. In August 1919, when Kun was overthrown by the Horthy regime, the von Neumanns were permitted to return to Budapest and their business. Ironically, the republican and the Kun governments were supportive of Hungary's Jews (Kun was Jewish) but detested bankers. The Horthy regime was rabidly anti-Semitic but liked bankers, even Jewish ones. The von Neumann family was in the position of having to flee a pro-Jewish government and being saved by an anti-Semitic one.

Despite anti-Semitic laws limiting the number of Jews allowed to attend the university, von Neumann was admitted to the University of Budapest, but he chose to spend most of his time at the University of Berlin, where he could listen to Albert Einstein and study with the mathematician Erhard Schmidt. Wigner, Szilard, and Gabor were also in Berlin. While still technically enrolled at Budapest, he took a degree in chemical engineering from the Eidgenössische Technische Hochschule in Zurich.[4] In 1926 Budapest granted him a Ph.D. in mathematics.

Von Neumann went off to the little German university town of Göttingen to further his education. The university already enjoyed a first-rate reputation; Karl Friedrich Gauss had built his observatory there in 1807. Göttingen was in an astonishing golden age of physics and mathematics under the leadership of the German mathematician David Hilbert. It is no exaggeration to say that practically everyone who influenced mathematics and physics in the first half of the century taught at, studied at, or spent some time at Göttingen. Max Born was in the physics department. Werner Heisenberg was a student and did his work

4. Herman Goldstine explained that chemical engineering was something of a fad at that time. "All mommies and daddies wanted their little boys to be chemical engineers," he told the author. "Chemical engineering was invented in Germany, and it came into its own during the First World War, so it was pretty natural that parents would read about all those great attainments in chemistry and assume that's what their little boy ought to be in." Wigner was also pushed into chemical engineering.

on quantum physics at Göttingen. Erwin Schrödinger published his work on basic atomic physics. As Jacob Bronowski wrote, "here is where the arguments took place. And from all over the world people came to Göttingen to join in." Szilard and Wigner were there. Einstein dropped by. Paul Dirac, Lothar Nordheim, Wolfgang Pauli, and Linus Pauling visited Göttingen. J. Robert Oppenheimer and Norbert Wiener came from America.[5] Von Neumann studied under and collaborated with Hilbert.

Von Neumann became a privatdozent in mathematics at the University of Berlin, and in 1930 Oswald Veblen invited him to come to Princeton University as a visiting professor. A year later he was offered a permanent job. In 1933 he went to the newly formed Institute for Advanced Studies, located down the road from the university, a scientific think tank funded by the New Jersey department store magnate Felix Fuld.

Describing von Neumann's mathematical work in any detail is difficult and irrelevant to the story of the computer, but some mention of it is necessary because it is important for an understanding of, first, the world in which von Neumann's remarkable brain resided and, second, the enormous regard in which he was held in the scientific community when he enters our story.

Modern mathematics, for all intents and purposes, began in 1910, with the publication of the *Principia Mathematica*, by Bertrand Russell and Alfred North Whitehead, which held that all mathematics was derived from logic and was without contradictions. Russell and Whitehead went into great detail to prove that this was so.

Hilbert and his followers believed that mathematics should be separated from their meanings, that is, the number 7 meant the number 7 and had no meaning drawn from experience. A positive number was a positive number was a positive number. Hilbert tried to dissociate the number from the logic; he even harnessed the methods of Russell and Whitehead to prove his point. Their method, he wrote, was itself consistent and free of contradictions.

5. One of Hitler's first acts was to install a political hack to run the university. The department of mathematics, possibly the best in the history of the world, quickly dispersed, mostly to America.

In 1927 von Neumann got into the act with a famous paper supporting Hilbert's position. All analysis, von Neumann argued, could be proven to be without contradictions.

Three years later the position of Hilbert and von Neumann was demolished by the young German mathematician Kurt Gödel, whose famous theory holds that "in any sufficiently powerful logical system, statements can be formulated which are neither provable nor unprovable within that system, unless the system is logically inconsistent." The logical system he had in mind was Whitehead and Russell's, but he was saying Hilbert and von Neumann were also wrong.

A brief example of the kind of unprovable statement is Epimenides' paradox. Epimenides was a Cretan who said, "All Cretans are liars." Look at that statement long enough and you must realize that no matter how you handle it, the statement comes back on itself; if it is true, and Epimenides is a liar, then the statement is false, because he was telling the truth. It also works in reverse, in what Douglas Hofstadter called a "strange loop." A simpler statement might be "This statement is false." Hofstadter wrote that Gödel demonstrated that "provability is a weaker notion than truth."

This was the world in which mathematics became metamathematics and leaped across into philosophy. Von Neumann lived in this world comfortably. He wrote his paper when he was twenty-four.

Von Neumann was a pioneer in game theory, and wrote, with Oskar Morgenstern, a paper adapting game theory to real-life strategic situations, including military matters.

His place in science is secure as one of the first to take theoretical mathematics and marry it to practical physics.

The anecdotes about his mental prowess take up more space than we have to relate them, but a few must be mentioned.

Goldstine once asked von Neumann to recite *A Tale of Two Cities*. Von Neumann began, "It was the best of times, it was the worst of times. . . ." Fifteen minutes later, when it was clear he was prepared to recite the entire book from memory, he was begged to stop. He had not read the Dickens classic in twenty years.

He never forgot jokes and could recall them at just the right moment in any conversation. His brain, which could perform calculations at a speed virtually unmatched by any other living human, was also the repository of possibly the world's largest collection of dirty limericks.

Von Neumann had memorized all twenty-one volumes of the *Cambridge Ancient History* and the *Cambridge Medieval History,* and was an expert on all the royal family trees of Europe.

His lectures were a chore for his students. He believed in using only a small portion of the blackboard. He would write down an idea, and immediately erase it, so that he could go on to his next idea. Students had to race to see whether they could write down the first thought before the eraser flew and von Neumann was writing something else. By common acknowledgment, his style was brilliant. Goldstine wrote:

One of the difficulties people experienced in listening to one of his lectures on mathematics was precisely its sheer beauty and elegance. They were often so taken in by the ease with which results were proved that they thought they understood the path von Neumann had chosen. Later at home when they tried to re-create it, they discovered not the magical path but instead a harsh, forbidding forest.

His ability to compute in his head made him the target for innumerable practical jokes. Von Neumann was frequently asked to help a colleague through a difficult problem, which he usually could do without pencil and paper. Several times he was asked to solve problems the colleague had already solved, just to see how good he was. He invariably succeeded. Occasionally, however, the colleague pretended to have arrived at the answer while von Neumann was still thinking. Upset that someone could be faster than he was, he was known to sulk for weeks until he was let in on the joke.

He had a passion for children's toys and was wont to scrap with five-year-olds to see who could get at the toy first.

His biographer Steve Heims has written that von Neumann's personality was complex. He enjoyed sex, for the pleasure of it, but without emotional involvement. If he entered an office with a good-looking secretary, he was known to find an excuse to bend over to look up her dress. He was sometimes described as emotionally underdeveloped.

He was married twice. Heims relates one instance in which his second wife was sick in bed. She asked von Neumann for a glass of water. He went downstairs, but returned emply-handed fifteen minutes later.

"Where do we keep the glasses in this house?" he asked. He had lived in the house for seventeen years.

He carefully nurtured his Hungarian accent, and at least one acquaintance caught him speaking perfect, unaccented American. When he checked himself, the accent returned.

He destroyed a car per year on the streets of Princeton, and several friends described him as an astonishingly poor driver, given to roaring down a one-way street in the wrong direction. "Von Neumann couldn't even change a tire on an automobile. He was a complete idiot, mechanically," one friend said.

In his later years, Johnny, as he was known to all, showed an almost childlike fascination for people in uniforms (or anyone else with power) and became a leading proponent of nuclear armament. He was frequently criticized for being a shill for the government, and his attitude was called a loss to science; he was impressed by honors and fame. One critic wrote, "I regret, personally as well as scientifically, that honors and duties have ascended to your entertaining head. It would be good to see and hear you again—just for the fun of it." All who knew him were impressed by his sense of invulnerability and his sense of survival.

Von Neumann signed on to become a consultant to the Manhattan Project in 1943, and to Aberdeen at about the same time. He was fascinated then by hydrodynamics, useful because air acts like a fluid when extreme pressure (such as an explosion) is applied to it. His particular interest was implosions, which involved the ability to produce a symmetrical shock wave that compressed the fissionable material (U-235) so that it exploded in a predictable fashion, producing a maximum effect. Von Neumann and James L. Tuck developed a "high explosive lens" that made the atomic bomb work.

He had been interested in mechanical computing. In January 1944 he wrote to Warren Weaver at the Applied Mathematics Panel, asking what facilities the government had for computation. Weaver told him about Aiken, Stibitz, and Wallace Eckert at Columbia. He did not mention the Moore School, apparently considering their work naïve.

Von Neumann commuted between Los Alamos, Aberdeen, and Princeton. One day in June 1944, he was standing on the train platform at Aberdeen when Goldstine spotted him.

"I knew him in a very perfunctory sort of way," Goldstine later said. "A couple of years before I went into the army, the American Mathematical Society had a session at the University of Michigan on modern theories of integration, and I was asked to be the reporter for the meeting. . . . One of the speakers was von Neumann. . . . Now, to think that von Neumann remembered me is dubious, but at least I had met him, and I knew what he looked like."

Goldstine went to von Neumann and introduced himself. Von Neumann was charming, as usual, and casually inquired what Goldstine was up to. Goldstine described ENIAC, telling von Neumann the machine was capable of 333 multiplications per second. Von Neumann's eyes lit up. What began as a casual conversation turned into what Goldstine described as something like the oral examinations for a doctorate. Von Neumann was clearly taken with the idea.

A day or so later, von Neumann telephoned Goldstine and asked to see the work at the Moore School. Von Neumann did not have the proper security clearance, but that was simply ignored.

"We first heard about this sometime around the first of August," Mauchly remembered, "that there was going to be an eminent mathematician to come up here and talk to us, and he might be a great deal of help to us because he was about the most eminent mathematician in the world. . . . I was as anxious as anyone to meet this man and find out what he could do for us."

"His clearance to come there . . . was arranged by about September 7. . . . He came to the Moore School, and Goldstine introduced him around, and I showed him the two accumulators. . . . They could compute a little faster than Dr. von Neumann could. . . . He looked at our exhibit, and we were told to show him anything, tell him anything. We then settled down in a room someplace and talked in front of a blackboard.

Von Neumann was told about the new machine the Moore School people wanted to build, and he clearly understood the ramifications of this kind of computing ability. He certainly saw the possibilities of using a machine like ENIAC on his Los Alamos problems.

"He was really racing far ahead and speculating as to how you build better computers, because that's what we were talking to him about," Mauchly said. "We said we don't want to build another of these things [ENIACs]. We've got much better solutions in many ways."

Von Neumann arranged to be taken on as a consultant to the ENIAC project, and he visited Philadelphia many more times. He now became an avid supporter of the Moore School's work, legitimizing it in the eyes of the scientific establishment, and he was helpful in its getting the EDVAC contract. He was in frequent conference with Mauchly and Eckert. His forte was clearly the logical makeup of the machine; his abilities as a logician were unique. The technical issues now took on a more formal air. Nancy Stern has written that before his arrival Eckert and Mauchly provided most of the direction by means of informal conversations. After von Neumann entered the picture, there were regular staff meetings with recorded minutes. Von Neumann was highly active in the meetings, making suggestions, acting as a sounding board. Goldstine wrote to Gillon:

As far as EDVAC is concerned, Johnny von Neumann has been working for us as a consultant and has been devoting enormous amounts of his prodigious energy to working out the logical controls of the machine. He has also been very much interested in helping design circuits for the machine.

Burks told of a time when the group was discussing adders; Eckert and Mauchly had developed several using ten tubes. Von Neumann announced he could do it with five.

"No," Eckert said, "it takes at least ten tubes."

"I'll prove it to you," von Neumann said, and drew an adder on the blackboard.

"No," said Eckert, "your first tube can't drive its load in one microsecond, so an inverter is needed, then another tube to restore the polarity."

"You're right," von Neumann admitted after further argument. "It takes ten tubes to add—five tubes for logic, and five tubes for electronics!"

The main problem with ENIAC, and the main task facing the designers of EDVAC, was the creation of a stored, programmable memory. To be truly useful, EDVAC needed to remember instructions and to be able to have those instructions changed at the will of the operator without all the unplugging, dialing, button-flicking work of the ENIAC.

The best candidate for a storage device was the mercury delay tube, something Eckert knew a great deal about.

The principle is traceable to the work of Pierre and Jacques Curie in 1880. The Curies found that if they applied an electric current to a quartz crystal, the crystal could be made to vibrate at a known rate. Conversely, if they could make it vibrate, it would produce electric current at a known frequency.[6]

William Shockley[7] of the Bell Labs was working on the concept that sound waves travel through a liquid at a much slower rate than electricity travels through a wire. If one could measure the rate of travel through any liquid, then by building a tube of that liquid of a known length one would produce a predictable delay in the transmission of that impulse. He built a tube containing water and ethylene glycol and proved the concept.

A better tube was built a few years later, one using mercury as the fluid. Sound travels through mercury at the known rate of 1,450 meters per second. A tube 1.450 meters long (four feet, nine inches) would produce a delay of one millisecond. The builder of the tube? J. Presper Eckert for the Radiation Laboratory at MIT.

Eckert's solution for the computer problem was a combination of the two discoveries. He put a quartz crystal at one end of

6. This is the same principle used in quartz watches.
7. The same Shockley who went on to co-invent the transistor.

a mercury tube. It oscillated when given a jolt of electricity. The vibration traveled the length of the tube to another crystal, which absorbed the pulse and oscillated in response. This oscillation produced another electric impulse. If the end crystal was connected to the beginning crystal, the impulse could theoretically be kept going through the tubes almost indefinitely. Actually, friction and resistance gradually weakened the signal, but Eckert suggested a box with ten vacuum tubes to amplify and shape the signal. In ENIAC, one number stored required one tube. In EDVAC, 1,000 binary digits could be stored with ten vacuum tubes and a delay line.

No controversy involving the history of the computer matches what happened to this idea.

Tension was already high at the Moore School. Eckert and Mauchly had won their fight over the ENIAC patent. They understood that the work they were doing on EDVAC should also be patentable. They were technologists and had a clear understanding of the commercial possibilities of their machines. Many persons at the Moore School did not, or did not think any one or two people should benefit from them. Von Neumann was on the side of the latter, believing the work was for the war but also for pure science. He represented, to an extent, the academician who opposed the technologist. Talk of patents seemed to upset him.

On June 30, 1945, a 101-page document arrived at the Moore School from von Neumann in Los Alamos. It bore the title "First Draft of a Report to the EDVAC" and was credited to John von Neumann. The paper contained a brilliant and complete exposition of all the thinking that had been done at the Moore School on the new computer. Von Neumann had taken this work and fashioned it in a unique way, describing the logic and makeup of the machine, which he called "a very high speed automatic digital computing system" and "an automatic computing system." The machine he described had a stored, programmable memory. Instructions for its operation were extensive.

Von Neumann was influenced by the work of Warren McCulloch, a neurophysiologist at the University of Illinois, and

Walter Pitts, a mathematician, who in 1943 published a paper describing the physiology of the human brain and the "logical calculus" of brain activity. Von Neumann's paper on EDVAC was replete with references to neurons and other parts of the human nervous system, comparing them to the automatic computer. Besides offering the first example of anthropomorphizing the computer, the paper took on the unmistakable characteristics of a von Neumann creation. No one in the world could have done it as well.

Goldstine and Warren had the paper reproduced and distributed it all around the Moore School. Goldstine proceeded to send copies to interested scientists around the country and to Britain. When the scope of the distribution became apparent in the Moore School, there was considerable consternation. Eckert and Mauchly were outraged.

Their anger was based on three things. First, the work at the Moore School was still classified, and by publishing and distributing the "First Draft," Goldstine was violating security regulations.

Second, if the two men were going to apply for a patent on EDVAC, there could be no doubt about their primacy; no lawyer would be able to challenge their right to say the idea originated with them. They feared that publication would harm their chances of obtaining and holding a patent.

Third, and most important, von Neumann's paper contained almost no reference to the work of the other Moore School researchers, and they feared that because of his fame credit would accrue to von Neumann for what was not his. They both knew the axiom in science holding that if a group of scientists gets together to discover something important, the most famous of them will get the credit. The axiom held in this case as well. Moreover, in science the first person to publish usually gets the credit. Eckert could not publish his ideas outside the Moore School, because EDVAC was a military secret.

There is no evidence that von Neumann intended to take credit not due him, and his reference to the work as a "first draft" would seem to indicate that he intended the paper to be distributed among the researchers for comment and corrections before a final paper was distributed. Goldstine's action, however, made publication a fait accompli.

On the other hand, it must be said that at no time did von Neumann try to correct the record, disown sole authorship of the ideas, or disavow credit. The "First Draft" was the first publication that outside scientists had seen containing the outline for an electronic computer with a stored memory, and the natural assumption to be made from such a publication was that the idea had originated with von Neumann.

The paper has become, arguably, the single most important document in the field. Almost every history written about the computer, or about von Neumann, credits him with the idea of a stored memory computer. Among scientists, computers are to this day known as von Neumann machines.

Von Neumann was not the originator of the stored-program computer. As we have seen, the idea for such a machine was being discussed at the Moore School a year before von Neumann arrived on the scene, and Eckert had written a memo on the subject almost six months before von Neumann had even heard about the Moore School project.

Goldstine has defended his actions and stoutly maintains that von Neumann deserves credit for the stored program.

This report represents a masterful analysis and synthesis by him of all the thinking that had gone into the EDVAC from the fall of 1944 through the spring of 1945. Not everything in there is his, but the crucial parts are. . . .

It is obvious that von Neumann, by writing his report, crystallized thinking in the field of computers as no other person ever did. He was, among all members of the group at the Moore School, the indispensable one . . . only von Neumann was essential to the entire task.

Why did von Neumann let the record stand? Eckert had a story and a theory, although it must be kept in mind that Eckert is not a disinterested witness.

"We were in a railroad station, and a bunch of us were getting a meal," he related, "and when they were supposed to bring separate checks but didn't. When the girl arrives with this check, and people said, 'Von Neumann, you're the mathematician,' and handed it to him as a joke. He looks it over and checks it out, and says, 'They forgot to put my crab shells on the bill. Other than that, it's all right. And this raises an ethical problem.' They said, 'What's that?' And he said, 'To take the saving myself or divide it among the rest of you.' Of course, he ignored the third possibility.

"I began to believe those were his ethics."

Von Neumann's dislike of Eckert and Mauchly, particularly of their inclination toward commercializing the computer, was growing at the time, and that might have had something to do with his attitude.

Some historians have written that there is space on the title page for more names, but this is debatable. In fact, there are two title pages. The first, which gives only the title, contains von Neumann's by-line and has room for other names. The second, more complete page has no room for more names.

Von Neumann's contributions to EDVAC are real and important, and his overall contributions to the early computers, as we shall see, are not minor. But the publication of the "First Draft" soured the atmosphere at the Moore School and has seriously distorted the history of the computer. As will become evident, the legal ramifications to Eckert and Mauchly fulfilled their worst nightmares.

Work on ENIAC continued. The war was ending, and the Moore School engineers knew ENIAC would not be ready in time to help in the war effort. They had another project, EDVAC, in mind, and they were sure their computer was worth pursuing.

The army still wanted its machine, and in May 1945 a contract was signed between Aberdeen and Penn arranging for ENIAC to be moved to Aberdeen when it was ready. A computing annex was built for ENIAC. Goldstine, now a captain, created a corps of people who would be permanently assigned to the machine, with John V. Holberton in charge.

The machine was generally finished at this stage; only the square-rooter was not yet installed.

"Somebody gave us a whole stack of blueprints, and these were the wiring diagrams for all the panels." McNulty remembered, "and they said, 'Here, figure out how the machine works and then figure out how to program it.' This was a little bit hard to do. So Dr. Burks at that time was one of the people assigned to explain to us how the various parts of the computer worked, how an accumulator worked. Well, once you knew how an accumulator worked, you could pretty well be able to trace the other circuits for yourself and figure this thing out.

"We then proceeded to program a trajectory to go onto this machine. We had barely begun to think that we had enough knowledge of the machine to program a trajectory, when we were told that two people were coming from Los Alamos to put a problem on the machine."

Von Neumann had arranged a test of ENIAC. The two men from Los Alamos were Stanley P. Frankel and Nicholas Metropolis, both theoretical physicists. The test was not what Brainerd had in mind for ENIAC; he wanted the machine to begin with something simple and work its way up. But von Neumann and Goldstine convinced him that something more important was involved.

No one actually knew where von Neumann worked when he was not in Philadelphia, but several people, including Burks, surmised it was out West (he once drove to Philadelphia with his daughter and said it took "several days"). Goldstine wrote that he simply had to trust von Neumann when he said that it was important, because although the equations were not classified, the problem they would help solve—the hydrogen bomb—certainly was.

Edward Teller said later that it was von Neumann

who persuaded us in Los Alamos to use computing machines. First the IBM equipment, which at the time was mechanical and magnetic, rather than electronic . . . was, indeed, exceedingly clumsy. . . . Johnny also made us aware . . . that this type of activity had a tremendous future. Particularly it had such a future because of the availability and increasing availability of electronic equipment which could and would speed up computing so as to surpass the rapidity of execution what the human brain can do.

Frankel and Metropolis were not seeking the answers to a problem; they were trying to find out whether the problem, which had to do with the trigger to the hydrogen bomb, was answerable. They arrived in Philadelphia in the summer of 1945 to check out the new machine. Enrico Fermi, intrigued by von Neumann's description of the machine, had tried to make the trip but could not get away. Adele Goldstine and the new women programmers helped explain the machine to Frankel and Metropolis and show them how the problem had to be addressed. By October the two men had programmed their problem on huge sheets of paper and brought them back to Philadelphia. The equations were carefully concealed to keep their nature from being detected.

The women then went about the task of programming the problem into the machine. ENIAC was totally untested at the time, and "no one knew how many bad joints there were, and how many bad tubes there were and so on," McNulty said.

"John and Pres were like mother hens—they were mother hens! Of course they were. They stayed with that computer night and day, and whatever went wrong, they went in there. There were a couple of engineers assigned to do the work, but [Eckert and Mauchly] were completely involved in every aspect of that operation—not in the problem itself. I'm not even sure they were told what the problem was."

One million IBM cards were used. Because of the limited memory of ENIAC, intermediate results had to be printed out, new cards punched, and these cards submitted back to the machine—a cumbersome process. Nonetheless, ENIAC worked splendidly. Within a month the results were in, and Los Alamos knew the problem was solvable. The director of Los Alamos sent a thank you to the Moore School, suggesting that the problem would not have been workable without ENIAC. "It is clear that physics as well as other sciences will profit greatly from the development of such machines."

Frankel and Metropolis were not the only visitors. By now most of the scientific community (at least those with security clearances) had traveled to the Moore School to see the new gadget. Veblen was there, the mathematician Mina Rees came by, Warren Weaver of the Applied Mathematics Panel from Bush's office came through. So did Jay Forrester, of MIT, who would later invent the magnetic-core memory, crucial to the usefulness of computers. From RCA came Vladimir Zworykin and Jan Rajchman, who had cooperated with the Moore School engineers (but had declined to take part in the contract, because Rajchman felt the Moore School engineers "extraordinarily naïve" and because Zworykin doubted the machine would work). Indeed, ENIAC was becoming a tourist attraction for the scientific community. Word spread throughout the country that Penn had an electronic computer that looked as though it would work. Even the classification of the project was dropped a notch to "restricted," as the usefulness of the more extensive classification was obviously in doubt.

A public unveiling was scheduled for February.

Mauchly, in the meantime, was trying to drum up business. He wanted to finish EDVAC, and after the war the army was no longer the best source of funding. He went to Pender for suggestions. Pender said he didn't really know where the money might come from; he suggested trying the American Philosophical Society, in Philadelphia, a small group of social scientists and philosophers[8] that gave out grants of a few hundred dollars each. That did not sound like a good idea to Mauchly.

Mauchly thought he knew of more likely candidates. He had been spending some time in Washington on a part-time job with the Naval Ordnance Laboratory. "I was down there . . . because of the fact that I could get no assurances from the Moore School that I would have a job thereafter; I was trying to keep a few irons in the fire so that if things turned out very badly at the Moore School, I would have another place to go."

"They wanted me as a statistician for underwater mines working on the acoustic principle, and all the tests they were making," he said. Mauchly said the invitation was arranged by, of all people, John Atanasoff, who had left Iowa State and was working for the navy in Washington. Mauchly's first trip to Washington was postponed because it conflicted with von Neu-

8. The society was founded by Benjamin Franklin. It is housed in a building in the Independence Hall complex and still meets once a year.

mann's first visit to Philadelphia, but Mauchly eventually went to naval ordnance. As with everything involving these two men, there exist two entirely different stories about their third encounter, each telling in its own way.

Mauchly:

"I tried to find out whether anything had come of his attempts at building a computer out at Iowa, and he didn't seem to want to talk about it. He wasn't interested in it, as far as I could tell. I came to regard this in the same way Ike Auerbach has ... he was a computer dropout. He just didn't seem to have any interest in computers.

"I told him we were working on a method where we would use a crystal, which would convert electric waves into sound waves and send them through mercury and back to electrical. I understood that the navy had some new crystals ... which were good for this kind of effect. He knew all about that, he thought he could tell me a lot about that; he made some calculations and he went on on how useful he could be if we would just give him some kind of work order which would transfer funds to him for doing work on it. We didn't have any way of doing that, of course."[9]

Atanasoff:

"I couldn't understand why he was there [at ordnance]; he seemed to have something to do with computers. Finally one day he ... told me, 'What you've done is old hat, and we've got a brand-new method of computing that's far improved over yours.'. . . He couldn't [tell] me, because it was classified. I didn't want to see it; I just wanted him to tell me about it. . . . He seemed to have so much time to come down to see me. My boss, Dr. Roy Weller, said it's his conclusion he came down just to watch me. He knew his ideas came from me." Atanasoff said he found work for Mauchly.[10]

Mauchly used his time for something more important than watching Atanasoff: he looked up friends who might provide funding for computers.

"My friends were in two places, the Weather Bureau and the

9. Interview with Esther Carr.
10. Interview with the author.

Census Bureau," he told Esther Carr. "I went down to the Census Bureau. I found that my friends were very interested; they were very receptive to the idea, and they said they'd try to do something more about it." The U.S. Weather Bureau also expressed interest. He could not tell them much about the machine, because of the secrecy. But ever the amateur meteorologist, Mauchly understood that weather forecasting would never approach being an exact science until high-speed computing was possible.[11]

Apparently, von Neumann understood this as well. On January 11, 1946, one month before the cloak of secrecy was to be lifted on ENIAC, someone brought a copy of the *New York Times* to the Moore School. Under the by-line of Sidney Shallett, from its Washington bureau, the *Times* reported:

> Plans have been presented to the Weather Bureau the Navy and the Army for development of a new electronic calculator, reported to have astounding possibilities, which, in time, might have a revolutionary effect in solving the mysteries of long-range weather forecasting. Official sources confirmed today that a conference was held in Washington yesterday, under the sponsorship of the Weather Bureau, at which representatives of the bureau, the Navy and the Army Air Force Weather Service heard the proposal outlined by the scientists who developed it.

Who were the scientists who developed this wondrous gadget and presented the plan to the government? Von Neumann and Zworykin. The story then went on to report that the "electronic calculator, as conceived by Drs. Von Neumann and Zworykin," was capable of performing a multiplication in eleven microseconds, and could solve 100,000 different equations in one minute. There were attempts in the past to produce high-speed computing, it noted, "but none of the existing machines . . . is as pretentious in scope as the von Neumann-Zworykin device."

This time everyone at the Moore School was upset, Eckert and Mauchly most of all. After all, the existence of such a machine was still classified information. Now, not only was the idea out in

11. Mauchly's dream remains unrealized. Although the fastest computers in the world, ILIAC and the CRAY, have been put to work, weather is far more complicated than Mauchly dreamed. The kind of long-range weather forecasting using computers that he talked about is still not here.

the scientific community, but the general public knew about it and the invention of the machine was being credited to others. Even more important, again, the machine was the work not of von Neumann and Zworykin but of Eckert and Mauchly and the team at the Moore School. Von Neumann had nothing to do with ENIAC and was part of the team involved with EDVAC. Zworykin, RCA's resident inventor,[12] had nothing to do with either. His laboratories helped with some of the peripheral equipment. The *Times* story did not mention that such a computer had been built, but it stated clearly that the concept was the work of von Veumann and Zworykin and that no one except the famous duo had a thing to do with this advance.

"What was I to think?" Mauchly remembered. "Here we were being very careful in 1946 to keep the secrets for the army, not only with respect to the military secrets and things affecting the national interest, but also to keep their public-relations secrets. We weren't even telling everybody there was such a machine until they had made an announcement."

What angered Mauchly most, however, was that the plan presented to the Washington meeting sounded suspiciously like the one he himself had presented a few months earlier. He had told von Neumann and Goldstine about the meeting, he maintained. The situation was "ultra curious," he said later.

Goldstine was on the telephone to Gillon to see whether something could be done about the leaks. Mauchly tried to reach Shallet, but could not. Then they tried to reach von Neumann in Princeton, but a telephone strike hampered communications. They sent telegrams instead. The next morning, a telegram arrived at the Moore School from von Neumann saying he would be glad to meet with the Moore School team. Although it was a Sunday, Eckert, Mauchly, and Goldstine made the one-hour drive to Princeton. Von Neumann acknowledged he and Zworykin had met with the Washington people. He said his only contact with a reporter had come when someone from the *Times* (presumably Shallet) called to tell him the story was going to appear in the

12. Zworykin, a Russian immigrant, was one of the inventors of television. He is known for his development of the iconoscope tube. RCA's television patents are based on his work.

newspaper and asked him for a comment. He told the group he had declined to say anything to the reporter. The meeting, von Neumann said, was initiated by Francis Reichelderfer, head of the Weather Bureau, who had heard of a meeting between von Neumann, Zworykin, and Rajchman about the computer. Mauchly hopped on a train to New York and went to the Times Building to see whether any more articles on computers were forthcoming and to try to discourage the *Times* editors from doing any more. Satisfied that no more stories could be expected, he and Eckert took the train to Washington to find out who had leaked the story and to see whether his suspicions about the von Neumann-Sworykin plan were founded. Shallett had apparently been tipped off by a naval officer. Mauchly met with Harry Wexler, the head of research at the Weather Bureau, who said, "Well, this all sounded strangely familiar, John. Of course I felt that this sounded just like [what] you had been hinting at. You didn't tell me as much about it as they did. You didn't tell me anything about how many tubes, how much floor space, or all the other things that they were telling us. But I knew that what you told me about was classified, and so there was nothing more that you could say. So I felt that I couldn't say any more either."

Another man at the meeting told Mauchly he had assumed that von Neumann and Zworykin were talking about Mauchly's project and that they were speaking for Mauchly.

Gillon expressed his displeasure to all parties, including Reichelderfer.

In fact, von Neumann was speaking for himself. He had decided long before this that the computer was a major technological advance in scientific research, and he wanted to build one at the Institute for Advanced Study. Zworykin, whose lab was up the street, wanted a piece of the action. Both von Neumann and Zworykin were now urging Eckert and Mauchly to move from Penn to RCA to continue their work. On November 27, 1945, von Neumann offered Eckert (Mauchly only by implication) a post at the Institute for Advanced Study.

"It was clear that there were forces pulling us toward Princeton two ways," Mauchly said, "the Institute for Advanced Study was very close to RCA in Princeton, and Dr. Von Neumann started talking about how he would have the help of the RCA laboratory, Dr. Zworykin's people, in trying to build a machine up there. It would be an attractive feature for us to go up there and help him.

"The only trouble with that attraction was that Dr. Zworykin told a different story. When he talked to me about coming to join the RCA laboratories, he sort of talked as if the whole show was in his laboratory, [and] wouldn't it be nice because of the fact that Dr. von Neumann had volunteered to be a help to us. Further, when I said, 'That's nice. Just where will the patents lie?' he said, 'Well, everything gets assigned to RCA. That's always the practice.' "

Security by now was a joke. On the Fourth of July, 1945, Douglas Hartree had been in from England to take a look around. He went home and started pushing his government to finance computer development. By October 1945 Gillon had given permission for some of the Moore School people to discuss ENIAC and EDVAC at a meeting at MIT. Eckert and Mauchly seemed to be the only two people cowed by the security rules.

The time finally came when the wraps could be taken off ENIAC. The army, justly proud of what it had brought about, decided to hold a public display. Two hundred people—government and military dignitaries and reporters—were invited to the University of Pennsylvania for dinner and to hear speeches.

"As I remember it, the president of the National Academy of Sciences at that time [Frank B. Jewett], who was also director of the Bell Labs . . . he had a talk in which he said he hardly knew how to use a slide rule anymore, and he couldn't imagine what this machine was ever going to be good for," Mauchly told Esther Carr. "I think he meant that as a joke, but on one knew how to take it. It was a letdown for some of us." Maj. Gen. Gladeon M. Barnes, the head of research and development service of the Office of the Chief of Ordnance, gave a speech and pressed the button starting the first demonstration program, "formally dedicating the machine to a career of scientific usefulness."

"We went over to the demonstration where Art Burks and others demonstrated in slow motion the things which ENIAC could do, such as add a number of numbers, and counting, and things of that sort," Mauchly remembered. "Then in high speed, and it was all over before you could see and know what you were seeing. We don't know how well they [the audience] understood what was going on."

At a press conference, the engineers rigged up ENIAC with small frosted lamp bulbs in place of the visible neon bulbs, which were hard to see, and impossible to record on newsreel film. Each had a number or a plus or minus sign painted on it. The machine was run very slowly so that the film might record the activity: at full speed even the human eye would fail.[13]

Only one problem developed—a multiplier malfunctioned—but Burks fixed it before the visitors arrived. The demonstration programs had been set up by the Goldstines, Holberton, and "his girls."

The public demonstration was a huge success. Clearly, the importance of the event did not elude those invited to it. The *Times* put the story on the front page, written this time by T. R. Kennedy, Jr. The headline read, "Electronic Computer Flashes Answers, May Speed Engineering."

PHILADELPHIA, Feb. 14—One of the war's top secrets, an amazing machine which applies electronic speeds for the first time to mathematical tasks hitherto too difficult and cumbersome for solution, was announced here tonight by the War Department. Leaders who saw the device in action for the first time heralded it as a tool with which to begin to rebuild scientific affairs on new foundations.

Such instruments, it was said, could revolutionize modern engineering, bring on a new epoch of industrial design, and eventually eliminate much slower and costly trial-and-error development work now deemed necessary in the fashioning of intricate machines. Heretofore, sheer mathematical difficulties have often forced designers to accept inferior solutions of their problems with higher costs and slower programs.

Kennedy's story reported that ENIAC was a thousand times faster than any other computer (it was actually faster than that) and had been used "on a problem in nuclear physics." After giving a brief description of the machine, the story jumped to an inside page. There readers saw photographs of the machine and

13. The Moore School people all went to the movies to see whether their bulb-switching stunt worked. They never saw a report on ENIAC.

of Eckert and Mauchly, whom the Times called its "inventors." In another reference to the secret H-bomb test, the reporter quoted someone as having said that "a very difficult wartime problem" had been sent through ENIAC. The problem, which would have taken 100 trained men a year to solve manually, was solved in two hours.

Dr. Arthur W. Burks of the Moore School explained that the basic arithmetical operations, if made to take place rapidly enough, might in time solve almost any problem.

"Watch closely, you may miss it," he asked, as a button was pressed to multiply 97,367 by itself 5,000 times. Most of the onlookers missed it—the operation took place in less than the wink of an eye.

To demonstrate ENIAC's extreme speed, Dr. Burks next slowed down the action by a factor of 1,000 and did the same problem. Had the visitors been content to wait 16⅔ minutes they could have observed the answer in neon light. The next was multiplication—13,975 by 13,975. In a flash the quotient appeared—195,300,625. A table of squares and cubes of numbers was generated in one-tenth of a second. Next, a similar one of sines and cosines. The job was finished and printed on a large sheet before most of the visitors could go from one room to the next.

The ENIAC was then told to solve a difficult problem that would have required several weeks' work by a trained man. The ENIAC did it in exactly 15 seconds.

The story also quoted Goldstine and mentioned Gillon. It did not refer to von Neumann.

The computer age was born.

The total cost of ENIAC was $486,804.22.

The importance of the machine was not lost on the scientific community. A week before the public demonstration, Frankel and Metropolis had written to Goldstine, advising him they were leaving the Manhattan Project for the University of Chicago, and asking whether they could rent time on ENIAC. Fermi had also expressed interest and invited Goldstine out to speak to some scientists at Chicago. The army agreed to provide time free of charge. Frankel and Metropolis showed up to do an experiment called the "liquid drop model of fission," based on the works of Niels Bohr and John Wheeler. Hartree came in from England to run a problem on compression. A. H. Taub and Adele Goldstine did a computation on shock waves, and J. A. Goff, of Penn, ran a problem in thermodynamics.[14] D. H. Lehmer, of Aberdeen, and his wife came to do a problem in mathematics involving prime numbers, and Mauchly's wish to do weather computation came true when a weather mathematics problem was run on ENIAC—by von Neumann.

Someone studying shock waves would have done well to study the staff of the Moore School at this time. Onto the scene came Irven Travis, who had been in the navy during the war.

"Irv Travis was the best undergraduate teacher I ever had," Eckert said. "I liked him very much. . . . He had a lot to do with computers for fire-control purposes [in the navy], and they thought, 'Well, he's an expert on the computer. Put him in charge of all the guys working on computers.' They put him in as my boss. I didn't mind that; I thought he was a great guy."

Eckert's opinion changed quickly. Travis, now placed in command of all the Moore School research, was unhappy about the accounting practices at the Moore School and wanted to emulate Johns Hopkins and MIT in their business practices. Moreover, Travis and others felt that individuals should not benefit financially from work performed while they were on the faculty or staff of the university. Travis and Pender also thought that the publication of von Neumann's "First Draft" and the *New York Times* leak demonstrated insufficient control over affairs at the Moore School. Having had no part in ENIAC or EDVAC, Travis seemed singularly unimpressed with the accomplishments of the school. "I set about to put the house in order," he said later, "to get an organization and a structure which would allow the soliciting of sponsored contract work for both governmental and industrial sponsors and to build a strong research organization."

"He was trying to be a big shot in a hurry and get a lot of contracts, and he figured if he had these patents that he could fold in with the contracts, he'd be a bigger shot in a hurry," Eckert said. General Electric was already talking about $1 million contracts, although the university was decidedly hesitant about

14. The Soviet government inquired whether it could purchase a "robot calculator" from the university. The army suggested that Penn decline the offer.

making such an agreement with a business corporation.

To do this, Travis felt he needed a patent release from all his people. He made the announcement at a staff meeting on March 15, 1946. Several Moore School engineers disagreed vehemently, especially Eckert and Mauchly, who already had an agreement signed by the president of Penn, granting them the ENIAC patents and, they believed, implying that EDVAC patents would be theirs as well. Even Carl Chambers, the supervisor of research and no radical, thought this was out of line. Eckert, Mauchly, Shaw, Davis, and the engineer C. Bradford Sheppard refused to sign. Travis gave them some more time to think it over.

The parties met several times to discuss the issue. The minutes of one meeting between Eckert and Travis showed that Travis agreed that Eckert could disclose any of his new ideas to the Moore School at his own discretion. Travis later added in the margin, "Except that we do not encourage him to spend time here."

Mauchly described another meeting:

"I don't want any of this nonsense that we've been having about patents and all that stuff," Travis told him. "I want you to sign these agreements."

"Well, patents are no issue," Mauchly said. "We've signed an agreement with the university. It's all settled; don't worry about it."

"No, it isn't settled," Travis said. "If you want to continue to work here at the university, you must sign these agreements."

Eckert and Mauchly were adamant about their rights. No one else at the university seemed to see a problem regarding patents. During the discussions on the ENIAC patents, they had visited the university's fine medical school, which dealt with the issue of patents all the time. The administration there assured them there had been no difficulties. Travis, now supported by Pender, remained firm.

"Travis gave Mauchly and I [*sic*] a month to make up our minds," Eckert said. "We said, 'That's foolish; it doesn't take a month to make up our minds about something we've already made it up on.' He said, 'Take a month.' A month later we came

back, and he said, 'Take a week.' A week, and he came back and
said, 'I'll give you a day.' "

On March 22 Eckert and Mauchly received a letter written
by Travis and signed by Pender, insisting they sign a patent
release, agree to remain at the Moore School for two years, and

certify that you will devote your efforts first to the University of Pennsylvania and will during the interval of your employment here subju-
gate your personal commercial interests to the interests of the University.

Because of the urgent need for planning by the Moore School of its
research program and because of the lengthy discussions which have
been conducted over the past weeks, it is necessary that acceptance or
rejection of these conditions be given by 5:00 p.m., March 22, 1946.

The letter was delivered in the morning, and Travis was giving them until that afternoon to sign over the ENIAC patent
and any claims on EDVAC.

"Everything we thought we had gained by rather unseemly
struggles before that, trying to settle things with the university
about who got what, suddenly was shot up," Mauchly told Carr.

By 5 P.M. Travis had gotten his answer. Eckert and Mauchly
delivered identical letters, lamenting the fact the conditions of
their employment had been changed.

Up to this time we had believed that the interests of all concerned were
compatible—that is, that there was no conflict between our desire to do
the best possible job for the Moore School and the Army Ordnance,
and our interest in the ultimate commercial development of electronic
computing devices.

Dr. Travis has now stated that, in his opinion, there is an essential
conflict of interest in this regard.

I am therefore forced at this time to choose immediately between
two alternatives—to abandon entirely the possibilities of ultimate commercial enterprise, or to retain and further my interests in this respect
by severing my connections with the Moore School project. I am intensely
interested in the development of better electronic computing devices
for scientific as well as industrial and commercial purposes. Moreover,
I believe that in the development of commercial machines, there is the
greatest promise of aiding scientific work as well. It is under these circumstances that I tender my resignation from the project.

Eckert and Mauchly claimed they had been fired. Travis,
Pender, and Brainerd claimed they had quit. The latter expla-

nation smacks of disingenuousness. Besides violating a signed agreement and breaking the institution's word, Travis's order was not even fair. Although few universities grant their employees complete commercial rights, Penn seemed to be alone in demanding that their scientists give up all such rights. In one simple act, Travis destroyed the University of Pennsylvania's substantial lead in computer sciences and probably cost it millions of dollars in potential licensing fees and royalties, and unmeasurable amounts of prestige.[15] The university never recovered from the firing. In the history of American higher education, Travis's decision surely stands in a class by itself. At the Moore School, the ENIAC firings are to this day called the "great might-have-been."[16]

Eckert and Mauchly were about to be out in the cold. Von Neumann's feelers to Eckert had already caused a furor at the Moore School when Pender had found out that RCA and Zworykin were involved. He seemed to feel this was dirtying the university's hands in commerce. The issue became moot when von Neumann rescinded the employment offer, again over the issue of commercializing the computer.

During the last months it . . . became clear . . . that your further commercial interests in the automatic computing field on the one hand, and the requirements and the stability of the Institute research project, particularly in its basis of cooperation with our other partners [RCA, mainly], may not be easily reconciled. . . . Under these conditions I can no longer assume the responsibility to the Institute or to the project and our partners for delaying the organization any further, or by limiting it in any way which might have been justified if you had accepted our original offer. I must therefore, much to my regret, consider our past discussions with you and our offer made to you as null.

That closed the door to the institute. But Eckert and Mauchly were not without offers. IBM expressed an interest in hiring them.

15. The lead that Penn lost has been taken over by MIT, the University of California at Berkeley, Carnegie-Mellon, and Stanford. Penn itself long ago changed its policies, and the Moore School still teaches computer science and does research, but it has not been of the first rank since Travis forced Eckert and Mauchly out. Travis himself quit the university three years later to join industry.
16. *Pennsylvania Gazette* 81, no. 2.

IBM knew something about the project at the Moore School and had offered as much assistance as Penn had asked for. Thomas Watson, Sr., had ordered his people to devote themselves to the war effort, and had felt that helping the Moore School computer would be a good thing. Eckert said he felt Watson had ulterior motives. He said that when IBM sent a contract to the Moore School to lease the card punch machines, the contract contained a clause offering the machinery at no cost if Penn agreed to give IBM a nonexclusive license to any patent derived from any machine using IBM equipment. Goldstine rejected the offer. At one time Watson asked von Neumann to act as a consultant, and von Neumann actively pursued this possibility. Von Neumann, Eckert claimed, went to Eckert's patent attorney to ask whether this would be ethical, was advised that it was not, and delayed acceptance of the offer for a while to consider the matter.

With things at the Moore School at an end, Watson asked to meet with Eckert and Mauchly.

"The old man didn't make a great impression on me," Eckert recalled. "He said something I thought was true . . . he said he didn't think people invented things anyway: all ideas were put on earth by God, and we were discoverers. I think this is true. I thought it was kind of gutsy of him to say it.

"The stories about him were such that you were going to have to do it his way. . . . I don't think that was right. We were afraid they would try to suppress what we were doing and keep punch cards in forever. As it turned out, he didn't understand what we were doing well enough, and we could do what we wanted to without his knowing it. I didn't realize that big business was as backwards as it was; I didn't think they were that thick. . . . All the things the employees of IBM said had overtones that scared me a little bit," Eckert said. "I saw these signs hanging all over the place saying, 'THINK,' and I thought, 'Jesus! What's that all about? . . .'

"We said no."

Mauchly made the decision; he did not trust Watson to let them work independently. Eckert was more willing to give it a try, but his wife and his father sided with Mauchly. Had they said yes, their lives and the history of the computer might have been radically different.

The only solution for Eckert and Mauchly was to go into business for themselves. They had the know-how to build an EDVAC-type machine; they had the engineers. The Moore School gang was breaking up.

Von Neumann was being courted by Norbert Wiener at MIT, by Harvard, by the University of Chicago, and, still, by IBM. He wanted to stay at the institute, but only if it agreed to let him build a computer. MIT, for one, seemed to offer him anything he wanted. Wiener wrote him:

> Veblen told me about your post-war plans for hydrodynamics. I think your balance of pure and applied mathematics is the right one [but] how does all this fit in with Princetitute *[sic]*? You are going to run into a situation where you will need a lab at your fingertips and labs don't grow in ivory towers. Mind you, I could stand a little ivory tower myself, and don't see you in any hurry to get out of one. If, however, you see yourself in the position of effective loss of your own non-ivory-tower schemes for the future, I have a secret to convey. A few weeks ago, Harrison, dean of science at MIT, asked me what the math department at MIT would think about the possibility of you as head of the department. . . . I said, of course that would be delightful. . . .

He went on to offer the department chairmanship without the administrative problems that usually go with such a role, "leaving you the policies and your favorite projects." He gloated how that would drive Harvard "into some strange antics." Harvard, too, was recruiting von Neumann heavily, with letters to him from members of the department. The University of Chicago offered to set up an "Institute of Applied Mathematics" with von Neumann at the head if he went west. The Institute for Advanced Study—essentially a think tank—was not set up for this kind of research. But they wanted to keep von Neumann. Von Neumann did an excellent selling job. He wanted to build a computer because he saw, perhaps better than anyone, the usefulness of the machine as a research tool. He also felt computers could be socially useful. Nancy Stern has written that von Neumann was dedicated to establishing "the social utility of mathematics in general." Mathematicians, moreover, could get a piece of the

government-fund pie that he felt sure would become available
to the computer sciences. The institute met his terms. It produced $100,000 of its own money, and the army and navy put
in like amounts. Von Neumann entered into a joint research
agreement with RCA, which had just built a lab in Princeton.

Von Neumann went back to work at the institute full-time,
taking Goldstine with him. Other engineers considered going
with von Neumann; some considered staying with Eckert and
Mauchly. Travis tried to stem the flow, sending a nasty letter to
von Neumann when Travis was approached by Shaw asking to
be released from the Moore School so that he could go to work
in Princeton. Von Neumann told him that Shaw had initiated
the contact and that he intended to pursue discussions whether
Travis liked it or not. Shaw, however, elected to follow Eckert
and Mauchly.

Von Neumann's antipathy toward the two grew even stronger.
In October 1946 Frankel[17] tried to get a job with von Neumann
but was told he would first have to sever his relationships with
Eckert and Mauchly.

I have the greatest respect for Eckert and Mauchly's ability, for their
past achievements and for their future promise. It is no criticism on my
part, just an observation of facts, that they are a commercial group with
a commercial patent policy. On the basis of the information before me,
I have to conclude that we cannot work with them directly or indirectly
in the same manner in which we would work with an academic group
which has no such interests. . . . If you wish to maintain the same type
of close contact with Eckert and Mauchly [as you have with us]—which
is for you and you alone to decide—then you should not put yourself
into an incompatible position by communicating with us too. I would
appreciate your making your choice in this respect before we continue
our discussions further.[18]

This was written by the same von Neumann who was eager
to collaborate with Zworykin and RCA, and the same man who
helped formulate the institute's patent policy, which gave a commercial reward to inventors. Von Neumann's motives are

17. Frankel and Metropolis eventually built a computer for Los Alamos, called
the MANIAC.
18. Stern, Von Neumann Papers, Library of Congress.

ambiguous. He clearly did not eschew all commercial interests, yet he condemned Eckert and Mauchly for being commercial creatures. Perhaps the reason for his attitude toward the two men was personal dislike. Von Neumann never said.

Eckert and Mauchly were still hanging in midair. Before they could get organized, they had one other function to perform at the Moore School, teaching a six-week summer course on computing organized by Chambers and entitled "Theory and Techniques for Design of Electronic Digital Computers." Since the wraps were off ENIAC and since everyone knew about EDVAC, almost everyone in the world interested in computers made a pilgrimage to Philadelphia. The list of institutions represented included the army, the navy, MIT, the National Bureau of Standards, Cambridge University, Columbia, Harvard, the Institute for Advanced Study, IBM, Bell Labs, Eastman Kodak, General Electric, and National Cash Register.

The conference served as a reunion for the Moore School crowd. Eckert and Mauchly gave talks, as did von Neumann and Goldstine. The Moore School Lectures, as they are known, were seminal events in the history of the computer: they provided the first great exchange of ideas on electronic computing, and the participants spread out all over the world carrying the message. Maurice Wilkes, of Cambridge, for one, went back home and built EDSAC (Electronic Delay Storage Automatic Calculator), a stored-memory computer that was operational before EDVAC. The National Bureau of Standards was impressed enough by the technology discussed at the Moore School Lectures to go out and start building its own computers.

"We performed, I think, about as good a function as we could," Mauchly told Carr, "getting people educated and spreading the word as to what was possible. We presented different ideas, not just one way of doing things. For instance, with the memory and storage problem, we rather thoroughly discussed the use of cathode-ray tubes for electronic beams directed to storage on the face of the tube, as well as the kind we thought was the most helpful at the moment, the storage of patterns in these mercury liquid sound waves."

The meeting was a total success, but Eckert and Mauchly faced

more pressing matters. They needed some government contracts to pay them to build computers and get their company off
the ground. They formed a partnership, and Mauchly began to
sound out his contacts in the government. He and Eckert were
no longer the colleagues of the faculty of the Moore School and
of the computer people at the institute—they had become their
competitors. They would find that the world of business bears
little resemblance to academe. The latter is much simpler and
easier to understand.

The army, meanwhile, had a working computer in Philadelphia and decided it was time to bring ENIAC "home" to Aberdeen. The move was delayed because the facilities at Aberdeen
were not finished. Technically, the army "accepted" ENIAC on
June 30, 1946, after a five-volume report was written and submitted by the University of Pennsylvania. Adele Goldstine and
Harry Huskey wrote much of the report. ENIAC was turned off
on November 9, 1946. The Moore School had to knock down
walls to get the machine out of the building. ENIAC was trucked
to Aberdeen.

Von Neumann had come up with an idea to give ENIAC
rudimentary storage capacity, he and Adele Goldstine worked
out a system of giving instructions to the machine, and Richard
Clippinger modified their system. The army had awarded the
contract to make the modifications to the Moore School.

"This is one of the queer things," Kathleen McNulty said.
"Eckert and Mauchly, who had just started in business and really
needed money desperately to operate, had put in a bid to do this
modification. There was nobody better prepared than they were,
because they had the engineers from ENIAC who went with them.
But instead, the intelligent powers that be at Aberdeen said, 'Oh,
the Moore School did such a wonderful job, they would also do
a good job of doing this modification.' The Moore School, when
they got the contract, . . . didn't really have any personnel to put
to work on it. . . .

"In a sense you couldn't work without working directly with
the machine, and seeing how it worked. We were working with
the Moore School, so they chose me out of the programmers of

ENIAC, and Clippinger. .... Once every two weeks, after we designed a few different things, we would go up to Princeton, to the Institute for Advanced Study to consult with von Neumann. McNulty found things had changed.

"[When] von Neumann used to come to the Moore School . . . and when it would come to be lunch time, we would all go out to lunch. Von Neumann was an extremely fascinating and wonderful person, and had all these great stories. Loved women; he always liked to be surrounded even though we didn't contribute a whole lot. . . . He would regale us with stories, and we had a wonderful time, and we were on wonderful terms with him."

Now, she found, when she went to consult with von Neumann, Goldstine would greet them. He would ask what they had for them that week, and the women would give their report. He would then go in to see von Neumann and tell him what the women had said. He would return and say, "All right, you can come in to see Johnny." Von Neumann would give them instructions, and Goldstine, now playing doorman, would show them out.

"Here we were in the presence of God," McNulty remembered. "We were really shocked. We had come over from Aberdeen to Princeton. It had taken us five hours to get there."

ENIAC was turned on again on July 29, 1947, von Neumann's modifications having been made.

The machine continued to work reliably until 11:45 P.M. on October 2, 1955, when it was turned off for good and dismantled. Although the government at first wanted to sell the machine for scrap, saner heads prevailed. The machine was split into four unequal parts. The largest was sent to the Smithsonian, where it was outfitted with large bulbs and put into action as a flashing display. A small section was sent to the U.S. Military Academy, at West Point. Burks rescued four units, including two accumulators, one-third of the high-speed multiplier, and one-half of the master programmer, which is now on display at the University of Michigan.

The Moore School received two accumulators, a function table, and several main panels. At this writing, they are sitting in an empty room on the first floor of the Moore School. The University of Pennsylvania has tried to obtain funding for a computer museum, where they could display ENIAC, parts of the differential analyzer, and several other computing devices. The university failed to raise the money to build the museum, and except for a dusty plaque at the Moore School entrance, the school's share of the world's first electronic, general-purpose computer sits alone and dead at the place of its birth.

8. UNIVAC

There are two times in a man's life when he should not spec-
ulate: when he can't afford it and when he can.

MARK TWAIN

THE BRITISH were perhaps the most enthusiastic about the computers after the revelation of ENIAC. Douglas Hartree, who ran
a problem on the machine, went back to Britain spreading the
gospel.

Several centers for building computers sprang up in the first
years after the war. Maurice Wilkes, working with a team at
Cambridge, put together the first stored-program computer—
EDSAC, a direct descendant of EDVAC. Wilkes's idea was to
build a computer quickly so that scientists at Cambridge and
elsewhere could immediactely take advantage of the new technology. Consequently, EDSAC was not an effort to push the state
of the art but what scientists call a "quick and dirty" solution to
the computing problem. EDSAC made use of mercury delay lines
(relying on experiences by the British admiralty's signals section)
and could store 576 binary digits in each five-foot tube. EDSAC

used thirty-two such tubes in its main memory and others in the central processor. Input was a tape reader; the results came out on a teleprinter. EDSAC contained 3,000 vacuum tubes.

Wilkes's machine could perform addition in 1.4 milliseconds. Users of the computing service[1] programmed the machine by means of the English alphabet and one of the first computer assembler (or translator) languages. The machine converted the letters into binary digits. The Cambridge group also developed a library of programming procedures called subroutines, for various uses (another first), and eventually Wilkes coauthored the first book on computer programming.

Funding came from the university and from a chain of tea shops, J. Lyons & Company, the first commercial sponsor of an electronic computer. Lyons wanted to use computers in its office and contacted Goldstine in America for advice. Goldstine told them to look up Wilkes. By 1949 Lyons was building its own computer, LEO (Lyons Electronic Office), based on the EDSAC design. LEO was actually working in the Lyons office doing clerical work by November of 1951.

When the Bletchley Park project dissolved after the war, many of the scientists and engineers who had broken Hitler's code spread out, taking with them the knowledge they had acquired in building COLOSSUS. One was F. C. Williams, who had developed a unique method for storing information using the standard cathode-ray tube. The Williams tube had a significant advantage over the mercury delay tube and other forms of memory in that it gave the user random access to the information. It was not necessary to go through all the stored information in the memory to get at what one wanted; one could go directly to the right place in the memory. Williams took his idea to Manchester University.

By 1947 Williams had built a prototype of a computer using the cathode-ray tube, which ran successfully a year later. Williams's team, working with the mathematician Max Newman, built a larger machine, the Manchester Mark I (or MADM), and took out forty-two computer patents in the process. The Mark I was

1. The world's first using an electronic computer.

solving mathematical problems by April of 1949. It could store 128 forty-bit words[2] on the tubes and had a supplemental memory on magnetic drums. Eventually, the electronics firm of Ferranti received a contract to build nine improved versions of the original Mark I.[3]

Following a pattern set by ENIAC, the Ferranti Mark I from the start served military needs. One of the first problems run on it, by Alec Glennie, concerned the British atomic bomb.

In 1951 the Manchester team built an improved version of the Mark I, the Mark II (or MEG, for megacycle engine), twenty times faster and much easier to use.

Hartree was directly responsible for yet another team. In the summer of 1945, the British government, at Hartree's instigation, founded the National Physical Laboratory, at Teddington, Middlesex, an organization similar to the U.S. National Bureau of Standards. Sir Charles Darwin, grandson of the biologist, was its director. A number of scientists and engineers from Bletchley Park, Alan Turing among them, quickly joined up.

Turing went to work immediately. On February 19, 1946, he presented a paper containing the complete design for an electronic stored-program computer. He called it the Automatic Computing Engine (ACE). The British historian Simon Lavington has written that Darwin probably thought of ACE as the machine that would serve the computing purposes of the entire country—a national computer. Since the National Physical Laboratory did not have the facilities for constructing a large machine, Darwin sought out the post office, which employed such pioneering electrical engineers as T. H. Flowers and A. W. M. Coombs. Flowers had been to the Moore School in 1945. But the post office was too busy trying to restore Britain's telephone sys-

2. A "word" is any cluster of bits, or binary digits, grouped together so that the machine can use them.

3. According to Lavington, one experiment run on a Ferranti was a "love letter" produced by the use of random numbers to signify random words. The letter, perhaps the first ever written by a computer, went as follows:

Darling Sweetheart,
You are my avid fellow feeling. My affection curiously clings to your passionate wish. My liking yearns to your heart. You are my wistful sympathy: my tender liking.
Yours beautifully,
M.U.C.

tem after the destruction and disruption of the war.

Darwin approached Wilkes, at Cambridge, and Williams, then at the Telecommunications Research Establishment (TRE). Wilkes had attended the Moore School Lectures in the summer of 1946, while Williams was working on his memory device. Williams left TRE for Manchester University. When the NPL proposal arrived in Manchester, he turned it down. Williams had funds to do his own computer research, he did not like Turing's design, and he did not like Turing.

Meanwhile, at Cambridge, Wilkes was already building his EDSAC, and he wasn't interested in ACE. He, too, was unimpressed with Turing's design and shared Williams's opinion of Turing. This left Darwin on the spot.

Turing left the National Physical Laboratory in 1947, and it decided to build its own prototype of the ACE, called the Pilot ACE. Based on Turing's design, it was a radical departure from any other machine under construction. Only von Neumann had anything as extreme in his head. In many ways, Pilot ACE was too far ahead of itself; most of the British computers stayed with the original EDVAC-based design, and it was years before the British computer makers caught up with Turing. The internal clock, which timed the electronic pulses, was 1 megacycle, faster than anything else in Britain. Addition could vary between 64 microseconds and 1.024 milliseconds, depending on where in the memory the orders were placed. Lavington has written that the main memory contained 128 thirty-two-bit words in mercury delay lines (expanded to 352 words a few years later, and to an additional 4,096 words in 1954). The machine used 800 vacuum tubes. Pilot ACE went to work for the first time in May of 1950, but it had some reliability problems that kept it from full-time operation until two years later. NPL finished Turing's ACE in 1957.[4]

The British code busters were not the only ones interested in continuing to make use of what they had learned about elec-

---

4. Turing's design was that far ahead of everyone else's. Even von Neumann's machine lacked some of the sophistication of Turing's, which has had a profound influence on the fastest and largest of modern computers.

tronic machines. A group of Americans who had helped break the Japanese codes for the U.S. Navy during the war were also out of work. During the war they had worked at a top-secret facility at 3801 Nebraska Avenue, N.W., in Washington. Their machines came from such industrial giants as Eastman Kodak, National Cash Register, and the Bell Labs. After the war, these firms showed a singular preoccupation with getting back to making consumer goods and taking advantage of the coming boom. They had no desire to keep producing a few secret machines for the military.

Two of the navy engineers, Howard T. Engstrom and William C. Norris, decided it would be a good idea to get into the business of providing the government with electronic cryptography machines. A third officer, Ralph L. Meader, who headed the Naval Computing Machine Laboratory at the NCR plant in Dayton, Ohio,[5] joined them.

The initial problem was a total lack of interest by the investing community, exacerbated by the fact that the men could not describe to potential investors what they wanted to build except in the vaguest terms. Their machines would be top secret. To the rescue came a Minnesota businessman, John E. Parker.

Parker owned Northwest Aeronautical Company, in St. Paul, a builder of the wooden gliders used by the army. After the war, Northwest had no markets; Parker needed something else to invest in. Meader put him in touch with Engstrom and Norris. Parker was willing to accept the idea that the two men could not describe the machine in any detail, but he wanted assurance from the navy that if he built the machines, the navy would buy them. A meeting was arranged in which the navy, still as vague as possible, assured Parker they needed the mysterious devices.

Parker, Norris, Engstrom, and Meader formed Engineering Research Associates in St. Paul to produce electronic cryptography machines in the old glider factory on Minnehaha Avenue. When the government seemed unwilling to grant contracts to a

5. According to Auerbach, there was one installation at NCR in Dayton that was so secret that when the war was over, the military bricked up the door rather than empty the room. Eventually the room was cleared out, but Auerbach claims the work done in that room is still classified.

new, untested company, Parker arranged for the deal to go through Northwest Aeronautical. Eventually, after ERA's reputation had been made, Northwest went out of business, and ERA began producing the special-purpose, top-secret electronic computing machines.

In February 1946 the Moore School employed almost all the computer scientists in the world outside Britain. Within several months, most of them had been driven out by Travis's stand on principles.

Where to go became a serious problem for the Moore School engineers and scientists. Three groups appeared. A few engineers, including Sharpless, remained at the Moore School to work on EDVAC. Others gravitated to one of the two warring parties, either to Eckert and Mauchly or to von Neumann.

The decision for Goldstine was an easy one. He associated himself closely with von Neumann and saw no future with the Moore School. He wanted to continue work on computers.

Of course, the most obvious choice for a location for this work was at the University of Pennsylvania, but unfortunately this was not a good time in the life of that institution for innovation. Perhaps institutions as well as people can become fatigued, or perhaps it is the fatigue of the leaders of an institution that gives the place itself that feeling.

It is not easy even today to analyze exactly why the Moore School became unsuitable for this type of project. However, some of the factors can be distinguished.

Goldstine wrote that most of the senior staff at the Moore School, except Brainerd, did not appreciate what had been accomplished there or what the importance of ENIAC and EDVAC was. Few of the regular faculty participated in the projects; most, if not all, had heard about the dissension and the bitterness and were "turned off by the disruptive aspects they had witnessed," Goldstine wrote. Some might have felt that the project would interfere with the primary purpose of the Moore School: the education of engineers. The school appreciated that it had a contract to finish EDVAC, and, thanks to the guidance of Warren, it did so; but the central processor was not completed until 1949, and the input-output system never worked. No one hired for the computer project was offered a permanent position at Penn. Goldstine wrote that the university seemed happy to get rid of them all. Goldstine claimed that another principal reason for the Moore School's loss of dominance in the field of computers was the departure of von Neumann, whom he described as "the greatest thinker of our times on computers and computing." Von Neumann's leaving had little to do with it; Goldstine tended to overemphasize von Neumann's importance. The Moore School, which had Eckert and Mauchly and all the engineers, destroyed its position all by itself. By the time von Neumann made his major contributions to the logic of the computer, the ENIAC team had already departed the Moore School and the university had already fallen behind in the technological race.

Goldstine watched von Neumann play the Institute for Advanced Study against MIT and Chicago, and when the institute finally, if reluctantly, agreed to let von Neumann team with Princeton University and RCA to build a computer, Goldstine, still technically in the army, signed on. Burks was also offered a job with von Neumann and left the Moore School on March 8. Goldstine negotiated with Eckert and the Moore School engineer C. Bradford Sheppard for a while, but when Eckert decided to go into business, Sheppard joined him.

By the end of March, the institute team was being gathered and Julian Bigelow had been named chief engineer. Bigelow had his task cut out for him: the institute was a center for pure intellectual research, a playground for genius. It had no laboratories or workshops, and except for those who mowed extensive lawns and replaced light bulbs, it had few people who did anything but think. Nonetheless, von Neumann knew clearly what he wanted to do.

The purpose of this project is to develop and construct a fully automatic, digital, all-purpose electronic calculating machine. . . . Furthermore while the machine is to be definitely digital in character, it is important to provide it with some continuous variable organs, essentially as alternative inputs and outputs. . . .

The overall logical control of the machine will be effected from the memory . . . by orders formulated in a binary digital code. . . . These orders form a system which gives the machine a very considerable flexibility. It is expected that it will be able to deal efficiently and at extremely high speeds with wide classes of problems. . . . In this sense the machine is intended to be an all-purpose device.

Von Neumann, perhaps more than anyone, recognized the importance of the computer. He clearly understood that the machine would revolutionize mathematics and experimentation in such fields as hydrodynamics, quantum physics, electrodynamics, and astronomy. He had already used the word *revolutionize* several times in an early memo.

The project was called the Electronic Computer Project for the Institute for Advanced Study. Here von Neumann's technical contributions are manifest and beyond controversy. The machine he designed would be faster than anything else in the world, and although difficult to set up, and not particularly suitable for commercial use, it was designed specifically as a general-purpose scientific tool. While all the other computer makers were generally heading in the same direction, von Neumann's genius clarified and described the paths better than anyone else in the world could. Moreover, many of the developments in programming and in machine architecture at the institute profoundly influenced future computer development. While everyone else was building slower serial machines, von Neumann was building the first practical parallel computer. While others were using crude digital instructions for their machines, von Neumann and his team were developing instructions (what scientists call codes) that would last, with modification, through most of the computer age.

In June 1946 von Neumann, Goldstine, and Burks issued a long paper outlining their machine. A second paper came out a year later.[6] The material was placed in the public domain, which meant it would not be patented. Goldstine called the papers "in many ways, the blueprint for the modern computer," and to some

6. The first paper was entitled "Preliminary Discussion of the Logical Design of an Electronic Computing Instrument." The second, published after Burks had left for the University of Michigan, bore the title "Planning and Coding Problems for an Electronic Computing Instrument."

extent that is so. The papers clearly laid out how a computer should be organized and built.

The machine itself (called the IAS, after the institute) was the source of some controversy within the institute—many there felt the institute had no business building machines—but enjoyed the support of the new director, J. Robert Oppenheimer, who also understood its potential.[7] Because of Bigelow's meticulous standards and the growing list of potential users, all of whom made suggestions, the IAS machine was not finished until 1950.

In the meantime, von Neumann had become the principal spokesman in the United States for computers. His contributions in this regard may equal the technical innovations he produced. Von Neumann was a zealous evangelist for the cause of computers. His reputation assured that the scientific establishment in the United States and abroad paid attention to what he was saying. Von Neumann converted the skeptics[8] and made scientists take the machine seriously.

He was everywhere, touting the machines, proclaiming the revolution, recounting the benefits to science of the machines he hoped to build. His publications not only laid the foundation for further computer development but also guaranteed that his name would forever be associated with the machines. This created a painful situation for Eckert and Mauchly.

"Small wonder, I guess, that people started talking about von Neumann computers," Mauchly told Carr, "especially further, that our new helper, von Neumann, as soon as he had the ideas fully under his belt, you might say, well adjusted and organized for himself, started accepting invitations from almost anywhere about the wonders of these computers and what could be done with them. It was something I just didn't know how to cope with when I'd hear from my friends in Washington that von Neumann was going to speak on computers down at the Navy Building so-and-so tomorrow.

7. Not everyone expressed an opinion. Goldstine said that Albert Einstein was apparently aware of what von Neumann was doing but that he seemed to have no interest in electronic computing.
8. Aiken, for one, was once quoted as suggesting that six of his Mark I's were all the computers the United States needed, that his machine could handle all the computing any scientists wanted to do.

"I said, 'Well, I guess I'll be there.' I get down there. I was perfectly welcome to come in; it wasn't a closed meeting at all. I would sit, perhaps in the front row. Von Neumann got up there, smiling and jovial face, telling all about the wonders of these computers. He never even mentioned the fact that he saw me in the audience. I thought that was a little peculiar.

"I didn't know how to react; I didn't know what to do about this. I just took it, you might say, I just relaxed and figured surely people will gradually know what's going on here. But there's no question about it: he was a charming and logical speaker, and he carried the interest of the audience. Everything made him the number-one promotion man, spreading the word about how useful these computers could be in the scientific work, and I think, as far as he was concerned, that was the main thing, the scientific work."

Mauchly, a sensitive man, was deeply hurt by von Neumann's spreading reputation as the inventor of the stored-memory computer and by von Neumann's refusal to acknowledge his debt to Mauchly and Eckert. The hard feelings could only intensify.

The dispute came to a head over the EDVAC patent, precipitated again by von Neumann.

Eckert and Mauchly left the Moore School with the issue of the EDVAC patent still unsettled. Penn was obliged to produce patents for the army under the contract, but who owned them? Von Neumann forced the issue. On March 22, 1946, a year after the Moore School team had disbanded, von Neumann and Goldstine had an impromptu meeting with two men from the army's legal branch in the Pentagon. Von Neumann told them he thought he had some patent rights and asked how to file for them. He was given an Army War Patent Form to fill out and was told he had to submit evidence to support his claim. He completed the form and submitted the now famous "First Draft" as evidence.

Eckert and Mauchly, who believed they had invented EDVAC, were furious. Pender, at the Moore School, was beside himself; he could not turn over patents he did not control. The army's legal branch was now in the middle, an uncomfortable position to be in. Goldstine and von Neumann accused them of favoring

Eckert and Mauchly. The legal branch denied any favoritism and tried to clarify its position. Writing to Goldstine, it said, "The attitude of the Ordnance Department in this matter is not so much that of arbiter as it is one of desiring to assist in the resolution of any differences which may exist between the parties concerned over right and title to the various patents involved."

A meeting was finally arranged for April 3, 1947, in Philadelphia, at which all sides were represented. The government, in its invitation, wrote:

Since the government has a right to the use of the patents, it is naturally concerned that the patents be filed at an early date in order to reduce to a minimum the possibility of being put to the expense of establishing its right in connection with the patents should some party other than those presently involved file a patent which would infringe on those with which we are now concerned.

It was an unpleasant gathering. The army pointed out that patents were valid only if they were filed within one year of the publication of the innovation. It ruled that von Neumann's "First Draft," distributed widely by Goldstine, was technically, a publication. Since it was dated almost two years previously, the one-year time limit had passed; that put EDVAC in the public domain. The army told von Neumann, "It is our firm belief from the facts that we have now that this report of yours dated 30 June 1945 is a publication and will prohibit you or anyone else from obtaining a patent on anything that it discloses because it has been published more than a year ago, and a statute provides that if you don't file disclosures within a year it constitutes a bar to patenting that device." The army, which behaved honorably throughout the affair, was not settling the question of who had invented EDVAC; it merely stated that no one—not von Neumann, not Eckert and Mauchly—could take out a patent on the machine.

The action probably prevented a colossal patent lawsuit, but it displeased all parties. Although those innovations not covered by von Neumann's publication were still patentable, the bulk of the machine was now in the public domain. The two sides, tempers high, exchanged charges. The army, still trying to mediate,

asked both parties to share future disclosures with each other
for the sake of the advance of science. Von Neumann said he
was done filing disclosures. Eckert and Mauchly said they would
consider the suggestion, but they never sent anything to von
Neumann. The meeting ended. Everybody lost.

The EDVAC patent, however, was the least of Eckert and
Mauchly's problems. They needed money for their new business, and obtaining that money and the contracts to build computers proved to be infinitely harder than they ever dreamed.
Their naïveté would make things worse.

Eckert and Mauchly scoured the area looking for some
investment money, what is now called venture capital. They found
none.

"We went to see a lot of people around here, but Philadelphia was dead . . . in its tracks," Eckert said. "The real reason
for that was that Philadelphia was the center of industry at one
time for the United States, but it was heavy industry, Baldwin
Locomotives and Midvale Steel, and circuit breakers, and GE
and Westinghouse, real heavy stuff, you know. We were talking
about little bitty chicken stuff. There can't be much money in
that.

"The other thing was, they didn't understand it; it was completely over their head. I think both the university and the bank-
ing crowd in this area were dead."

The two went to the New York investment houses, some of
which had invested in large electronics firms such as Philips of
the Netherlands. "These people were backing electronics people," Eckert said, "but they were backing people who were already
established. We were too early for getting backing for venture
electronics. If we had come a few years later, we would have had
the money poured all over us, but we were just too early for
that."

They tried connections. Mauchly knew someone who knew
Ernest Cuneo, the lawyer and conservative newspaper columnist. Cuneo represented show business and journalism people
like Walter Winchell and Drew Pearson. Cuneo thought Eckert
and Mauchly had a bright idea and "tried to get us in a number
of places." Cuneo did not do well, and Eckert's father was unhappy

with the idea of his son's business being owned by others, particularly a group of New York Jews. The elder Eckert signed a note to borrow $25,000, and Eckert and Mauchly were able to raise "a few hundred thousand," mostly from friends in Philadelphia.

They needed a name for their machine. In the early discussions, the computer they wanted to build was simply known as an "EDVAC-type machine." That wouldn't do. Several suggestions were made. Mauchly, tongue in cheek, came up with Indiscreet Numerical Fudger and Computer, or INFAC. At a meeting, Eckert suggested Universal Automatic Compater, or UNIVAC. They later found that the name also belonged to a British vacuum-cleaner company and a false-tooth adhesive, but the lawyers assured them there was no problem. The name stuck.

They needed contracts to sell their UNIVACs. Mauchly, who had gone to visit his friends at the Census Bureau for the Moore School, now was stalking the halls for his own company, competing with the Moore School and with von Neumann at IAS. Other companies were also pawing the ground, waiting to jump into the field. Travis had invited a representative of Reeves Instruments to the Moore School and had also contacted Burroughs.[9] Both companies were tempted to go into the field themselves and, not incidentally, less likely to invest in Eckert and Mauchly.

The people at the Census Bureau were sympathetic. Under federal law, however, they could not spend money on research and development, but they knew that the National Bureau of Standards could act as a conduit.

The National Bureau of Standards, or NBS, was one of two government agencies eager to get involved with computer technology. The other, the Office of Naval Research, under Mina Rees, had already funded computer development at MIT and Harvard. A branch of the Commerce Department, NBS was established in 1901 primarily as a regulatory agency with some research. During World War II, however, it expanded its research functions (over the objections of Vannevar Bush). In 1945 Edward U. Condon, a theoretical physicist who had refused to serve in

9. Ultimately, Travis went to work for Burroughs, building computers.

the Manhattan Project because he thought it immoral, was named director of the bureau. Condon overturned the old establishment at NBS and went into research at full speed. He was eager to fund young scientists and new ideas. Such a man seemed custom-made for Eckert and Mauchly.

The Census Bureau met with NBS on March 28, 1946. It wanted to transfer $300,000 to NBS for a computer. The bureau specifically asked NBS for "(a) an appraisal by experts in electronics on the practicality of the equipment Drs. Eckert and Mauchly indicated they can build, (b) assistance in writing specifications to be included in a contract for building such equipment if it is seemed advantageous to negotiate such a contract." Transferring the money proved to be a bit difficult, as the fiscal year was about to expire, but the funds were attached as a rider to another bill, Mauchly said.

NBS agreed to the funds transfer, but announced it would require a 15 percent share for overhead. The $300,000 was now down to $255,000. The decrease "was considerable, as far as we were concerned," Mauchly told Carr. Nonetheless, they had a solid lead.

The two men had formed a partnership, at first called Electronic Control Company, because of Eckert's belief that the computer's first major contribution would be in the control of mechanical or manufacturing processes. Several of the Moore School engineers, including Shaw and Lukoff (back from the navy) joined them. They set up shop on the second and third floors of a building at 1215 Walnut Street, in Center City Philadelphia, above the Kent Clothing Store.

One of those joining the company was Isaac Auerbach, a former student of Aiken's at MIT. Auerbach already had a degree in electrical engineering from the Drexel Institute of Technology[10] and was working for a master's degree in applied physics when he met Eckert, who offered him a job. Auerbach moved back to Philadelphia and inspected the offices of Electronic Control.

"It was terrible," he said. "It was a dance studio at one time.

10. Now Drexel University. Drexel's campus is adjacent to Penn's, in West Philadelphia.

They had a big mirror, a kick bar in one area, The front office that Mauchly and Eckert occupied and the conference room were reasonably nice. A couple of secretaries. Then you walked behind that, and it was just one big open area, where all the engineers had desks. They were pushed up, close together as you can get them. Drawing boards stuffed in. We had a drawing board in this corner. One over there. On the floor above that, we had a laboratory and a stock room. The bathroom was the chemistry lab. The large room that existed above that was a laboratory. The fourth floor was just storage."

The front of the offices had large windows that faced out onto Walnut Street, an expensive shopping area. Once every month the windows would be washed, and for days afterward, Lukoff wrote, "there would be disturbing thuds as pigeons tried to fly through the glass."

The Census Bureau transferred the money to NBS in April 1946, but the contract remained unsigned. As was customary, NBS needed an outside consultant to provide recommendations. Whom should they pick? George Stibitz. Again, the Washington scientific establishment seemed comfortable only with one of their own. That Stibitz was singularly unqualified to act as judge of Eckert and Mauchly's new machine went unnoticed. A fine mathematician and innovator at Bell Labs, he had been dead wrong about the electronic computer in 1943, and he was wrong again three years later. In a memo that covered only lightly the fact that he did not understand what Eckert and Mauchly were doing, Stibitz wrote, "I find it difficult to say much about the Mauchly-Eckert proposal. There are so many things still undecided that I do not think a contract should be let for the whole job." He said the proposal was "promising enough to let a contract to study the problem, leading to a solid proposal and schematic." The "old-boy network" struck again.

Astonishingly, NBS, following the lead established by army ordnance during the war, proceeded to ignore the advice. Government organizations that one would have expected to be staid and conservative seemed perfectly willing to fly in the face of conventional wisdom and take a chance on new technology. Instead of the three-tiered contract Stibitz recommended, John

Curtiss, the assistant director of NBS, ssued a two-tiered contract—one for research and study, the other for development. Stibitz, who refused to take Eckert and Mauchly seriously, suggested soliciting bids from major companies, but J. C. Capt, the director of the Census Bureau, was afraid the big firms would undercut Electronic Control. Curtiss thus sent requests to only a few. Two responded—Raytheon Manufacturing and Hughes Tool. Only Raytheon actually submitted a bid, but it was well above Eckert and Mauchly's.

Electronic Control was in business.

Eckert and Mauchly had just made their first serious mistake, a kind of mistake indicative of their lack of business sense. The terms of the contract with NBS were impossible. The contract was for a flat fee, $255,000. As we saw, they had asked for $300,000 and the Census Bureau was prepared to give that much, but the National Bureau of Standards took 15 percent off the top for overhead. Yet Eckert and Mauchly had guessed that their costs for building UNIVAC would be $400,000. If that guess was close to the mark (which it was not), their young, undercapitalized company had agreed to absorb a loss of more than $100,000. The two men assumed that this kind of loss was worth the effort to get their company going.

But companies with experience in government technology contracts knew better. Building high-technology machines is complex, and Murphy's Law (holding that if anything can go wrong, it will go wrong) was first enunciated by an engineer on just such a contract. Pushing the state of the art in technology always takes longer and costs more than the pushers think at the beginning.

Eckert and Mauchly did not have to look outside the computer field for an example of how the game should be played. NBS was not relying solely on Electronic Control for computers. The Office of Naval Research wanted a computer, and NBS provided technical support. Again NBS let out bids, and the winner was Raytheon, an electronics company apparently serious about getting started in the computer business. Raytheon, with years of government contracts behind it, insisted on and received a cost-plus contract. Cost-plus contracts—in which the buyer, the government, pays the cost of building the machine plus a reasonable profit—were standard in government work.

Eckert and Mauchly knew all about cost-plus contracts, or should have, but they elected not to ask for one, because of Eckert's obsession with patent rights. Under fixed-fee contracts all the patents go to the developer; under cost-plus contracts most of the patents usually go to the developer. Eckert did not want to take a chance on losing any more patents; his experience with Penn and von Neumann had left scars. According to Auerbach, the attitude was "Oh, yes, we'll build one of those. And when we build it, we'll demonstrate it to you, and you'll pay us for it. You only pay when the system is demonstrated and works." That attitude was disastrous.

The contract raised other questions as well. Under law, the government could not put its money up front; payment could be made only after certain things had been accomplished. The best NBS could do was pay in stages. Certain checkpoints were written into the contract, and only after Electronic Control had passed those checkpoints could any money be disbursed. NBS was doing all it could to encourage the new company, even going to other government agencies and encouraging them to buy UNIVACs (several, including the Air Comptroller's Office and the Army Map Service, agreed), but the NBS contract could in no way provide the kind of capital Electronic Control needed to start building computers.

Nonetheless, NBS was concerned about the little company and called a meeting of potential commercial customers to discuss its financial health. Mauchly wrote:

John Curtiss has stated that our financial position is what worries him most. If he was sure that we were well financed, he would be disposed to give us more machine contracts. He is apparently afraid that we will go broke, and the more orders he gives us, the worse it is for him if we fail.

NBS hoped to be the principal government supporter of developments in computer science, the storehouse of computer information. It even set up its own computing facility, the National Applied Mathematics Laboratory. Curtiss wrote to Eckert and

Mauchly that the bureau intended to "ensure free exchange of technical and progress reports between itself and all its contractors in the machine computing field." Curtiss said he hoped the Moore School, the Institute for Advanced Study, and army ordnance could be brought into the network.

In the spring of 1947, NBS went a step further. Curtiss went to a meeting of the National Research Council, a branch of the prestigious National Academy of Sciences, the Parthenon of the scientific establishment, and asked that a subcommittee be appointed to evaluate all the computer projects NBS was funding—UNIVAC, Raytheon, and EDVAC. Curtiss hoped the subcommittee would also look at the academic machines— von Neumann's IAS and MIT's new machine, Whirlwind—as well as at the computer activities at Bell Labs. The subcommittee was formed, and the reader can probably guess by now who its members were: Aiken, of Harvard, Caldwell, of MIT, Stibitz, and, of course, von Neumann. The first three had been burned by backing the wrong technology in the early 1940s and had been embarrassed by the Moore School; the last was hardly a supporter of the efforts of Eckert and Mauchly.

The subcommittee established itself under the name Subcommittee Z on High-Speed Computing. Curtiss assured Eckert and Mauchly that the subcommittee would be doing good work.

It appears advisable to let you know exactly what arrangements have been made by the Bureau to secure the technical assessment of the NRC Committee on High Speed Computing *[sic]* on the evaluation of designs for electronic digital computing machines. . . . Since the design evaluations will probably include the EDVAC, the IAS machine and the computer designed by the Servomechanism Lab at MIT, in addition to the UNIVAC and Raytheon machine, it is obvious that the designs compared will have been aimed at different applications.

Subcommittee Z didn't see its mandate that way. After taking its time drafting a report, it restricted its analysis to the NBS machines, omitting any mention of the machines being built by members of the subcommittee, despite the fact that none of these machines were secret and that one, MIT's Whirlwind, was extremely expensive.[11] Since they were scientists supposedly dedicated to a free exchange of ideas, their omissions are conspicuous. Nancy Stern has written that this omission "suggests not only a possible effort on their part to inhibit the exchange of ideas, but also a belief that academic ventures were simply not comparable to commercial ones, despite the seeming similarity of design efforts."

Moreover, their analysis of UNIVAC, EDVAC, and the Raytheon machine was incorrect and useless. The report noted:

A detailed technical discussion of these reports at this place is not what is primarily called for . . . since the mathematical and logical bases for machines in the speed and capacity range involved have already been extensively discussed in technical meetings and in the generally accessible literature . . . a considerable body of reasonably homogeneous scientific and technical "public opinion" on many of the major questions that are involved is already in existence.

The three machine plans differ from each other in many details, in particular regarding certain important characteristics of the codes used, the arithmetic system and operational procedures used, the methods of checking, etc. It seems, nevertheless that in the basic principles that control these arrangements they have a great deal in common. The members of the subcommittee are unanimous in their opinion that these divergences are not of primary importance. . . . It would therefore seem that these three proposals do not represent three really different and independent intellectual risks but that all are predicated on essentially the same estimation of what the most promising engineering approach is. . . . In view of these facts it appears to the subcommittee that a choice between the three proposal reports on a primary technical basis is hardly possible.

In other words, all the machines were basically alike and there was no point giving a detailed analysis.

The statement is so boldly incorrect that the motives of the authors are apt to be questioned. The machines were not alike, any more than the academic machines ignored in the report were alike.

11. The MIT engineers, stunned by ENIAC, finally concluded that digital machines were the way of the future, and began converting their computer operations to Whirlwind, which was their first digital computer.

As Stern has pointed out, computer designers, at the time the subcommittee was reporting that all the machines were alike, were having roaring public arguments about the virtues of serial architecture versus parallel, binary versus arithmetic, cathode-ray memory versus mercury delay lines. Moreover, Eckert and Mauchly had developed a high-speed magnetic-tape input-output device that made UNIVAC's accessibility considerably faster than anything else, a vital point for the commercial use of computers.

Although the design of UNIVAC was superior in a practical sense to anything else planned, the subcommittee gave Eckert and Mauchly no credit. The subcommittee earned none either.

The subcommittee report did its damage. Several government agencies, such as the Air Comptroller's Office, had altered their plans and decided to proceed slowly in their purchase of new machines from Eckert and Mauchly.

To make matters worse, Mauchly failed a security clearance. In a country slowly moving toward the age of McCarthy, guilt by association, even indirect association, was taken seriously. Mauchly, it seemed, had gone to a meeting of an organization in the 1930s which had a Communist connection, although he did not know it. Several of his employees also had alleged Communist ties, and his secretary's boyfriend was suspected of being "a card-carrying Communist." The security issue was eventually straightened out, but not before several other government agencies, tender about their security, had gone elsewhere.

Between the time of Eckert and Mauchly's leaving the Moore School and their signing the UNIVAC contract for NBS, Electronic Control had been paid $75,000. As Mauchly pointed out, building UNIVAC was the easy part; raising capital was the problem. They were forced to turn to business contacts to try to get more contracts.

Apparent relief came from the Northrop Aircraft Company, in Hawthorne, California, which was building a top-secret missile called the Snark. Northrop needed a small computer to fly in an aircraft to guide the Snark to its target. Northrop hired Mauchly to see whether such a computer was feasible. Mauchly persuaded them it was. Northrop asked for a general-purpose computer but specifically wanted a machine

to prove the feasibility of a particular method of navigation. It should be less than 20 cubic feet, in volume, and weigh 700 lbs. or less, and be capable of operating from 117 volts, 60 or 400 cycles. Ultimately, a compact, airborne computer will be wanted. Please submit a quotation or quotations on the cost of developing an experimental computer which will accomplish the aims outlined in this letter.

On October 9, 1947, Northrop and Eckert and Mauchly signed a contract for a machine to be called BINAC (Binary Automatic Computer). Northrop agreed to pay $100,000 for the machine— $80,000 immediately, the rest when BINAC was completed. The due date was the following May.

The contract provided Eckert and Mauchly with some of the capital they needed to keep going, but it was a bad pact for several reasons, the main one being that they had again underestimated the time and cost of constructing such a machine. Furthermore, they did not really have their hearts in the BINAC project, which distracted them from building UNIVAC.

For Northrop, the contract was a constant source of irritation. Northrop had several engineers who felt they could build their own computer and who resented their company's going outside for that expertise.

By this time Electronic Control had outgrown its Walnut Street offices, and the fire inspector found the premises unsafe: the engineers had disconnected the fuses. Auerbach said the inspector put his hands against some of the walls and could feel the heat from the wiring.

"I went . . . and found space, up at Broad and Spring Garden Street, that was used by the Red Cross," Auerbach said. "There was blood all over the floor, so we had to clean up all the blood, and clean the floor up. We always moved into space that was in terrible condition because we always got it cheap."

It was "unclean, unpainted, and uncared for," he said.

Electronic Control went to work on BINAC.

"I was told it would have to fit through a bomb bay door of

an airplane," Auerbach remembered. "I said, 'What?' They said, 'It has to fit through a bomb bay door.' I said, 'You're crazy. I was in the navy in electronics. It'll rattle to death. There's no way this machine will fly.' "

"The specifications are that it's got to fit through the bomb bay of an airplane," he was assured. "Yes, Sir!"

One problem was the power source. The computer would use a heavy iron transformer, but the specifications required the machine to have a light aluminum frame. Auerbach said he did not think the frame would hold the transformer and was advised to mind his own business. Since the frame bent when the transformer was placed on it, the engineers strengthened the frame—and thereby increased its weight.

BINAC was to be a small version of EDVAC, with some differences. It had a storage capacity of 512 thirty-one-bit words and used delay lines. The machine had two processors, each with 700 tubes, and could perform 3,500 additions or subtractions, or 1,000 multiplications or divisions per second. The two processors (essentially two computers 'linked to each other) were unique, because they gave BINAC the capacity to check itself for accuracy. The two processors performed a function, and if the results agreed, the computer executed the appropriate command. If they did not agree, the computer shut down and awaited further instructions. It was entirely binary, which set it apart from UNIVAC. More important, it was a stored-program computer, the first completed in the United States.[12] It was also the first machine to use a tape input, although the BINAC tape device was quite inferior to later devices for UNIVAC. Timing was originally to be 4 megacycles, but it was cut by Eckert to 2.5; the engineers felt that 4 megacycles was pushing things too far. It contained the best example to date of what is called machine coding, the basic binary instructions that give these machines the instructions to be a computer. Mauchly and Grace Hopper did the coding for BINAC, and Mauchly, Betty Holberton, and others did the original programming.[13]

12. The British EDSAC preceded it by a few months.
13. For reasons no one has been able to fathom, the best early programmers in computer history, going back to the countess of Lovelace, were women. This is

The part of the machine that handled the logic was made with germanium diodes, probably the first application of the newly invented semiconductors in computers.

According to Auerbach, the hardware people were generally ahead of the software people, or programmers,[14] "but both were very primitive. You have to remember that the war developed all of the digital technology with radar, so we knew more about how to build circuits, to deal with pulse circuits, than the programming people, because they had never done anything like this before. They were a number of years behind building the floor, building the shoulders on which to stand. . . . They were highly creative and very, very industrious and highly productive people."

Eckert and Mauchly could not produce BINAC on time; the machine was not ready for acceptance for almost a year and a half after the deadline. It was also well over budget. Northrop agreed to pay $100,000 for the machine, but Eckert and Mauchly spent $278,000 building it—money they did not have. Eckert and Mauchly tried to get the contract renegotiated, but Northrop, which had just taken a bath of its own in building experimental jets, was in no mood to bail them out.

"On many occasions paychecks were written and deposited in the safe," Auerbach said. "My paychecks were in the safe regularly. I'm sure others' were as well. So we worked for love. But it was very exciting. There's no question it was one of the most exciting periods of my life. I worked ninety hours a week—Saturdays, Sundays, all the time."

During the construction Eckert and Mauchly decided to incorporate themselves as the Eckert-Mauchly Computing Corporation (EMCC). Fifteen thousand shares were authorized, of which Eckert and Mauchly each received 6,750 shares, and 1,500

---

true not only at EMCC but in almost every computer lab. Hopper and Holberton are credited with writing one of the first assembly languages, a basic form of communicating with computers, a significant achievement.

14. Computer people are divided into hardware people and software people. The former are in charge of the machinery, everything you can touch, feel, or kick. The latter deal with the instructions, the programs, the codes. Douglas Hofstadter defines software as anything you can send over the telephone.

as company assets. The shares were valued at $1 per share. To raise more capital, Mauchly tried to interest a group of Boston venture capitalists, American Research and Development Corporation, in buying stock that would be valued at $40, but the investors declined.

The company picked up a few small contracts during this time, which permitted the staff to cash some of the paychecks, "but here again, there was no savvy from a business point of view," Auerbach said. "All the contracts were fixed-price contracts. They did not want to give away the technology. . . . That was an obsession. The obsession helped the downfall."

Dissension had erupted at EMCC over what to do next. The company was still failing because of undercapitalization. "Mauchly and I felt that the way to salvage the company was to slow the BINAC down to one megacycle, because we were just pressing the art too much," Auerbach said. He wanted to build a smaller, slower machine, a modified BINAC, "to make some money for the company so we had some money for our bills."

"We didn't have any money. . . . I used to buy crystals. We couldn't pay for the damn crystals. We brought them in from Western Electric. We made a partial payment here, a partial payment there. We couldn't buy what we wanted to buy."

Mauchly agreed. He found a number of companies that expressed an interest in a small computer, including General Motors and the Arthur D. Little Company, in Massachusetts. The University of Illinois and the NBS facility in Los Angeles were also interested.

He wrote:

From the business point of view it seems to me that we should be much more interested in selling BINACs than in selling UNIVACs at this time. If we can assume the modifications necessary to make the BINAC suitable for many engineering and mathematical uses are not incompatible with our obligations regarding UNIVACs, and that we can offer BINACs for delivery in something like 6 to 8 months, then we have in the BINAC a product which can bring us income approximately one year earlier than any income and profit derivable from UNIVACs. Moreover, the sale of a BINAC will in most cases not compete with the

sale of a UNIVAC; that is, the customer who buys a BINAC either is
not in the market for a UNIVAC or will probably buy one anyway when
they are available.

Auerbach said he went to Eckert: "Pres, I'll tell you what. I
think I've got a brilliant idea. Why don't you give me a few guys.
I will build a machine, one megacycle. I'll use paper tape input
and output, and we'll sell the machine to the universities. We do
that, at least we'll have money with which you can then build
UNIVAC and stay alive. If you don't do that, you won't stay
alive."

"That argument went on hot and heavy for a period," Auerbach remembered, "and one night we stayed up until God knows,
three or four o'clock in the morning. A man named Jim Weiner
was there at the time, the company secretary [Gene L. Clute[15]]
. . . Eckert, Mauchly, and I. We constituted the 'executive committee' of the company."

Eckert would have none of it. He wanted to build UNIVAC
and would not tolerate any further distraction. He would also
not tolerate dissent.

"Mauchly and I came out on the short end of the stick,"
Auerbach said.

"Eckert and I have long since mended this, stayed colleagues
of sorts. When I'm interviewed and asked if he was a good business man, I say, 'No, he was not.' He was an extremely temper-
amental man, and I voted against him; therefore I was no longer
a member of his coterie; I was out. That was that, I was out. I
found that I was no longer being talked to. This man used to
call me up at nine o'clock on Saturday night, nine o'clock on
Sunday morning, eleven o'clock on Sunday night, in the middle
of Thanksgiving dinner, middle of a holiday dinner—he wanted
to talk. All of a sudden he didn't even know that I existed."

Auerbach left the company shortly thereafter and joined
Burroughs.

Mauchly later defended the decision, although he probably
knew it had been wrong.

15. Clute had been brought in by Eckert from Northrop to try to straighten out
the firm.

As I see it, the decision to go ahead or not go ahead with BINAC modification must rest with the facts and opinions supplied by the engineering department. The statements made by Eckert and the sentiments
expressed by members of the Executive Committee last Tuesday pointed
definitely to the abandonment of BINAC modification and construction.

The engineering department, with Eckert at its head, was
running the company. Mauchly, who knew the customers and
knew what would sell, subordinated his knowledge to the needs
of the engineers; but he was right, and they were wrong. Stern
has written that Eckert was generally content to let Mauchly run
the business end. But his stubbornness over the BINAC issue
appeared to show there was a limit to Mauchly's authority. EMCC
would not be the last computer company to sink when the engineers dominated marketing decisions; it might very well have
been the first.

It needed an angel, and the angel arrived. His name was Henry
Straus, vice-president of the American Totalizator Company, the
manufacturers of pari-mutuel betting machines at horse-racing
tracks.

That racetracks needed computers should not be surprising.
They must total up the money bet, figure the odds on the horses,
and compute the winnings. Until this time, the racetracks used
mechanical means, and the largest purveyor of this kind of technology was American Totalizator. Straus, an engineer, had
invented that technology.

In 1927 Straus and some friends were visiting the racetrack
at Havre de Grace, Maryland. They bet on a horse named Cockney, a nine-to-one shot. Cockney won, but because the betting
had been so heavy, the track was delayed in paying off; and when
the payments were made, the winners received much less that
the posted odds indicated. A near riot ensued. A friend suggested Straus could produce a machine that eliminated that kind
of trouble. Straus put together some ideas and went to General
Electric, which assigned the project to Arthur J. Johnson, a racing buff. Straus and Johnson produced a relay computer that
would do the job. Even after witnessing a demonstration, however, American racetrack owners were not willing to take a chance

until Straus went to England and sold several.

Straus had competition. Another machine had been invented in Australia and imported by Charles A. and Gurnee Munn, millionaire businessmen in Palm Beach, Florida, who installed it at Hialeah in 1931. The machine failed, and the Munns asked Straus to fix it. He did, and the Munns and Straus went into business together, using Straus's machine.

"They were doing pretty well without a computer," Eckert said. "They had built machines which were, in effect, computers of a limited form, out of relays, which were fast enough for the limited thing they were doing. There were about fifty racetracks in the United States at the time. But at any one time, I think, only about ten racetracks were open. They had these things mounted in trucks, and they simply drove them from track to track. That was their way of avoiding having a lot of dead ones sitting around. . . . The same way with window machines, they loaded those in trucks. . . .

"This was, of course, a real-time system; it had to work instantly. In New York, Jamaica [racetrack] had 1,000 window machines in those days, 1,000 real-time windows feeding into the relays. A couple of their machines were rigged up to compute the odds automatically. Most of their machines were just adding machines. They would accumulate twelve horses . . . in different registers, because some were coming from $100 windows, some from $2 windows, and they accumulated them into a single register so you would get a total for each horse, and then a grand total. They were using a small desk machine. They could do that fast enough; they would post them on the board with pushbuttons."

Sometime in 1946, Bryan Field, manager of Delaware Park, just south of Philadelphia, decided he wanted to break the potent American Totalizator monopoly. Even at Delaware Park, a small racetrack, Totalizator was charging $150,000 a month for the machines. After seeing the story of ENIAC in the *New York Times*, Field invited Eckert and Mauchly to visit a racetrack to see the problem. Because Delaware was closed, they went to Havre de Grace, and spent their time behind the windows showing them how the system worked. Field assured Eckert and Mauchly that the owners of the track would back their venture. Eckert and Mauchly turned them down because Field wanted a special-purpose machine, and the men did not want to be distracted from building their universal computer.

In 1948, as things were getting worse, EMCC's patent attorney, George Eltgroth, decided to revive the pari-mutuel possibility. Eltgroth knew a number of executives at American Totalizator's Baltimore headquarters, and convinced Straus that Eckert and Mauchly had something he needed to see. The computers that Eckert and Mauchly were building would serve Totalizator's needs superbly. Besides, Eltgroth pointed out, if someone else got his hands on these machines, Totalizator might find it no longer had the racetrack monopoly that had made Straus a very rich man.

Straus proved to be the ideal partner. He felt EMCC should remain in the control of Eckert and Mauchly. He therefore proposed a deal in which he and three others nominated by Totalizator became members of a nine-man board of the computer company. Eckert and Mauchly would retain 54 percent of the voting common stock, and 6 percent would go to EMCC's employees. Straus put up $500,000 for the remaining 40 percent, including an advance of $50,000 when the contract was signed and a loan of $62,000, to be repaid in two years.

On June 15, 1948, the changes were made in the board of EMCC, expanding the board by two seats, to a total of five. Eltgroth and Wistar Brown, the sales manager who came from IBM, got the two openings. Four more directors were added on August 6—Straus, the two Munns, and the secretary Gene Clute. The charter of the company was changed to require a two-thirds vote of the board to do anything major; this was Straus's way of holding ultimate control. He apparently also saw that Eckert and Mauchly did not run their business very well. This meant that in order to raise a salary by more than $6,000 a year, pay a bonus, spend more than $1,000 for a capital item, or sign any contract for more than $50,000, Eckert and Mauchly had to get the backing of at least one of Totalizator's directors. It was unlikely the Totalizator vote would split. Totalizator also retained exclusive rights to any equipment EMCC made for use at racetracks.

The company moved once again, to 3747 Ridge Avenue, in North Philadelphia, a two-story former knitting mill. Directly across the street was Mr. Laurel Cemetery (where, the staff joked, they could bury their mistakes). Next door was a junkyard. The building was located at the bottom of a hill, dubbed "Death Valley" because of the summer heat that settled there.

The EMCC engineers labored to get the two processors for BINAC working first separately, then in tandem. "Short routines were now being run for minutes," Herman Lukoff wrote. "Data put in the memory was holding for hours; sometimes, however, it would mysteriously disappear." The engineers finally got both processors to run together, but never for long. The staff was put on two shifts, as the machine ran test programs all night long. Jack Silver was put on the "graveyard shift" to watch all the flashing lights, mark down the time when the machine failed, and restart it. Silver found the task boring and eventually hooked up a radio to keep him awake. He found that when BINAC was running, odd noises came from the radio. He eventually put this phenomenon to good use; he turned the radio's volume up high. This permitted him to walk around the building and stretch his legs. If the computer failed, the static suddenly cleared up.

While work on UNIVAC and BINAC was going on, several EMCC engineers were busy with two other developments important in the history of the computer. Ted Bonn's task was the tape input device. Metal tape was tried first; magnetic tape player and recorder heads were thought at the time to be too crude to provide the kind of accuracy needed to store important data. A chemistry lab was set up to produce a metal coating that could be electroplated. Eventually Eckert decided to switch to magnetic heads. The engineers had to figure out how to stop the tape after one recorded character (a binary digit) and restart it without losing the next character. Marv Jacoby figured out a way to move the heads back and forth at high speed; "dithering," he called it. Lukoff has described the work:

Magnetic heads were also under development. To get the high data rates, we realized that the tape had to contain many parallel channels.

There were many problems to be solved in developing the magnetic heads, such as physically squeezing the many transducers in, contouring the head to maintain contact with all channels on the tape, and selecting materials hard enough to give the head a decent life. . . .

Tape recording and playback test vehicles were constructed to handle endless loops of tape. Experiments were conducted with various recording techniques, the objective being to select one that gave highest density with high readback reliability. A sequence of pulses was recorded on the tape, and each time the loop of tape circulated, the read back signals were compared with the original information recorded. The objective was to read back many thousands of times without error.

The system worked, and became a standard input-output method for computers until the 1970s, when magnetic disc and drums and electronic keyboards replaced them.

Lukoff was working on a cathode-ray memory system. Eckert (and von Neumann, at IAS) hoped to use a system invented at RCA called a Selectron, but that did not work out. The problem of the memory seemed, at first, to be simple: all that needed to be stored was a 1 or a 0, or something and nothing, or two things that would stand for a 1 or a 0. The bit had to be kept on the screen long enough for the computer to use it; it couldn't fade away before its turn came. Lukoff contacted the Waterman Products Company, in the Kensington section of town, which made oscilloscopes with a small screen.[16] These did not work the first time; but when Lukoff plugged in a set of earphones, he discovered the reason—music. A nearby radio-station transmitter was interfering with the operation of the screen.

Lukoff next ordered a two-inch screen from Waterman and got that to work. The goal was a screen that would have 1,024 positions for each bit in thirty-two rows and columns. To stand in for 1's and 0's Lukoff first tried dots and dashes. That was a mess. Then he tried big dots and little dots, and that worked much better. "The big dot was obtained merely by defocusing the beam to form a blur," he wrote. Unfortunately, each big dot threatened to wipe out the dot next to it. He went to dots and circles and found that this solution was just right. Although his system was not ready for the first computers, this technology was

16. There Lukoff met his wife, Shirley.

much ahead of what anyone on this side of the ocean was working on. The little company was constantly pushing the state of the art.

When BINAC was done, Eckert and Mauchly threw a party. All were fed hors d'oeuvres and cocktails. The computer provided the music. Taking Silver's discovery one step farther, an engineer found that by attaching a loudspeaker to a part of the computer, the machine could be made to produce predictable tones. The party ended when the computer actually laid an egg: a hard-boiled egg that had been placed in the innards rolled out at a certain command.

EMCC called a press conference and demonstration. Eckert and Mauchly used the opportunity to publicize UNIVAC—the demonstration was a splendid chance to attract a crowd. The Moore School had begun announcing the expected completion of EDVAC, and Eckert and Mauchly wanted to counter the publicity. The next day, representatives from business were invited and most of the major corporations in America sent people, including Remington Rand, which sent Gen. Leslie R. Groves, the father of the Manhattan Project, who was now an executive with that company. Eckert demonstrated the magnetic tape input machine developed for UNIVAC which could be accelerated to a high speed and stopped within one-hundredth of a second without damage. Groves's assistant snipped off a piece of the tape and put it in his pocket, but Eckert saw him and demanded it back. "Nice try," said Groves. On the following day, government officials took the tour.

BINAC, with its stored memory, ran its first program a few months before EDSAC and the Mark I did in Britain, but it was not officially completed until later. The Mark I had a limited stored memory. EDSAC deserves to be called the first full-blown computer.

Although BINAC was a technological achievement of the first rank, its completion was not the high point in the brief history of EMCC. The machine was sloppily constructed, and there has occurred a long debate over whether it ever really worked properly.

On August 22, 1949, EMCC held its acceptance test for

Northrop in Philadelphia. The machine was operational for seven
hours, with forty minutes "down time" to replace malfunction-
ing parts. Northrop accepted the machine, crated it, and packed
it off to California. It is not clear whether the machine ever worked
in Northrop's hands.[17] Even before the delivery, Northrop engineers visiting Philadelphia were unhappy about the sloppy
workmanship and the use of cheap parts in some instances.
"Economizing and poor workmanship indicated," one engineer
told the headquarters. Officials of the company were also unhappy
with the quality of the workmanship, and complained that once
the machine had arrived at headquarters, Northrop could rarely,
if ever, get it to work reliably.

   In part, the problem may have been that the machine did not
survive its trip to California very well (Northrop engineers said
it arrived in "deplorable condition"). That was Northrop's
responsibility. Also, it is possible the Northrop people in California did not know how to assemble it properly, or run it correctly.
Nancy Stern has written that some Northrop engineers may have
been primed to dislike the machine because they had not been
permitted to build it. Whatever the reasons, Northrop engineers
debated for years whether BINAC ever worked. The company
found twenty-eight major problems in the first five months.

The following items refer specifically to redesign, replacements or work
never completed in which the reliability of BINAC was involved. . . .
New circuit never completed—old one operative but unreliable. . . .
Original circuit unsatisfactory. New circuit partly wired in but not finished or checked.

   One Northrop engineer, Jerry Mendelson, many years later
wrote an article defending the machine, asserting that it did work
at Northrop; he himself ran problems on it.

What was not foreseen (this is my opinion, not absolute fact) was the
miserable state of the equipment and its drawing when it was shipped.
The two machines [processors], which were supposed to be identical to
each other and run in exact synchronism, had major differences in their

17. It certainly never flew in an airplane. Northrop engineers had rigged up an
analog machine that solved most of the problems; as far as Northrop was concerned, BINAC was a wasted effort.

components and wiring. Neither machine corresponded to the drawing package that accompanied it.

Another engineer said the fault was in the original construction. The vacuum tubes, she wrote, were "just standard radio tubes purchased from the factory without any quality control." Only about 25 percent of the tubes seemed to be suitable. She said, "BINAC, seemed to operate well on sunny days, but poorly on rainy days; the windows were normally open in the BINAC room."

Actually, the vacuum tubes probably did not come from the factory. EMCC people frequently went into the surplus-store section of the city, off Market Street, and purchased tubes from those outlets because the company did not have the money to buy them any other way.

The problem seemed to lie in the fact that Eckert's heart was not really in BINAC. Eckert wanted to build UNIVAC, and he did not much appreciate the necessary distraction of the other contracts, including BINAC. One observer remarked at the demonstration that the machine was a mess and did not look like "a machine ready for delivery."

Eckert and Mauchly felt BINAC was merely a prelude to building UNIVAC. Stern has written that the men had three things in mind in building the device for Northrop: first, it would prove to the world that their company was capable of building an electronic computer, and this might attract new business; second, the company, by demonstrating its competence, would convince potential UNIVAC customers that they could build a larger machine; and third, they hoped to sell time on BINAC to commercial concerns to raise more money. As Mendelson wrote,

It became clear that there were going to be severe problems with Eckert and Mauchly because at that time they were building or trying to build the UNIVAC 1. Their key people were assigned to that machine, and they were, in my opinion, and in the opinion of others, delaying, holding the BINAC in a partially completed state because it was the only piece of hardware they had to show any potential customer.

Northrop did not want its machine to be used either as a floor sample or as a facility for Eckert and Mauchly to rent time. All those things would delay delivery.

The National Bureau of Standards had agreed that the acceptance run of BINAC would serve as a benchmark for the UNIVAC contract, and NBS accepted it as such. In that respect, BINAC served its purpose. Again, Northrop was unhappy because it worried that the arrangement would delay delivery, which it did. NBS was unhappy because it felt that building BINAC delayed construction of UNIVAC, which is also true. NBS, in fact, was so unhappy, it decided to build its own interim machine, a small digital computer called Standards Eastern Automatic Computer (SEAC). No one was happy.

The company had by now acquired some other customers for UNIVAC. All insurance companies need computing help, and the Prudential Insurance Company, in Newark, one of the largest in the world, needed the help badly. Congress had just passed the Geurtin Act, which required more complex computing of actuarial tables; the resulting mass of work was more than Prudential could handle. It had considerable experience with mechanical card sorters and counters, using IBM equipment. One of its actuaries, Edmund Berkeley, had done research into alternative computing methods and worked in Aiken's lab when Berkeley was in the navy. Prudential asked him to investigate computers. He looked at Aiken's machines and a new machine being assembled at IBM, but he knew that UNIVAC was by far the best computer.

The company was more interested in high-speed input and output than in the actual processing. Mauchly had to convince them they needed all-around speed. Moreover, Prudential wanted to use punch cards, because they were familiar with them, and were a bit leery of Eckert's new magnetic tape input-output device.

Here something came into play that would rebound throughout the rest of the story of the computer: the Prudential management was afraid of souring relations with IBM. IBM was the largest and best of the office-machinery companies, and customers were afraid of the firm. Later, when other companies got into the computer business, they would find clients reluctant to cut the cord connecting them to IBM, a dependence that was fatal to many of IBM's rivals.

Prudential was also afraid of EMCC's financial situation, for it did not want to invest in a contract with a company that might sink at any moment. In a compromise, Prudential agreed to put some money into research and development, reserving an option to buy a machine later. The insurance company paid EMCC $20,000 for Mauchly to act as its consultant. EMCC had to issue monthly reports and was required to present a demonstration once Eckert had actually built the tape device. Eckert and Mauchly missed every deadline, but Prudential was impressed enough to keep extending the contract. On December 8, 1948, it signed a $150,000 contract for a UNIVAC. The machine had card-to-tape and tape-to-card converters so that Prudential could keep using punch cards (and remain a loyal IBM customer). The converters took time to develop. Since the whole purpose of the magnetic feed was to eliminate punch cards, Eckert must have cringed at the thought of building punch card converters.

The A. C. Nielsen Company, best known today for its television rating system, was then concerned mostly with market research and had a huge demand for data processing. In 1946 A. C. Nielsen, Jr., wrote to Curtiss at NBS asking Curtiss's advice on getting a computer. The firm was "running into a rather serious problem"—it was running out of room in its headquarters and couldn't expand on its present site. Curtiss wrote back that buying a computer might be a little premature but that the two best companies were Electronic Control and ERA, in St. Paul. Nielsen checked them both out and concluded that Eckert and Mauchly were about a year or two ahead of ERA.

I cannot help being impressed with the specific fact that Mr. Eckert is the man who developed ENIAC for the Army, and that Mauchly and Eckert seem to have the inside track with the Bureau of Standards at this writing. . . . The least that can be said is that some others in high and responsible places evidently have a great deal of confidence in these two men.

Eckert and Mauchly offered to sell Nielsen a UNIVAC for $100,000. Because Nielsen, too, was put off by the financial state of the company, the firm plunged in only partway; Nielsen took on option on a computer and offered both Eckert and Mauchly consulting jobs to keep Nielsen informed about the state of com-

puting in general and about UNIVAC in particular. The purpose, Stern has written, was to give Eckert and Mauchly more
business experience and a chance to get more time to solve the
capitalization problem.

Nielsen extended the contract several times and then went a
step farther: it offered to buy Eckert-Mauchly Computer. Nielsen was apparently convinced that his firm needed an electronic
computer and that Eckert and Mauchly could build one for him,
but that they did not know how to run a business. He thought
the contracts they had signed with Northrop and Prudential were
proof of that.

These agreements will, they feel, provide adequate financing with the
exception of the patent work required. They seem to feel that they
could charge these customers for the patent investigation because neither of these customers had the slightest interest in their getting patent
protection. My own view is that they did a bum job of planning and
negotiation in this respect because if patents are important to [their
company], they should put them in the price even if, like the proverbial
salesman's overcoat, they did not actually show up in the expense account.
However, they don't seem to feel that they are in a position to change
any of their terms with either of these prospective customers.

Eckert and Mauchly still wanted to go it alone; they turned
Nielsen down. Nielsen, swallowing his reluctance, signed a contract for a UNIVAC, at a sale price $151,400—$30,280 on the
signing of the contract and $7,500 a month. A year later Nielsen
signed a second, similar contract for another machine. Both
machines were tape fed; Nielsen was willing to abandon punch
cards. An honest man, he apparently believed in Eckert and
Mauchly's technical know-how. But there was a catch: the first
contract would not be executed until Eckert and Mauchly had
come up with two more customers and a capital fund of $240,000.

Mauchly found the customers and the capital. The NBS–
Census Bureau ordered another machine for $169,600, and a
consortium of Watson Labs / Teleregister ordered a UNIVAC
for $100,000. Both contracts were for partial payments each
month, with the remainder to be paid when the computers were
delivered. Eckert-Mauchly Computer had six contracts worth $1.2

million, and 134 employees. The firm, however, was still about $500,000 undercapitalized. Then disaster struck.

On October 25, 1949, Straus and an associate were killed when their twin-engine plane exploded in the air near Baltimore. Eckert and Mauchly's angel was gone.

"We just didn't have enough money," Eckert said, "and too much delays thrown in from the government wrench throwers. We were running right on the edge of our finances. Straus knew this. We were just trying to finish up a little more on some of our demonstrations and things. . . . Straus was then going to use that BINAC to demonstrate the feasibility of that and get much more capital. He was going after many millions. He got wiped out.

"We didn't know how to go out and raise that kind of money. We had a hundred people to pay."

Two weeks after the plane crash, surrender flags went up over EMCC. The Munns, never completely enthusiastic about Straus's Philadelphia venture, sent Oscar C. Levy to replace him on the board. Levy asked Eckert and Mauchly about their efforts to raise more money or find a buyer. Eckert said Remington Rand had expressed an interest. Eltgroth and Brown indicated they had contacts with several firms, including, again, Nielsen. Mauchly said that Drexel & Company had been retained to act as broker. Two weeks later, at another board meeting, there were further reports on negotiations. There had been some contact with Thomas Watson, Sr., at IBM, but Watson was still not convinced of the future of electronic computers; on the other hand, his lawyers were certain that any alliance between IBM and EMCC would involve antitrust problems.[18]

Mauchly tried to get a loan from the Reconstruction Finance Corporation, with the help of friends at NBS and the Census Bureau. He failed. EMCC was running out of money and not paying its bills. Several companies were still interested, but Eckert and Mauchly had no more time; their company would succumb to the first reasonable offer.

James Rand, the son of the founder of Remington Rand,

18. He was interested in hiring Eckert and Mauchly, but the men would not abandon their operation.

moved first. On February 1, 1950, he agreed to pay American Totalizator $438,000 for its share of EMCC stock. Eckert and Mauchly received $70,000 for their patents, along with guaranteed salaries of $18,000 per year for the next eight years ($3,000 more than they were making at EMCC). Other employees who owned stock split $30,000, and EMCC employees also received raises. In addition, Remington agreed to pay EMCC, which was to be an independent subsidiary, 59 percent of the net profits received from patent royalties for eight years, with a minimum payment of $5,000 a year. The arrangement turned out to be a poor one, and Eckert and Mauchly both lived to regret having taken the advice of their lawyers.

"I have had very bad experiences with lawyers over the years," Eckert acknowledged.

General Groves was put in charge of the overall operation of the EMCC subsidiary, which now devoted itself to the construction of UNIVAC. The business community was singularly unimpressed. *Business Week* predicted that the machine would have little commercial use.

Remington began renegotiating the contracts EMCC had with the government, Nielsen, and Prudential. Remington's lawyers asked NBS to change all three government contracts to cost-plus. NBS replied that it would like to but that the law would not permit such a change. NBS asked Remington to come up with some ideas for getting around the obstacle. Instead, the Remington lawyers threatened to cancel the contract unless NBS relented. NBS threatened to countersue. Remington gave in and agreed to complete the three government UNIVACs.

The lawyers then went after Prudential and Nielsen, arguing that it would cost EMCC four times the purchase price to build their computers. They tried to get the two firms to cancel their contracts; when that failed, they threatened to sue, although they had no real grounds. If worse came to worst, they could always tie up the two firms with lawsuits, at least until UNIVAC became obsolete. Nielsen and Prudential canceled the contracts, and Remington gave back their money.[19]

19. The two firms eventually purchased IBMs.

Eckert and the technical staff continued working on UNIVAC. Mauchly[20] was assigned to the sales department, because he could not get a security clearance to work in his own factory—the old problem of the allegedly Communist group meeting he had attended in the 1930s had not been resolved.

The stage was now set for one of the shortest and most decisive battles in American corporate history.

20. Mauchly's life had changed in other ways. In 1946 Mauchly and his wife, Mary, went for a brief vacation for the Labor Day weekend at the New Jersey shore. It was late at night and they had no bathing suits, so they decided to swim naked. Mary stepped into a "hole" and disappeared. Mauchly tried to find her, but without his glasses he was almost blind; he therefore went for help, running up the streets of Wildwood Crest naked, banging on doors. Mary drowned. Two years later Mauchly married Kathleen McNulty.

9. The First Dwarf

Anybody can win, unless there happens to be a second entry.
GEORGE ADE

As 1952 drew to a close, James Rand, Jr., was facing the kind of business opportunity that comes to few men. He ran a large, well-respected office-supply company. Two years earlier he had purchased EMCC, along with its expertise and engineers. UNIVAC I had just been released and was a gigantic technical success. In 1952, he added Engineering Research Associates to his company. Under William Norris ERA had turned out a succession of excellent special-purpose electronic computers, including the 1101—the first computer with a magnetic memory, which he delivered to the Georgia Institute of Technology in 1950. Like Eckert-Mauchly, ERA found the shortage of capital too much and sold out to Rand. At the annual Christmas party that year, Norris bitterly handed out electric shavers in lieu of turkeys.

He even had the advantage of a competitor who was asleep.

Although IBM dominated the office-equipment field, Thomas Watson, Sr., was still unconvinced that electronic computers had much of a future; IBM was earning enough money and had enough power to leave Watson uninterested in making a heavy commitment to the new technology. It almost seemed as if Rand couldn't lose.

Rand had always been a go-getter. In 1915 he quit his father's bank-ledger company because he thought his father not aggressive enough. He went into business for himself, borrowing $10,000 to market a filing system, called Kardex, that he had invented. He paid off that loan, took out another for $50,000, and, after his mother acted as peacemaker, joined his father to form the Rand Kardex Corporation. They borrowed another $25 million and began expanding. Rand planned to build the "greatest office supply company the world has ever seen," putting together a conglomerate by buying up other companies. His acquisitions included the Library Bureau of Boston (the firm to which Hollerith had turned to start his business), the Powers Tabulating Machine Company (founded by Hollerith's archenemy), and finally the Remington Typewriter Company. The company changed its name to Remington Rand.

By 1952 Rand's company was producing the only commercial general-purpose electronic computer in the world, had the two men who had applied for the main computer patents, and employed two of the best computer engineers in the world, Norris and Eckert.

When Remington purchased EMCC, the old Powers tabulator was abandoned. Eckert and Mauchly had produced a machine that made the tabulator look like an engine from the Middle Ages. Eckert and Mauchly delivered the first UNIVAC I to the Census Bureau in March of 1951. For its time UNIVAC I was a wonder.

Memory was kept in mercury delay lines and held 1,000 twelve-digit characters. Eckert designed the computer with conservative serial architecture, but the machine cycled at 2.25 million cycles per second, making the machine fast enough to more than compensate for the design. The architecture eliminated some of the duplication required in ENIAC's parallel design. Besides enabling Eckert to use fewer vacuum tubes than were in ENIAC (5,000 versus 18,000), it also permitted him to produce a relatively compact computer; the main processor was 14.5 feet by 7.5 feet by 9 feet. Input and output was through the magnetic-tape system, itself a revolutionary innovation. No longer would customers have to wade through mountains of the ubiquitous Hollerith-IBM card. The tape was one-half inch wide and 0.001 to 0.003 inches thick, and 1,200 feet of it were wrapped on each reel. A reel held more than a million characters, about the same amount of data contained on tens of thousands of punch cards. Eckert and Mauchly also produced the converter that permitted customers who had data on punch cards to transfer the data to the magnetic tape.

The machine could read 7,200 decimal digits per second, which made it far and away the fastest device of its kind ever constructed. Eckert and Mauchly also produced a series of peripheral devices, all having the prefix UNI attached to them, as in UNITYPERS, UNIPRINTERS, UNISERVOS. (The UNITYPER was a typewriterlike gadget that permitted operators to enter the data on the magnetic tape using either digits or alphabet characters.) They developed, too, a device for duplicating tapes, what computer people have learned to call backups. Mauchly designed the coding, the binary instructions that ran the machine. In short, UNIVAC I was the best computer in the world.

UNIVAC almost became a generic name for computer, the way Xerox has become a synonym for photocopiers. This recognition came as the result of a daring public-relations stunt devised during the election campaign of 1952, between Dwight David Eisenhower and Adlai E. Stevenson.

According to Harry Wulforst, a publicist for the firm who wrote a history of the early days, the stunt was the result of a barter agreement between the Columbia Broadcasting System and Remington-Rand. CBS asked Remington for a few hundred typewriters and adding machines for election night. In return for the machines, CBS promised to poke its cameras over the shoulders of the election assistants to show the Remington-Rand logo. A public-relations man for the company[1] suggested to the CBS people that one way to keep the audience's attention during the otherwise tedious vote count would be to try to predict the winner using a computer. CBS agreed.

The CBS people apparently thought the computer would be a show-business gimmick, and Walter Cronkite, for one, assured other reporters that "we're not depending too much on this machine. It may be just a side show." But "then again," he added, "it may turn out to be of great value to some people."

As CBS prepared for election night, the engineers were busy programming UNIVAC I in Philadelphia. They produced algorithms to analyze election returns and voting patterns in the last two presidential elections, along with voting trends going back to 1928, a task that Wulforst correctly pointed out had no precedent. With the help of political scientists, they put all the information they thought might be useful onto the data tapes. Frightened of what they were trying to do, the Eckert-Mauchly engineers used three computers, one to process the data on the air, a second to check the first, and a third to serve as a backup in case something happened to the other two. Data were relayed back and forth to New York on a Teletype line. The engineers worked right up to air time, as Eckert hovered over their shoulders.

CBS went on the air at six Eastern time. The first results were Teletyped to Philadelphia in triplicate. Operators entered the data on three magnetic tapes. One tape was placed on the second computer to check for accuracy with the other two. Errors were flashed on a printer. If the three tapes matched, the data were recorded on a fourth tape. This was run through a program designed to make sure there were no logical inconsistencies—that, for example, no precinct could record more votes than it had voters or that each new total was higher than the preceding one. Only then were the data fed through the election program and compared to the historical data to determine the probable winner.

1. Wulforst doesn't say whether it was he who made the suggestion, but his book implies that it was someone else.

The stunt was a breathtaking gamble, and in the end the machine turned out to be superb; the humans experienced a failure of courage.

By 9:00 P.M., UNIVAC I had predicted a landslide victory for Eisenhower, a prediction that flew in the face of what the political pundits thought to be true. When CBS cut to Charles Collingwood, who was reporting on the computer, Collingwood told Cronkite that when he asked UNIVAC for a prediction, "he [UNIVAC] sent me back a very caustic answer. He said that if we continue to be so late in sending him results, it's going to take him a few minutes to find out just what the prediction is going to be. So he's not ready yet with the predictions, but we're going to go to him in just a little while."

Collingwood was either lying or being lied to. The engineers at Eckert-Mauchly were near hysteria, because UNIVAC would not change its mind about the prediction and because the engineers lacked the courage to believe what they were seeing. With only 7 percent of the vote in the machine, UNIVAC was insisting that Eisenhower would romp and take several southern states with him—something Republicans did not do. The computer operators checked the program over and over again as the CBS news department begged for something to put on the air.

According to Wulforst, Arthur Draper, Remington-Rand's director of advanced research, took matters in hand. He ordered the engineers to change the program to make the prediction match what the political experts were saying would happen. One factor, the one the computer used in extrapolating the returns into a final total, was altered. In Wulforst's words,

Fortunately, this was a simple procedure. One merely had to run the program to the breakpoint where the critical factor was computed, stop the run, type in a new figure from the supervisory control desk, and resume processing. Within two minutes, a new set of totals began rolling off the printer. A chastened UNIVAC reported 28 states and 317 electoral votes for Eisenhower. Much better, but not good enough for the thoroughly shaken crew in Philadelphia.

They "tweaked" the program again to make the computer agree with the experts. Now Eisenhower led by only nine electoral votes. Sure they had saved themselves from disaster, they went on the air with the prediction at 10:00 P.M.

An hour later, when the votes were rolling in and Eisenhower was running way ahead of Stevenson, even the manipulated program shrugged off human intervention and reported a landslide with odds of better than 100 to 1. CBS and Remington-Rand finally admitted on the air what happened.

"An hour or so ago, UNIVAC suffered a momentary aberration," Collingwood told the audience. "He [the computer] gave us the odds on Eisenhower as only eight to seven . . . but came up later with the prediction that the odds were beyond counting, above 100 to 1, in favor of Eisenhower's election. Let's go down to Philadelphia and see whether we can get an explanation of what happened from Mr. Arthur Draper. Art, what happened there when we came out with that funny prediction?"

"Well," Draper said, somewhat sheepishly, "we had a lot of troubles tonight. Strangely enough, they were all human and not the machine. When UNIVAC made its first prediction, we just didn't believe it. So we asked UNIVAC to forget a lot of the trend information, assuming it was wrong. . . . [But] as more votes came in, the odds came back, and it is now evident that we should have had nerve enough to believe the machine in the first place."

UNIVAC was an even better machine than the people who built it had thought it was. With 7 percent of the vote in, Wulforst wrote, UNIVAC gave Eisenhower 438 electoral votes. The official total was 442. The machine was off by only 1 percent.

As Edward R. Murrow said later, "The trouble with machines is people."

James Rand might have said the same thing. Within two years, Rand's computer operation had fallen in shambles and his company had become the victim of what is possibly the greatest failure in the history of American business.

Up in Armonk, New York, the home of IBM, things were stirring. The placement of the first UNIVAC at the Census Bureau shattered the calm. The descendants of Herman Hollerith, like their ancestor, had been thrown out of the Census Bureau by an upstart. That situation was intolerable.

Thomas Watson, Sr., had built one of the largest, most respected corporations in the world, with tentacles that stretched around the planet. IBM had a sales force that was the envy of every businessman, marketing experts who were recognized as the best anywhere, and a service organization that made the thought of buying anyone else's product anathema to most of its customers. Watson was not thrilled with the concept of electronic computing.

Some of his attitude may have stemmed from his unhappy experience with Howard Aiken at MIT. Watson had funded some university research in the 1930s, mostly Wallace Eckert's at Columbia, which had yielded a mechanical calculator for astronomers. The Eckert calculator had no real commercial value, but it was widely noted in scientific circles, as was IBM's sponsorship. Watson thought that was useful. One of the scientists who visited Columbia, Howard Aiken, believed that some of his ideas about computers were ahead of what he had seen at Columbia. He wanted to build an automatic computer. Aiken eventually got in touch with Watson, and a general agreement was reached whereby Aiken would build a machine under IBM sponsorship at IBM's Endicott, New York, plant. Several IBM engineers would assist in the construction of the machine, including Clair Lake and James Bryce. IBM eventually put up $500,000 for the machine, the Mark I.

World War II broke out and Aiken was drafted into the navy. The navy thought his work was important enough to assign him to Endicott to finish the computer. The electromechanical Mark I was demonstrated in January 1943 and then shipped to Harvard. In May of the following year, Aiken held a public demonstration of the Mark I, and Watson traveled to Cambridge for the event. Aiken proved ungrateful; he took all the credit for the machine and scarcely mentioned Watson or IBM at all. Since Watson had backed Aiken more for the public relations than for any commercial reasons, Watson was furious and a scene of epic proportions ensued.

"I'm just sick and hurt about the whole thing," Watson screamed at Aiken. "You can't put IBM on as a post-script! I think about IBM just as you Harvard fellows do about your university!"

He turned on James Conant, the Harvard president, and informed him that the Mark I was IBM's creation, not Harvard's, and that IBM would fund no more research at Harvard Square. Watson stormed out. His son later said that if Aiken and the elder Watson had had guns, they would have killed each other.[2]

IBM made out well in the war. In 1941 Watson had sent a telegram to Roosevelt grandly offering his company's total effort for the national defense. He actually had little choice in the matter, and even his son pointed out that it was a case of making a virtue out of necessity, but Watson was proud of his efforts. IBM equipment helped break the Japanese code and ease the paperwork problem that goes with modern warfare. IBM machines helped aim the guns in the jungles, as Watson frequently pointed out. He limited profits on military contracts to 1.5 percent and contributed that to a fund for widows and orphans of employees killed in service. Wives of IBM employees in service received one week's salary for every month the men were in uniform. IBM entered the war with revenues of $62.9 million and exited with $141.7 million. Earnings after taxes were $9.8 million in 1941; they were $10.9 million in 1945. The company's assets were $97.6 million in 1941, and $134.1 million in 1945.

During the war, IBM had its hand in a few computing projects and kept an eye on others, including those of the Moore School and ENIAC. Nevertheless, even after ENIAC was announced, Watson saw little need for IBM to enter the field. He had tried to hire Eckert and Mauchly but had been turned down. His son, Thomas, Jr., disagreed with his father about computing. Once a playboy who must have brought his father endless grief, the younger Watson came out of the Army Air Corps a sober, enthusiastic businessman, eager to carry on the family name in the family business.

2. The historian Katharine Davis Fishman relates the following anecdote. Twenty-five years after the shouting match at Harvard, the IBM chairman T. V. Learson walked into an exhibit of computer history sponsored by the firm. He walked along the display walls until he got to Aiken's picture. He was heard to mutter, "The sonofabitch!" and walk on.

The father had financed research into a new generation of electronic calculators, the model 600. The machines were successful, but they were a world away from what Eckert and Mauchly were building in Philadelphia. Some IBM customers were getting edgy, and it was all IBM's famous sales team could do to keep them from jumping ship. The salesmen related horror stories of what might happen if the businesses relied on electronic computers and the computers broke down. They urged the firms to study the matter carefully and perhaps form a committee, all in an effort to buy some time.

At IBM headquarters, however, the nervous customers were not yet making a great impression. One customer, Metropolitan Life Insurance, had informed Watson it had all the punch cards it could stand and needed to move on to tape machines. An IBM study group concluded that tape machines had no commercial value. Among the men within the firm who disagreed were James Birkenstock, Watson's executive assistant, and Cuthbert Hurd, one of IBM's newest researchers. They allied themselves with Watson, Jr.

The latter ordered Hurd to hire von Neumann as a consultant to help IBM get into electronic computation. Von Neumann signed on in 1951. Watson then arranged for some research money to flow to the researcher Ralph Palmer for work on a tape data machine. When the Korean War broke out, the elder Watson sent his customary telegram to the president of the United States, and the procomputer clique at IBM saw a golden opportunity and jumped at it.

Birkenstock and Hurd stalked the government, particularly the Pentagon, looking for work that might help in their campaign to build computers. "We spent several days walking around the Pentagon," Hurd remembered. "Every time we passed a door that said 'General' we'd go in." Everywhere they went, they heard about the need for computing power. They decided that no machine could satisfy all the demands of the war effort, but believed they could build one that would satisfy most of them. They would call it the Defense Calculator, and it would be a small electronic computer.

They took the idea to Watson, Jr.

"Hurd, Palmer and Birkenstock put their briefcases on the table and took out the drawings of the Defense Calculator," Watson said. "I was having pressures from all over the place—the anti-tape people were putting on pressure. I saw this machine, which was a black box with the number of calculations per second. It was all highly confusing, because mainly I was an airplane pilot."

The marketing people maintained there was no market. Watson, Jr., told his people to go find some customers. Marketing insisted that somebody set a price. "So we did the multiplications," Hurd said in an interview for the Smithsonian Institution, "and got a rental of $5,200 a month. Williams [the company treasurer] said, 'Let's round it off to $8,000 a month.' I made 40 photostats of Ralph's diagram and toured the country with them."

Birkenstock and Hurd came back with thirty letters of intent, but in the meantime the marketing division concluded that $22,000 a month was a more realistic price for the machine. Hurd and Birkenstock were in no hurry to go back to their customers and triple the rental fee, so the financial people agreed on $15,000. Several companies dropped out after hearing the news, but a few more signed on despite the price. Many of the customers were aircraft companies such as Douglas. The machine was renamed the IBM 701, the first IBM electronic computer. The 701 was announced with great hoopla; J. Robert Oppenheimer was the principal speaker at the first public demonstration.

The machine sold well despite the fact that it was a generation behind UNIVAC and was technologically inferior in every way except for the IBM name on the lid. The 701 was essentially a scientific computer. A commercial version, the 702, was also constructed, but it, too, was inferior to Eckert's UNIVAC. Watson, Jr., pushed his father to press forward, believing IBM would never catch up to Remington without more research and a large influsion of cash. The elder Watson, who had just promoted his son to company president, now backed him in front of the IBM board.

The Electronic Data Machine Division was established under Thomas V. Learson, who would later rise to the post of president, Albert Williams, and Louis La Motte. Funding came in part from profits from the Model 600 calculators. The first 702s were no sooner placed in industry than IBM announced two new models—the 704, a new scientific computer to replace the 701, and the 705, the first computer to use Jay Forrester's magnetic memory, and the replacement for the 702. The 705 was still not as good a machine as UNIVAC I, but it ranked much, much closer to it.

Remington Rand now had impressive competition. In reality it was no contest.

Things were not going well for Remington Rand. Norris, in St. Paul, did not get along with Rand in New York. The engineers in St. Paul did not get along with the engineers in Philadelphia. None of them got along with the front office in New York.

The dispute between St. Paul and Philadelphia was one of philosophy. Norris and his team in St. Paul wanted to build computers using the most contemporary technology. Eckert and the team in Philadelphia wanted to push the technology. Company legend holds that the engineers spent "20 percent of their time working on computers, and 80 percent of their time working on each other."

The regular sales force was divided and generally inept. Many knew nothing about computers and cared less—they were shaver and typewriter salesmen. Some were earning a fine living and did not want to upset their secure lives—something new technology has a way of doing. They had nothing in common with the computer experts from Eckert-Mauchly with their fancy Ph.D.'s. Remington had a special team of computer people, many of them engineers, who could discuss the finer points of the technology in great detail (sometimes in too much detail) but who had no idea how their potential customers ran their businesses or how computers might help. IBM, on the other hand, had salesmen who specialized in each industry and sometimes knew their customers' business as well as the customers did. Furthermore, when the Remington computer people did manage to make a contact, they could almost bet that the regular salesmen would never follow up. At least one computer salesman who cared said he dreaded going to work in the morning, afraid of the inevitable disappointment.

The sales department got no help from the executive suites. The computer division went through a long succession of incompetent presidents. Eckert, in an uncharacteristically kind mood, called them merely "ineffectual."

"Some," he said, "were former IBM salesmen and were supposed to be able to do wonders in no time, and of course didn't. . . . We would get a new president, and it would take two years to explain to this guy what the hell we were doing and what we really should be doing. By the time I had explained, they had plugged in a new president and we had to start all over. I did this lap after lap after lap. If I had it to do all over again, I would have lobbied to be president."

Rand was not the ideal person for what the computer people needed to do, and Eckert could complain that even as a division of Remington Rand, Eckert-Mauchly was undercapitalized.

"They never put enough money in it. Their business was very diversified; they didn't really have enough money to siphon off to us," he said. "The only way Rand could have done it was to go off and borrow a lot of money. Rand had already put together sixty-three companies when he got us . . . all kinds of things. That was hard to manage as it was, and he had gotten hooked once by an insurance company, that is to say . . . they were ready to take him over and only through a few friends who bailed him out at the last minute did he keep control of it. He was afraid to borrow too much."

"I think Rand was certainly as clever a man as Watson, in some ways cleverer, but the circumstances weren't as good. We didn't know this when we got in."

Eckert believed that Rand bought Eckert-Mauchly because it seemed to be a good idea at the time but that Rand did not really understand what those people in Philadelphia were doing.

In 1955 Remington merged with Sperry to form Sperry Rand. Harry Vickers of Sperry, an engineer, was named chief executive of Sperry Rand, and Gen. Douglas MacArthur became chairman of the new firm. Vickers's background was in dealing with the military, and life in the commercial world was not his strong point. He appointed a long line of computer-division presidents; each succession was preceded by internecine warfare and followed by retribution. Eventually, Dause L. Bibby, an IBM vice-president who had lost the political wars in Armonk, took over and was asked to institute the IBM philosophy at what was now called the Univac division. He was reported to be appalled by what he found: branches that hadn't seen head-office people in years; a bloated, impotent bureaucracy. Moreover, the technical staff from Sperry did not get along with the staff from Univac. Since one of Rand's hopes in the merger was to get some of Sperry's research people, the result was ironic: Univac's engineers were still among the best computer designers in the world, much better than the ones Sperry brought with it. Robert Sobel, the author of an unauthorized history of IBM, has suggested that Rand would have done much better had it merely hired away a few dozen IBM salesmen. Bibby did not do much better than his predecessors.

In 1957 Norris could stand it no longer. He took most of his ERA people from the Univac building and began his own computer company, Control Data, which specialized in extremely fast and large scientific computers. Even those Univac employees who did not jump ship bought Control Data stock as a hedge against disaster with Univac, a frightening example of how much faith they had in their company. Norris soon acquired a second specialty: harassing IBM, both in the marketplace and in the courts.

Two years later John Mauchly had enough. He set up his own business in Philadelphia. Eckert remained behind, but the time for his creative eminence had passed, and he seemed content to leave it that way.

Throughout this period IBM lagged behind Sperry Rand and everybody else in technology. Sobel has written that Sylvania, along with MIT, had produced a long-life vacuum tube far superior to any being used in a contemporary computer but that it passed up the opportunity to exploit the technology. Bell Labs produced the transistor, which revolutionized computers and the entire range of electronics, but Bell Labs was interested in telephones and did not take advantage of its lead. Philco, RCA, and GE began using transistors in their computers when they were available; IBM was still designing the 709 with tubes.

IBM had been committed to tubes from the beginning of their planning. They hired an engineer from the University of Illinois, Arthur Samuel, to run their own tube factory when they concluded that their vendors' tubes were inferior. Samuel told them not to waste their energy; transistors were coming. But Samuel also fought against moves to use more advanced solid-state electronics, because he felt they were not yet reliable enough. Every time IBM designed a new computer, Samuel had another battle with the engineers who wanted to use transistors.

Philco, in fact, was ahead of everyone, with a computer called the S-2000, but it squandered its opportunity, Sobel has pointed out. Other companies, such as NCR and Burroughs, merely dabbled in computers until the 1960s.

Although IBM was producing technologically conservative machines, it was second to none in its sales, servicing, and marketing. With this advantage and with the ineptness of its competition, it took IBM less than two years to dominate the market.

In 1953 a commercial firm wanting to buy an electronic computer bought a UNIVAC—it had no choice. Two years later, IBM sold more than one-half the computers in America, and Sperry Univac's share had dropped to 39 percent. A year and a half later, the computer industry was known far and wide as "IBM and the Seven Dwarfs." Sperry Univac was the first dwarf, second in the industry, but a distant second with 10 percent of the market.[3]

Before we take the story of Eckert and Mauchly to its sad, confused conclusion, we must take time out to follow the trail of the so-called Seven Dwarfs and to see how IBM, despite its reluc-

3. By 1965 the computer industry was made up of IBM and the eight dwarfs. The breakdown of the industry looked like this:

Position	Company	Share of Sales
1	IBM	65.3%
2	Sperry Rand	12.1%
3	Control Data	5.4%
4	Honeywell	3.8%
5	Burroughs	3.5%
6	General Electric	3.4%
7	RCA	2.9%
8	NCR	2.9%
9	Philco	0.7%

tance to take technological chances, managed to keep domination of the computer industry until the 1970s, when the industry
changed radically.

The story of the industry in the 1960s has less to do with
technology than with litigation. Charles Dickens once wrote that
"the one great principle of the . . . law was making business for
itself." In no other field is that dictum truer than in the modern
history of the computer.

Sperry Rand continued its chaotic ways until the middle of
the decade. It produced excellent computers but was unable to
sell anything like the numbers IBM sold or to exercise the kind
of control over the market IBM enjoyed. It was unable to meet
many of the orders it took, and unable to earn a dime in profits.
In 1964 J. Frank Forster, an old Sperry hand, was asked by Vickers to do something about Univac's South American operation.
He traveled to the offices on that continent and wrote a blistering critique of the whole operation, much of it true of the whole
division. When the present president of Univac was fired, Forster took over.

He streamlined the entire operation, putting it on a sound
fiscal basis, channeling research money to where it did the most
good, jettisoning the deadwood. To get the technical staff in line,
he appointed Robert E. McDonald, from the St. Paul office, to
run the technical staff. McDonald came to Sperry from ERA and
was one of the few to stay with Sperry (and resist buying Control
Data stock). He took firm control of both the St. Paul and the
Philadelphia operations; he was even daring enough to slip a bit
of research money under the table to engineers who thought
they had a bright idea but feared management would not allo-
cate resources for the follow-up.

By 1966 Univac had turned its first profit in the sixteen years
since James Rand had bought out the operation from Eckert
and Mauchly. Like IBM, it produced large computers, the so-
called mainframes, and a full complement of peripheral devices
and software. McDonald eventually took complete control of the
division, which was still hampered by poor marketing and insufficient research funding. As we shall see, that situation was
resolved at someone else's great expense.

Sperry never tried to take back the lead; instead, it sank into an uneasy relationship with IBM.

Control Data, however, fought like hell. In part this reflected the feisty personality of Bill Norris. As a founder of ERA, Norris had considerable connections with the military, so many that Drew Pearson, the muckraking columnist, suggested that some collusion was at work—that ERA was getting contacts without bidding on them. Katharine Davis Fishman has written that the column was one frequently given reason for the sale of ERA to Rand. The suggestion was that the navy, anxious to get Pearson off Norris's back, recommended to James Rand that he buy the firm to give it respectability. The other explanation is more likely; Fishman has noted that the firm needed capital to survive, and Rand offered the only alternative.

Norris was unhappy at Remington Rand almost from the beginning. His brusque manner did not suit Rand, and, more important, it was clear that Norris was upset over the incompetence of the company. His eventual departure was inevitable.

In 1957 he was approached by a management consultant who offered a deal that would permit Norris to run his own company. Norris and his friends from ERA seized the chance and formed Control Data to "design, develop, manufacture, and sell systems, equipment, and components used in electronic data processing and automatic control." Norris had no trouble raising the money: the stock offering was sold out almost instantly, Norris taking 75,000 shares at $1 per share.[4]

Control Data turned a profit in two years, which is astonishing considering how long it took all the other dwarfs to see black ink. Norris had several advantages. First, he decided he would not enter the commercial market right off; he would produce machines for sophisticated users—the military, the government, scientific laboratories. This meant he did not have to hold his customers' hands. Indeed, he provided little support and little software. His customers were savvy enough to do their own programming and did not need to call every time their computer burped.

4. Ten years later, Norris's stock was worth $55.5 million.

Second, Norris and his people knew their customers. They had worked with the government agencies for years. The market was limited, but Control Data knew where it was, and knew most of the people involved.

Third, Norris had a man named Seymour Cray, who had come with him from Sperry. Cray was, and is, one of the world's most innovative computer engineers. He is in a class by himself.

Cray thought being an executive was boring. He wanted to build computers, the fastest and biggest ones in the world. No one at CDC doubted he could do it, least of all Norris. When Cray announced he wanted to work in the woods in his hometown of Chippewa Falls, Wisconsin, Norris, who could grow angry at the idea of carpeting executive offices at CDC, promptly built Cray a lab in Chippewa Falls.[5] Norris visited only by appointment; Cray visited St. Paul occasionally. Visitors were given passionate lectures about computers, taken to a local diner for hot dogs, and abandoned while Cray returned to his lab.

Cray's first computer was the 1604.[6] Norris had to buy a factory to build it, and he partly financed the development by cutting everyone's salary in half. The 1604 was the most advanced large computer in the world, and Cray's reputation and CDC's ledger books benefited mightily. His next machine was to be the 6600, twenty times faster than any computer in the world.[7]

CDC was assaulting the one market IBM had ignored, the government agency or scientific laboratory that needed giant machines. IBM had dabbled in this field with a tube-operated computer called STRETCH, but the machine was a disaster, and

5. The notion of catering to genius, peculiar to the computer business, would reach the bizarre in the new complexes of Silicon Valley in the late 1970s. The notion is also one reason the industry has been as innovative as it has; genius is pampered and rewarded even if the pampering is not, on the surface at least, cost-effective.

6. Naming computers is an art form all its own. According to Sobel, the 1604 designation was arrived at by adding CDC's address, 501 Park Avenue, to the name of the machine Norris had built at Univac, the 1103.

7. Cray left CDC in 1973 to start his own company. He now produces what are believed to be the world's fastest computers, used by NASA and the Weather Bureau, the latter in a manner that would have pleased John Mauchly. Of all the manufacturers in the world, only the Japanese firm of Hitachi has apparently been able to keep pace with Cary's technology.

Watson, Jr., pulled the plug on it, taking a $20 million loss—petty cash to IBM. CDC thought it could do better, particularly with the new solid-state technology made possible by the invention of the transistor—a device that was much more reliable, was cheaper to make, used much less energy, and made it possible to attain much higher speeds.[8]

When the word of the 6600 leaked out, IBM went to work to counter the ploy, afraid that someone was challenging its dominance. The IBM strategy took two forms. One was to design a machine comparable to CDC's, the System 360/91, which IBM alleged to be faster than the 6600. The second was to make sure that all potential customers of the 6600 knew that good old IBM was going to produce a competitive machine. But while CDC was actually delivering 6600s, IBM's 360/91 stayed in the shop. This did not prevent the sales force from touting the computer and warning the unwary against straying from IBM. The main office supported their efforts by cutting prices. Norris found himslf both competing against a phantom computer and being obliged to cut the price of his 6600 as a result. Norris was furious at IBM, believing that the company never really intended to produce the 360/91 but that it was merely using it as a device to undercut CDC. In 1967 IBM abandoned the Model 90 series, agreeing to produce only those machines already purchased. Norris asked the Justice Department to charge IBM with antitrust violations, but the Justice Department, while taking evidence, did not move. Finally, in December 1968, Norris filed his own civil suit. The government moved into action a month later.

This opened an era of litigation in which millions of dollars poured into lawyers' pockets and in which major companies were sucked into lawsuits worthy of Dickens's *Bleak House*. On one occasion, Norris and a companion were standing by a window when a long line of black limousines went by. The man remarked that it must be a funeral.

"No," said Norris. "That's just the IBM lawyers going to lunch."

CDC filed thirty-seven different complaints of illegal activity, particularly charging that IBM had offered to sell computers

8. As usual, Univac was first with a transistor computer, the Model 80, delivered in 1958, at a time when IBM was marketing the vacuum-tube 650.

that did not exist. CDC asked for triple damages, routine in anti-trust suits.

IBM, of course, denied the charges, claiming that it had spent more than $100 million trying to develop the Model 90 series of computers and had encountered a lack of enthusaism in the marketplace. IBM also denied that its salesmen used unethical practices in selling the machines, pointing out, accurately, that its code of ethics warned the sales force against doing anything that smacked of "apparent monopolistic practices. Even though no one will probably start a lawsuit over any one of them, these acts may accumulate into an anti-trust action brought either by the government or by an aggrieved competitor." CDC claimed that although the alleged practices were not necessarily IBM policy, they were a part of the way IBM salesmen played the game.

IBM, always sensitive to the antitrust issue, employed legions of lawyers to keep it out of trouble. Now it needed legions to fend off lawsuits. With the filing of the CDC suit, almost every computer firm, peripheral manufacturer, or computer-leasing company filed suits. Sometimes the lawsuit was the only asset the firms had; failing businessmen sued IBM just on the off chance that IBM would settle. Lawyers took the cases on retainer, again in the hope that IBM would settle or lose. IBM defended every suit aggressively, frequently filing countersuits to keep its opponents off guard. Many of the suits were eventually dropped or thrown out of court.

But Norris would not let go. He was playing IBM's game and wanted what he felt was a fair shot at winning. He was already changing the nature of his company. He had acquired Commercial Credit, a finance company with more than $3 billion in assets. Commercial Credit handled the transactions when companies leased or purchased CDC machines. CDC also entered the service business as its machines eventually found their way to less sophisticated customers who needed support to run the machines.

IBM followed form and filed a countersuit against CDC, making its own charges of monopolistic behavior on the part of CDC overseas and within its own market, the large computer industry. The latter was a nuisance suit designed to clutter the picture as much as possible and divert CDC's lawyers. That charge was quickly thrown out of court.

Just obtaining the evidence proved to be a massive chore. CDC spent $3 million going through as many as 40 million IBM documents in an effort to prove the case. To keep some control over the evidence, it produced an index to the documents (using a computer, of course) which contained 75,000 pages. The index was made available to the Justice Department.

IBM, with 100 lawyers of its own, went over 120 million CDC documents to build its own case. But the firm was being harassed by hordes of lawyers around the country, all of whom smelled blood. IBM decided that it was in the company's best interests to settle with CDC. Negotiations between the two firms had progressed to the point where two IBM vice-presidents and two CDC vice-presidents were holding secret meetings. IBM executives suggested that the IBM president, Thomas Learson, was going to retire and wanted the CDC matter cleaned up. Norris and Learson eventually met. Two months later, in January of 1973, a settlement was announced.

Norris had won the battle. CDC was permitted to purchase IBM's Service Bureau Corporation, a division set up after a similar suit in 1956, which handled the servicing of computer customers. SBC had never been very profitable, and CDC bought it for $16 million. Norris had plans to turn CDC and his other service divisions into a national computer network in which customers would use telephone lines to plug into a CDC computer in Minnesota. The resulting network, Cybernet, made CDC the world's largest data-processing company. IBM also agreed to pay $101 million, most of which went to underwriting the SBS business, but included $15 million so that CDC could pay off its lawyers. IBM agreed to give CDC $30 million in research contracts and $25 million in business for SBS. Since IBM's legal fees probably exceeded $50 million, the victory seemed to be a considerable one.

What did IBM gain? Part of the agreement called for the destruction of the famous evidence index—to take place in the presence of IBM attorneys. The Justice Department, whose case was not affected by the CDC settlement, had been relying on the index for its prosecution. Now it was gone. The Justice Department considered this a destruction of evidence, but IBM and CDC held that the index was their property and that the documents indexed still existed. It would, however, take years to accumulate a new index. The government filed a motion ordering IBM to reconstruct the index or pay $4 million to have it done for the government. IBM was thereby given time for its lawyers to gain further delays.[9]

CDC had made the transition from being a computer manufacturer to being a computer services company, earning more from its services than from its computers.

Norris had come as close as anyone to taming the tiger.

Honeywell is the remnant of the Raytheon computer efforts. When the Raytheon engineers failed to produce a salable machine, Raytheon sold the computer division to Minneapolis Honeywell, in 1955. Like many of these companies, Honeywell centered on one man, in this case Walter W. Finke. Finke's strategy was to hit IBM directly, in the hope that IBM would not try to squelch his company out of fear of more antitrust action. Finke and Chuan Chu, an engineer hired from Univac, went after IBM's 1401 line, a small business computer. Honeywell produced a machine called the 200. It was twice as fast at the 1401 and went for about 5 percent less in monthly rental charges. Moreover, it could be obtained quickly, whereas a waiting list remained for the 1401. But the main selling point was that the 200 could use IBM software. Honeywell provided a device called the Liberator which permitted the 200 to read 1401 programs. The strategy was to make it "plug compatible," which meant that you could just plug IBM software into your computer. This made it more reasonable for a business to switch to a Honeywell computer, because the business could simply take its tapes, data, and programs and plug them into its new, faster, less expensive Honeywell. Since developing software soon became at least as expensive as pro-

9. Dickens would be pleased; the IBM antitrust suit lasted until early 1983, when the Reagan administration dropped the charges. An entire generation of antitrust lawyers made a living on the case and, like the barristers in Dickens's *Bleak House*, probably forgot what had prompted the suit in the first place.

ducing the hardware, companies like Honeywell could let IBM invest in writing new computer programs while they produced machines that could read the programs. A whole industry of plug-compatible machines grew up in the 1960s, and Honeywell was a pioneer. This stratagem killed the 1401.

By 1965 Honeywell was also earning a profit on computers. Finke, however, was replaced by managers who were more profit oriented, and he left Honeywell. Still too small to satisfy the needs of the new breed, Honeywell went looking for a partner. It found one in an unlikely place.

Two of the dwarfs would otherwise be giants. It has been written that IBM defeated Sperry in part because IBM was a much larger company, with greater resources. Yet two of the dwarfs were much larger companies than IBM. GE had sales eight times those that IBM reported, and RCA had double the sales. Both companies gleefully swung into the computer business, riding on the high reputation of their research labs, and both were eventually humbled by Watson and the Armonk team.

General Electric had been interested in electronic computers from the beginning. GE was the first customer for UNIVAC I, becoming the first commercial user of a computer in the United States. By 1958 it was being called the most computerized company in the world.

The GE approach centered on remote computing and time-sharing. GE engineers developed systems that enabled one computer to "talk" to another so that a company could increase its computing power without necessarily buying a larger machine. A company could also have computers at various locations which could communicate with each other. In addition, GE developed one of the first time-sharing systems in which several users could use the same machine almost simultaneously. GE built the Model 200 computer using solid-state circuits, and followed up with 400s, 600s (which incorporated the time-sharing system), and the 115; in short, it challenged IBM computer for computer.

But the costs were heavy. Although GE was the fifth dwarf, ahead of RCA and NCR, the losses were bleeding the company. In 1966 GE lost $100 million on its computer operation, in a year when its net income was $355 million. Earnings per share were depressed more than a dollar. A year later, losses were still high, around $60 million. A task force predicted that GE would have to lose another $685 million before it would turn a profit. GE gave up.

In 1970 GE announced that it had sold its computer operation to Honeywell for $234 million. GE would receive 18.5 percent interest in Honeywell's network, which Honeywell was obliged to buy back within ten years. The purchase put Honeywell into second place, temporarily ahead of Sperry Univac.

RCA's adventures in the computer wars are the stuff business-school case histories are made of. For generations RCA, under the Sarnoffs, father and son, had been preeminent in electronic research. Its labs were probably most responsible for the development of television, and RCA invented the system of color television that became the standard for the industry. That it should jump into the new field of computers was hardly surprising— after all, it produced the vacuum tubes that built ENIAC, and it was involved with von Neumann's efforts at the Institute for Advanced Study.

Its machines were competent, but RCA was out of its league. Unlike its competitors, who had a solid customer base from their office-equipment business, RCA sold mostly consumer goods and knew little about selling big-ticket items to other businesses. What little experience it had was in dealing with the military and the government. RCA rarely rose to the front ranks of the dwarfs. To prod the business, in 1957, David Sarnoff, the father, hired John L. Burns.

Burns had been an employee of Booz, Allen & Hamilton, the famed management consultants, and had worked with IBM. Burns's strategy was to keep technologically in step with IBM but to sell machines for less money. He was willing to do almost anything to get RCA computers into offices, even if it meant losing money on some of them. The assault on the computer market would be financed by profits from other RCA divisions, particularly television manufacturing and the National Broadcasting Company. The first machines under the Burns regime, the 501 and the 301, did not set sales records, but RCA had the capital to keep plugging away. Marketing was the name of RCA's game.

By 1964 RCA was turning a very small profit on computers. IBM had just come out with its 360 computer, the machine that would be the workhorse of the 1960s, and RCA decided to produce a plug-compatible competitor. RCA engineers took the IBM manuals for the 360 and designed a computer that did the same thing. The internal architecture was different, but outwardly its machine, the Spectra 70, was just like the IBM 360. RCA's total investment was $15 million, whereas IBM had spent $500 million to develop the 360. RCA could naturally sell a Spectra at a lower price than IBM could sell a 360. RCA also devised a system that permitted businesses to lease the machine, with the money going toward purchase of a Spectra. When RCA decided to push the software for the Spectra, it found the idea was too advanced for the commercial market, and RCA's computer operations were in trouble.

At this time, Robert Sarnoff, who had taken over from his father, hired a former IBM marketer, L. Edwin Donegan, Jr., as sales manager. This was not unusual. Many IBM executives and salesmen found lucrative jobs at other computer companies, thanks to the IBM mystique. The notion was that IBM was the best and that the people who work for IBM were also the best. If you hired them, the theory went, some of what made IBM so good would transfer to your company. Many, if not most, of the transferees failed. Working for IBM and running a competitor are not the same thing, Fishman has pointed out in her book *The Computer Establishment.*

IBM is so large that only the highest levels of management get to see how the complex factors of technology, marketing, manufacturing and finance are put together; below the level of division president or corporate vice-president, a man learns only his part and must extrapolate the rest. The history of the industry is dotted with stories of IBM'ers schooled in, say, marketing, who went out to manage other companies and fell down on production or finance.

Donegan's position at IBM had never been high enough to give him that experience.

Donegan was frequently described as possessing "charisma," as being totally dedicated to the task at hand, and as being deadly serious. He got the RCA computer division organized and was eventually promoted over two executives who had previously run the operation. He was facing a new competitor in the marketplace: IBM had just announced a new computer, the 370. RCA needed a machine to match it. RCA assumed that the 370 would be a modified 360, and, according to Fishman, Donegan felt that he could "put new covers on the Spectra, improve the prices and trot it out" as a new computer. Alas, IBM fooled him; the 370 was technologically superior to the new RCA machines, and cheaper to boot. Spectra users turned in their leased machines and flocked to IBM, a reversal of what was supposed to happen.

RCA constructed a $20 million facility in Massachusetts for its computer division and added a $16 million headquarters, moving the executive staff from the old building in Cherry Hill, New Jersey, across the Delaware River from Philadelphia, and having a corporate jet make the New Jersey-to-Massachusetts run twice a day.

IBM had announced a new system of storing memory using magnetic disks. RCA, following the old pattern, called "reverse engineering," ordered a disk in order to copy it. Fishman quotes an RCA engineer who said that the IBM disk unit arrived "beautifully packed, with all its elaborate documentation, and the sight of it just demoralized people."

According to Fishman, trouble broke out in the executive offices when several internal-revenue projections were challenged by whistle blowers within RCA. The dissension upset both Sarnoff and Wall Street, and rumors flew that RCA wanted to sell its computer operation. Sarnoff issued a press release saying, "RCA has no intention of selling its computer division. It has had no discussions with anyone in the past concerning such a sale. There are no discussions currently underway." Finally Conrad stepped in and ordered serious studies to determine just how much money the computer division was expected to lose. Estimates ran up to $100 million for 1971, if strict accounting procedures were followed. RCA's computer division could not break even again until 1975 and would need $700 million in capital to keep in the game. That did it; RCA went looking for a buyer.

Not many computer companies were interested in taking over

RCA's operation, which had lost between $250 million and $450 million through the years, depending on who was doing the counting. One of the individuals who were interested was Gerald Probst of Univac. He wanted RCA's customer base.

Sarnoff hung tough; he insisted that any buyer take over the whole operation—factory, machines, engineers, inventory, assembly-line people. Probst did not want all of that. He waited. The longer he waited, the less the property was worth but the more money RCA was losing. Sarnoff gave in.

On November 19, 1971, Sperry Rand and RCA announced the purchase by Sperry of RCA's computer operation. Univac hired 2,500 scientists and technicians and salespeople. The purchase price was $70.5 million down and 15 percent of the revenues from existing RCA computers. Univac acquired a customer base of 1,000 computers in 500 businesses and government agencies. All the machines were eventually replaced with UNIVACS.

RCA reported an extraordinary loss of $490 million on the sale that year.

There were two more dwarfs. Both Burroughs and NCR had staked out their own territory. Burroughs specialized in computers for banks; NCR, logically enough, specialized in business computer–cash register combinations that not only toted up sales but also kept inventory. Neither gave any thought to trying to take on IBM directly.

Burroughs built splendid machines and attracted a loyalty that even surpassed IBM's. The president of Burroughs, John Coleman, decided to enter the computer business early. He hired Irven Travis from the Moore School. Travis received several government contracts, but Coleman, not satisfied, bought a small company in California that made computers, and California and Michigan, Burroughs's home base, competed technologically.

What made the Burroughs computers so good was the then-unique idea that the software people, the programmers, needed to participate in designing the computers from the beginning. It is an overstatement to say that most companies designed their computers and then told the programmers to write the software, but only a slight overstatement. In most firms, engineers came first, programmers second. Burroughs went much further than the other firms in bringing programmers in quickly. The atmosphere was heady and intellectual. Fishman quotes one Burroughs executive as saying that the design team consisted of twenty-five men and that "six of them were outrageous geniuses." The machines were unusually easy to use; the programming made use of higher-level languages, which meant that the customers, frequently banks, talked to the machine in something resembling English. The first Burroughs machine, the B5000, had an operating system, a series of commands that acted like a traffic cop for data, that was unequaled in the business, and it could run more than one program at the same time.

NCR has one of the strangest corporate histories in America, largely because of one man—John Patterson, the king of American salesmen. Patterson was the mold in which all the table-thumping, slogan-spouting, glittering salesmen were formed. He would have understood an AMWAY distributors convention, for he invented that method of cheerleading salesmanship. He would not have understood Willy Loman, for selling was to him a religion, a joy. He ran National Cash Register with an iron hand, promoting protégé after protégé, then spitting them out when they got too powerful. Many of them went on to run some of the country's best and most successful companies. Thomas Watson, Sr., was one of them.

Watson, in fact, left NCR and joined the Computer-Tabulating-Recorder Company, the origin of IBM, under something of a legal cloud because of Patterson. Watson had joined NCR after the failure of his store in upstate New York. He quickly rose to the top of NCR's sales force in that region, catching Patterson's eye. He moved through the company's ranks, finally finding his way to New York City, where he set up a used-cash-register company whose sole purpose was to drive NCR's competition out of business. The company was set up deliberately by NCR's Dayton headquarters to that end. It worked. Watson used the same technique in Philadelphia, where again he wiped out the competition, and then took his act to Chicago. Such an operation was illegal, a violation of antitrust laws.

Watson used another Patterson ploy: his salesmen told

potential customers that NCR was going to produce a machine that was just as good as the competition's machine but that it would be cheaper. No such machine existed; it was a device to discourage anyone from buying elsewhere. When enough customers had been taken in by this, NCR was obliged actually to produce such a machine, but it quickly fell apart. Watson became Patterson's latest protégé.

In 1910, however, NCR's largest competitor, the American Cash Register Company, which housed several former NCR executives, all of whom probably hated Patterson, filed suit against NCR. The former NCR people knew where all the bodies were buried. Two years later, the federal government joined in the suit.

The Cincinnati trial was a showpiece as sentiment against trusts was running high. It produced mountains of evidence of illegal activities by NCR salesmen, and much of it focused on the operations that Watson ran for Patterson. The verdict was guilty, and Watson and Patterson were sentenced to spend a year in jail and pay a $5,000 fine. Both men appealed.

Then a flood devastated Dayton. Patterson moved into action, turning his company into a huge flood-relief project, producing rowboats instead of cash registers, opening the offices to the homeless, and feeding part of the city from the NCR cafeteria. Patterson became a hero, and sentiment moved to his favor.

The appeals court overturned the verdict on technical grounds and ordered a retrial. The public mood made such a retrial unlikely. Patterson had won. In the meantime, he had fired Watson.

Watson was bitter. "Now I'm going out to build a business bigger than John H. Patterson has." He did—using many of the things he had learned about running a successful company from that most successful of salesmen.

While Watson was building IBM, NCR was stagnating. This changed in the late 1940s, when NCR purchased a firm called the Computer Research Corporation.

Computer Research was the indirect result of the failure of Eckert and Mauchly to produce an airborne computer. When BINAC proved a bust, a group of Northrop engineers were given a crack at constructing such a machine. They, too, failed. But the engineers were so enthusiastic about the prospects of building computers that they quit Northrop and formed CRC, which was housed above a bakery in Torrance, California. When their backer died, in 1952, they sold out to NCR.

The company floundered until 1972, when a China-born Englishman, William Anderson, was named president. He shut down the company's mechanical-adding-and-accounting-machine operation and moved it into the field of electronics. He completely reorganized the old company, introduced new sales operations, and ordered the engineers to start turning out new computers. They did so, and NCR moved comfortably into the realm of computers for small businesses, where it remains to this day.

During these years, IBM was far from idle. It had become so big that two entire industries grew up just servicing its customers. One manufactured and sold peripherals to go with the IBM machines, usually less expensive than the IBM brand, and sometimes more advanced. The other industry was the computer-leasing business. These firms purchased large IBM machines and then leased them to customers for less than what IBM charged for the same machine. Moreover, IBM set the standard for software to such an extent that most of its competitors, as we have seen, produced plug-compatible machines that used what the IBM programmers produced. IBM, of course, bore the cost of the program design. And it still made prodigious amounts of money.

In the early 1960s, IBM took a daring risk and invested something like $5 billion in a new machine, the Series 360. *Fortune* magazine quoted one IBM executive as saying, "We call this project, 'You bet your company.' " The 360 was a third-generation machine, designed to make full use of the new solid-state technology, which had turned to integrated circuits, involving the implantation of transistors and diodes on silicon chips.[10]

The new technologies were not universally embraced within

10. The circuits originated in Bell Labs in 1955. Texas Instruments produced the first usable IC in 1958, and the technique was refined by Fairchild Camera in 1959. See Chapter 11 for more details.

IBM, which was doing fine by not pushing the state of the art. In 1961 IBM's logic committee, the firm's planning group, decided that integrated circuits (ICs) were going too far. They favored a computer that used transistors and diodes that were manufactured separately from the chip and then were soldered on. That was doing it the hard way. Texas Instruments was making ICs that had the devices built right on them. The hybrid design was more reliable, it was felt, but would become relatively more expensive if TI managed to learn to mass-produce the circuits and if other computer firms started using them.

The 360 was the first IBM computer whose construction required the efforts of the worldwide company, not just the domestic branch. It was also the first machine for which IBM produced most of the components and peripherals itself. It was, moreover, the first produced by Arthur Watson, Tom's younger brother, a vice-president. The machine was in trouble from the beginning. IBM had announced it too soon and then could not produce it, a situation that finally prompted the CDC suit.

The cost of writing the programming for the computer was immense, perhaps as high as $500 million. The machine proved to be far more complicated and difficult to build than any machine IBM had yet constructed, and the company was mired in the project for years, partly because of the tension between the engineers and the marketers, a state of affairs that even Tom Watson recognized and lamented. Marketing kept wanting to announce the machine; the engineers, knowing they did not have the machine under control, fought to keep the company from making any public announcement. One problem was the difficulty the engineers had in devising a time-sharing system, a problem that lost IBM several early customers, including MIT, which jumped to General Electric. IBM even had to hire outside programmers to help.

Honeywell had already announced its 6600, the match for the 360, and Watson was beside himself with anger, writing in a memo that the 6600 was developed in a lab containing thirty-four people, "including the janitor," fourteen engineers, four programmers, and one Ph.D. IBM management was shaken up several times.

Finally, in April 1965, the first of the series, the 360 / 40, was delivered, followed quickly by three other models. IBM had a huge backlog of orders. The machine was a great success and had a larger impact on the industry than did any machine since UNIVAC. The 360 become the dominant computer of the 1960s and brought computing to places where it had never been before.

The machine also secured for IBM the preponderant place in the industry well into the 1970s, when the nature of the business changed with the development of microprocessors and microcomputers.

One other company needs to be mentioned, the most successful spin-off from IBM.

In 1950, Kenneth Olsen, an engineering student at MIT, went to work for IBM's Digital Computer Laboratory and was assigned to the Whirlwind project to help design a large computer for the military that would have applications for such things as aiming missiles and running aircraft simulators. The key to Whirlwind was that it was to operate in real time; it would respond to things that were happening while the response was going on. The machine was so complex that Jay Forrester, one of the IBM engineers involved, had to invent the magnetic core memory to make it work. Olsen was one of those who helped with this invention. He also produced—on a bet—a small computer to test the memory of the Air Defense Command's SAGE computer system.

He then went to work on a joint project with MIT to actually build the SAGE computers. By the age of thirty-one, he had acquired a great deal of experience in designing and building the machines, and he began to think it was time to try his hand at running his own computer company. Along with a colleague, Harlan Anderson, Olsen began studying entrepreneurship.

He founded Digital Equipment Corporation (DEC) in 1957, using $70,000 he obtained from the venture capitalist Gen. Georges Doriot. (When Doriot sold his share in 1972, it was worth $350 million.)

Olsen and Anderson moved into an old woolen mill in Maynard, Massachusetts, after the two men had cleaned the place out, which included scrubbing the bathrooms. They hired a number of engineers, usually from IBM, and turned many of them into salesmen. DEC salesmen are the only ones in the computer business not on commission, because Olsen, who is known for his intolerance for many conventional business practices, thinks commissions are "demeaning."

Having begun with building circuit modules, DEC soon produced its first computer, named by Olsen the Programmed Data Processor, or PDP-1, which sold for $120,000, a fraction of what competing machines sold for. The design philosophy was that the machines ought to be simple and fun and that the people using the machines should not have to have engineering degrees to figure out how to run them. In 1965, DEC turned out the PDP-8, the first to use integrated circuits. The machine was an astounding success.

Because its machine was smaller than the mainframes, DEC called it a minicomputer, a name that stuck. Dozens of competitors jumped into the minicomputer market—a market untouched for years by IBM—and PDP-8s became standard equipment in scientific laboratories, small businesses, and factories. As the price of the machine fell and its capabilities improved, more and more businesses automated with minicomputers, usually DECs. The minis were built to do specific tasks and at the same time to work with large mainframes, a particular advantage in automation.

By the 1970s, DEC had become the world's second-largest computer company.

The industry was largely created by Presper Eckert and John Mauchly. They earned little from it. Indeed, by the mid-1960s, they were to endure the final indignity.

10. **Bleak House**

*If the world is full of people like this, why are we worried
about setting the record straight? Let's just live our lives and forget
these liars.*

J. PRESPER ECKERT

ONE WOULD THINK that if a man invented a machine that revolutionized the world, took out a patent on that machine, and had the full financial and legal resources of a major American corporation on his side, he would spend most of the rest of his life enjoying fortune and fame. Edison did, Bell did. By and large, Pres Eckert and John Mauchly did not. They tended to blame their plight on lawyers, but they deserve a fair share of the blame themselves.

Patents are specifically provided for in the United States Constitution to "promote the progress of science and useful arts, by securing for limited times to authors and inventors the exclusive right to their respective writings and discoveries." Things do not always turn out that way. Many inventors have learned to hate patents, patent law, and, especially, patent attorneys. Thomas

Edison, who held more patents than anyone else in America, once called patents "an invitation to a lawsuit." When General Electric asked his permission to file yet another lawsuit over one of his patents, he replied, "Say I have lost all faith in patents, judges and everything related to patents. Don't care if the whole system was squelched." He said later, "My electric light inventions have brought me no profits, only 40 years of litigation."

Several eminent scientists have refused to take out patents. One Stanford scientist calls patent attorneys destructive to the scientific process. He is seconded by Ike Auerbach.

"I made my last patent with Burroughs," he said. "I told the patent lawyer, 'You have now filed the last patent you will ever file in my name. I will make claim to nothing, because what you are doing is destroying a group that has the capability of producing great things. You're divisive.' "

His advice came too late for Eckert and Mauchly. They applied for their ENIAC patent in 1947. The application, apparently the work of Eckert and Eltgroth, was poorly drawn. "I was there and took part in those discussions," Auerbach said. "I'm not a supporter of what they did. They diddled and delayed the patent; they added this gimmick and added that gimmick; they threw the whole kitchen sink in, they tried to incorporate any ideas that were just sitting there at the time. There was a lot of manipulating going on." Auerbach said the patent process was deliberately delayed to produce the maximum amount of profit later. Eckert and Mauchly paid dearly for this badly drawn and processed patent in the end.

Over the years Eckert and Mauchly, working for Remington Rand and later Sperry Rand, applied for other patents on UNIVAC. If granted, these patents would have required almost every manufacturer of computers, including IBM, to pay royalty fees to Sperry, and would theoretically have made Eckert and Mauchly rich men.

"We had assigned the rights to a corporation to raise money," Eckert pointed out, "and when they bought the corporation, [Remington Rand] got them as part of the assets of the corporation."

"In the original [sale] contract," Mauchly explained, "they were

loath to put out much money in cash. Well, we said, 'Okay . . .
put it in futures, you might say, and we'll be happy with a royalty
agreement if we get a percentage of the royalties.' When it came
time that it began to look like there might be a significant amount
of money some time in the future, they said, 'Well, let's negotiate.' "

In late 1952 the federal government filed an antitrust suit
against IBM, which IBM lost. In a consent decree, they agreed
to sell their office machines as well as to lease them, and to divest
themselves of some of their punch card facilities. The decree
also required IBM to permit any competitor to receive a license
to build machines as long as IBM was paid. Remington, watching the suit, and knowing it had valuable patent applications
pending, filed a brief asking complete access to IBM patents.
During negotiations, the IBM lawyers countered by demanding
access to the ENIAC and UNIVAC patents, finally offering a
cross-licensing agreement and $2 million if Remington agreed
to drop its suit. Remington's lawyers refused, and IBM countersued, charging Remington had violated some of its tabulating-
machine patents. IBM also challenged the important computer
patents still pending.

Remington's lawyers ran scared. They apparently feared the
challenge to the original patent applications. They agreed to the
cross-licensing. IBM agreed to pay royalties of 1 percent for all
machines built after October 1, 1956, if Remington received the
ENIAC and UNIVAC patents. IBM agreed to pay $10 million
over an eight-year period, the money to go as an advance against
the royalties.

Eckert and Mauchly believed they were getting the short end
of the deal; the money was so spread out that their percentage
would yield negligible amounts. They also thought that the royalties for machines built before 1956 would be substantial, and
Remington had given them away. Remington's lawyers told them
to keep quiet.

"I was supposed to get 5 percent of that," Eckert said, "but I
didn't get 5 percent. They spread out the payments in such a
way that John and I got a small percentage."

"The money we were after was what IBM was paying Remington as royalties," Mauchly said. "They [the Remington lawyers] said, 'Oh, it really isn't royalties. We just phrased it that way. What it really is is damages, because Remington sued IBM for unfair trade practices.' They sued and countersued and out of all that, the stuff that their agreement says is $10 million worth of royalties, that isn't royalties at all. I said, 'But the agreement says it is.' They said, 'well, we can't push too far.' "

"This has more to do with the ethics of attorneys than it has to do with patents," Eckert said. "The whole patent system is a piece of junk. It's really medieval stuff."

The two men would get about $300,000 over eight years for their patents. When the patents were finally issued, it was instantly clear that the money IBM would have owed Remington without the agreement would have been even more by tens of millions of dollars and that Eckert and Mauchly's share would have been much greater. Because of the agreement, neither Remington nor Eckert and Mauchly ever got full value for the patents. In fact, the cross-licensing gave IBM another boot up: the Remington patents were far more important than the IBM patents, and they wound up with access to Remington's superior technology.

The ENIAC patent, No. 3,120,606, was issued on February 4, 1964. The patent itself consisted of 200 pages of text and 148 separate claims. It had been amended several times. It was assigned to Illinois Scientific Developments, a wholly owned subsidiary of Sperry Rand.

In 1967 Illinois Scientific brought suit in the District of Columbia, charging that Honeywell had infringed on the ENIAC patent. Honeywell, followed the time-honored practice of responding to a lawsuit with a lawsuit, and went to federal court in Minnesota,[1] charging that the patent was held by fraud and that the cross-licensing agreement between Sperry and IBM vio-

1. Eckert maintained that there was a good reason why Honeywell brought the suit in Minneapolis instead of responding in Washington: "There's only been one patent, and that a year earlier, in which the Eighth Court . . . ever upheld a patent. That's why Honeywell fought to try it there. They had a lot of farmer judges that didn't know a patent if they saw it." On the other hand, Honeywell was based in Minneapolis, as was its law firm.

lated the Sherman and Clayton antitrust laws. Both cases were combined and were heard in Minneapolis by the district court judge Earl Larson.

The countersuit, filed by Honeywell's law firm of Dorset, Windhorst, Hanaford, Whitney & Halladay,[2] came as a shock. It alleged, among other things, that the patent had been applied for after the statutory one-year period following the machine's development and, most stunning of all, that Eckert and Mauchly were not the inventors of the electronic computer—that John Atanasoff was.

Several others jumped into the case. A foundation from Iowa State University representing Atanasoff's interests tried to stake a claim but was denied by Larson on technical grounds. His decision was upheld on appeal. Burks, Shaw, and Sharpless also entered the suit, claiming they shared in the invention of ENIAC. The judge eventually denied that claim.

Almost everyone who had participated in the early history of the computer either testified or filed affidavits with the court. The Honeywell lawyers launched a full-court attack on Eckert, Mauchly, and Sperry. Sperry's lawyers, however, seemed to take only parts of the attack seriously and defended only against those aspects with their full resources. That proved to be a mistake.

The trial lasted for almost a year. Honeywell produced 30,000 documents in evidence, Sperry 6,000. The trial transcript consisted of 50,000 pages. The trial portion ended on March 13, 1972. On October 19, 1973, Larson issued his "Findings of Fact, Conclusions of Law, and Order for Judgement." Sperry Rand was routed.

Larson found for Honeywell, citing four reasons: first, that ENIAC was put into public use more than one year before the patent was applied for; second, that there was sufficient publication of the nature of ENIAC to constitute "prior art" and invalidate some of the patent claims; third, that the lawyers involved in the patent delayed the process and withheld important information from the Patent Office in a way that constituted

2. Henry Halladay was the senior partner in charge.

misconduct; and fourth, that Atanasoff really was the inventor of the electronic computer.

Larson ruled that since the patent was applied for on June 26, 1947, the statutory date before which the machine could not be put in public use was June 26, 1946. He ruled that the Los Alamos experiment run in December of 1945 constituted "public use" under the meaning of the law and that, therefore, the patent application was six months too late. He rejected Eckert and Mauchly's claims that the hydrogen bomb test was experimental.

The ENIAC machine, disclosed and claimed in the ENIAC patent, was constructed, fully tested and successfully operated in December, 1945, and was also both on sale and sold to Army Ordnance more than one year prior to the filing date of the ENIAC patent application. . . .

The pre-critical date uses of the ENIAC machine were not made under the surveillance of Eckert and Mauchly, and for the purpose of enabling them to test the machine and ascertain whether it would answer the purpose intended, and to make such alterations and improvements as experience demonstrates to be necessary. . . .

The judge ruled that the machine was constantly being shown off to visiting scientists and military officers and that, furthermore, "all so-called testing, de-bugging and trouble shooting was normal operation and continued throughout the useful life of the ENIAC machine."

On "prior art," Larson cited von Neumann's "First Draft." Larson called the paper an "anticipatory publication" which contains an "enabling disclosure of the ENIAC." This, he ruled, disqualified some of the claims in the patent.

While the First Draft Report does not include a detailed disclosure of the specific hardware to mechanize the machine disclosed within the report, it does include a disclosure sufficient to teach one skilled in the art how to accomplish the logical control of a high-speed automatic digital computing system.

The machine is "either anticipated by or obvious in view of" the von Neumann paper, he wrote, thus fulfilling Eckert and Mauchly's worst fears about the "First Draft." The paper was every bit as destructive to their interests as they had been afraid it would be.

(Eckert and Mauchly came close to losing this aspect of the case on other grounds as well. At about the crucial time, Burks had written two papers that could also have undone them. One popular paper came out one day before the one-year date. Another, more technical one was written two months before the critical date, but no published until a year later. Larson ruled that the first paper "did not reveal enough to invalidate the patent," Burks wrote. The second paper, which was more detailed, did not count, because of the date. Here again, everyone published papers but Eckert and Mauchly. As engineers, they did not seem to grasp the importance of publishing what they were doing, and perhaps were too impressed with the security problems. Others, the scientists, did understand why publishing was important and did not feel constrained by the security.)

In his ruling on misconduct, Larson was brutal. While he ruled that there may not have been actual fraud by Eckert and Mauchly's attorneys, he cited several "derelictions." He ruled that when the application was amended in 1963, the lawyers were engaged in an intentional and improper instance of "late claiming," going back into the patent and expanding its claims to widen the rights of the inventors.

> The 1963 amendment to broaden the scope . . . was unreasonably delayed, and was not merely a logical development of the original application but an exigent afterthought to capture the subsequent contributions of others already in the public domain.

When they weren't filing late claims, the Sperry lawyers were doing their best to delay the proceedings.[3] Here, Larson said, all the delays were to the advantage of the patentee (Sperry). "Deliberately extending the expiration of a monopoly is a serious violation of the Constitution and the patent laws," he wrote. The delay here was "unnecessary and unreasonable," and he pointed out that the problem was not slow lawyers. In contrast

---

3. Patents last for seventeen years. The longer a patent grant can be delayed, the longer an inventor can gain from his invention.

"is the speed with which a substantial number of lawyers acted in 1963 in filing the amendments and the repeated pressure on the Patent Office in 1963 to issue the patent." In other words, Sperry's lawyers could move quickly when they wanted to. He also ruled that the lawyers withheld certain information from the patent claim, particularly about the work of others.

Larson ruled that the conduct of the Sperry lawyers was not gross enough to disqualify the patent on grounds of undue delay, but it rendered the patent, for all intents and purposes, unenforceable.

The delay in filing the patents goes all the way back to the reluctance on the part of the Moore School to get involved with this decidedly commercial procedure. As we have seen, despite a contract to file patents for the government, little was done until Eckert and Mauchly pushed. In an interview with Nancy Stern, Eckert blamed Brainerd for the delay.

"He failed to act," Eckert said. "A date was arrived at which the patent lawyers said, "Look, we've got to know who to put on the patent." It is a factual matter of patent law that the patent must be taken out in the name of the inventors or inventor. Any deviation of this, either by adding people that weren't involved or substituting people who were involved invalidates the patent. . . . It was a legal necessity. . . .

Yet Eckert himself is partly to blame after that, according to Auerbach, who said Eckert and Eltgroth delayed and manipulated to buy more time, and when they did file a patent, it was far too broad.

Moreover, part of the problem was a series of maneuvers before the Patent Office to settle legal disputes between Sperry and Bell Laboratories. Nonetheless, the patent application was not made with great haste, and Sperry's lawyers were more interested in making the patent as broad as possible than in getting the patent out as quickly as possible.

Finally, there is the matter of John Vincent Atanasoff. Larson wrote categorically that Atanasoff was the inventor of the electronic computer and that much of the idea for ENIAC came from him.

Larson wrote:

The subject matter of one or more claims of the ENIAC was derived from Atanasoff, and the invention claimed in the ENIAC was derived from Atanasoff. . . . Eckert and Mauchly did not themselves first invent the automatic electronic digital computer, but instead derived that subject from Dr. John Vincent Atanasoff, and the ENIAC patent is thereby invalid. . . . The utilization of ideas in a device prior to the time of the alleged invention, whether or not the device was subsequently abandoned, is evidence that when those ideas are incorporated in a later development along the same line, they do not amount to invention. . . .

After correspondence on the subject with Atanasoff, Mauchly went to Ames, Iowa, as a houseguest of Atanasoff for several days, where he discussed the ABC [Atanasoff-Berry Computer] as well as other ideas of Atanasoff's relating to the computing art. . . .

Honeywell has proven that the claimed subject matter of the ENIAC patent . . . is not patentable over the subject matter derived by Mauchly from Atanasoff. As a representative example, Honeywell has shown that the subject matter of detailed claims 88 and 89 of the ENIAC patent corresponds to the work of Atanasoff which was known to Mauchly before any effort pertinent to the ENIAC machine or patent began.

The court has heard the testimony at trial of both Atanasoff and Mauchly, and finds the testimony of Atanasoff with respect to the knowledge and information derived by Mauchly to be credible.[4]

No other part of the judge's decision has generated as much debate or heat as his claim that Atanasoff was the real inventor of the computer. Almost everyone involved has taken sides. Arthur Burks has proven to be Atanasoff's leading proponent. A history of ENIAC published in 1981 in the *Annals of the History of Computing* by Burks and his wife, Alice,[5] asserting Atanasoff's claim, has sent many of the surviving participants back to their typewriters to hurl ballistic blasts at each other. Eckert and Mauchly, deprived of the wealth that patent rights to a computer might have brought them, found that the judge's decision also deprived them of the historic credit for such an invention— a credit they firmly believed their due.

4. The issue is somewhat confused because elsewhere Larson's decision notes that "the application for the ENIAC patent was filed by Mauchly and Eckert whom I find to be the inventors" and then states that apparently the invention was a "team effort." The bulk of the decision, however, denies the invention to Eckert and Mauchly. The confusion has never been cleared up.
5. A former "human computer" at the Moore School.

Who invented the electronic computer? An answer to that question is vital to the story. It is possible, as Goldstine and Burks have urged, to accept Larson's decision as the most reasoned and impartial statement of fact. But judges and juries in a trial can decide only on the basis of evidence presented to them within the constraints of the law, statute, and case. If, for some reason, some evidence is not presented or if legal procedures prohibit the presentation, they must make their decision on the basis of what they heard and saw. Furthermore, their decision is rooted in the law; what is legally right is not always what is just. Consequently, judges and juries do not always find the truth, nor are they always just; they merely do the best they can under the circumstances. Larson, sitting without a jury, faced an extremely difficult task in trying to sort out the varying claims in *Honeywell* vs. *Sperry Rand*. His decision was probably correct as a matter of law.

The dispute centers on what Mauchly and Atanasoff did in Ames, which is, as we have seen, a matter of considerable debate. Third parties have had no trouble reaching conclusions about what happened during that meeting. Goldstine wrote:

During the visit the two men apparently went into Atanasoff's ideas in considerable detail. The discussion greatly influenced Mauchly and through him the entire history of electronic computers. . . . Atanasoff also apparently had ideas for a more general-purpose electronic digital computer and discussed his nascent ideas with Mauchly on this occasion.[6]

Correspondence between Mauchly and Atanasoff was plentiful both before and after Mauchly's June visit to Ames. Both men were, at least initially, free with each other in exchanging ideas. Atanasoff, for instance, told Mauchly in a letter on May 31, several weeks before the visit, about his idea of turning his computer into a variation on the differential analyzer.

As you may surmise, I am somewhat out of the beaten track of computing machine gossip, and so I am always interested in any details you

6. Goldstine wrote his book while the Honeywell suit was in the trial stage, and some, if not all, that he reported could have been based on Atanasoff's testimony.

can give me. The figures on the electronic differential integraph seem absolutely startling. During Dr. [Sam] Caldwell's last visit here, I suddenly obtained an idea as to how the computing machine which we are building can be converted into an integraph. Its action would be analogous to numerical integration and not like that of the Bush Integraph [at MIT] which is, of course, an analogue machine, but it would be very rapid, and the steps in the numerical integration could be made arbitrarily small. It should therefore equal the Bush machine in speed and excel it in accuracy.

His idea of turning his rudimentary machine into more of a general-purpose computer antedates even the Mauchly visit. In 1940, in a memo written to raise funds, Atanasoff noted:

It is the main purpose of this paper to present a description and exposition of a computing machine which has been designed principally for the solution of large systems of linear algebraic equations. . . . Linear algebraic equations are found in all applications of mathematics which possess a linear aspect.

Yet what he proposed was not a general-purpose computer; rather, it was an electronic machine that substituted for the differential analyzer.

But were his ideas useful to Mauchly? In testimony before the court, and in statements to others years later, Mauchly said they were not. He maintained that Atanasoff's computer was economically inefficient and of little real value.

He was asked in the trial whether Atanasoff had told him what kind of vacuum tube he was using.

"Well, the particular kind of vacuum tube would be of very little interest to me. The cost might have [been]," Mauchly testified.

"In any event, Dr. Mauchly, you knew . . . in December 1940 before you ever went to Ames, Iowa, that a computer which could use vacuum tube technology to solve 29 equations and 29 unknowns . . . would represent a considerable advance in the computing art?" the Honeywell lawyer asked.

"Not necessarily."

"You didn't recognize that?"

"It depends on how efficient and how easy it is to use and

how much it costs and so on. It's a matter of economics too. . . . Without some consideration of cost, utility, availability, whatever you want to call it, there is no advance really at all."

"And you are unable . . . to eliminate the question of cost in determining whether it would be an advance in the computing art in your own mind?"

"Yes."

Atanasoff's machine did not make efficient use of the technology, Mauchly maintained, and was worthless to him.

He had not always felt that way, however. There exists evidence in his own handwriting that he was somewhat more impressed by what he saw in Ames, at least shortly after the visit, than he wanted to admit later.

In a letter to H. H. Clayton, shortly after his trip, Mauchly wrote:

Immediately after commencement here, I went out to Iowa State University to see the computing device which a friend of mine is constructing there. His machine, now nearing completion, is electronic in operation, and will solve within a very few minutes any system of linear equations involving no more than 30 variables. It can be adapted to do the job of the Bush differential analyzer more rapidly than the Bush machine does, and it costs a lot less.

My own computing devices use a different principle, more likely to fit small computing jobs.

Note his reference to "a different principle." In a letter written to Atanasoff several months later, Mauchly still seems excited about what he saw.

A number of different ideas have come to me recently anent computing circuits—some of which are more or less hybrids, combining your methods with other things, and some of which are nothing like your machine. The question in my mind is this: Is there any objection, from your point of view, to my building some sort of computer which incorporates some of the features of your machine? For the time being, of course, I shall be lucky to find the time and material to do more than merely make exploratory tests of some of my different ideas, with the hope of getting something very speedy, not too costly, etc. Ultimately a second question might come up, of course, and that is, in the event that your present design were to hold the field against all challengers, and I got the Moore School interested in having something of the sort, would the way be open for us to build an "Atanasoff Calculator" (a la Bush analyzer) here?

Atanasoff wrote back quickly:

Our attorney has emphasized the need of being careful about the dissemination of information about our device until a patent application is filed. This should not require too long, and of course, I have no qualms about having informed you about our device, but it does require that we refrain from making public any details for the time being. It is, as a matter of fact, preventing me from making an invited address to the American Statistical Association.[7]

We have seen in great detail the work Mauchly had done at Ursinus College experimenting with flip-flops and vacuum tubes. Mauchly had spent a considerable amount of time in cosmic-ray research labs, with his father or his father's friends, and seen them count electronically. He had observed researchers at the Bartol Research Foundation at Swarthmore using scaling circuits. He had constructed several devices, all of which are still in his house in Ambler, Pennsylvania. He had signed up for courses at the University of Pennsylvania specifically to learn how to build a computer with these tubes. What Atanasoff had accomplished may have confirmed in his own mind that he was right in assuming vacuum tubes could count and compute, but it is doubtful that he needed much confirmation.

Why wasn't Judge Larson impressed by this work? Sperry's lawyers did not see the issue as very important, and little of this testimony appears in the court record. Since Mauchly did not write scientific papers or keep a diary, there was little written confirmation of this work; had there been, the Sperry lawyers would probably not have had this evidence admitted, for they appear to have taken this part of the trial less seriously than they took other aspects.

Kay Mauchly says she was puzzled by the lawyers' attitude on the whole Atanasoff issue.

"I said to the Remington Rand [*sic*] lawyers, 'Why was all this great importance placed on Atanasoff?' It was so obvious that

7. Atanasoff never received the funding he needed and never filed a patent. He abandoned the machine before it was finally working and moved to Washington.

there was no relationship at all between what John was designing and what Atanasoff was. This is the answer I got from the . . . lawyers: Atanasoff was a 'red herring' thrown in there to distract the judge; they never dreamt that he would buy the whole thing."

There were many witnesses to Mauchly's work at Ursinus, particularly among his students, yet the lawyers did not see fit to bother with this issue.

No invention is produced in isolation; all inventors stand "on the shoulders of giants," in the words of Newton. This is the case with the computer. Many people came before Mauchly and Atanasoff, including Charles Babbage, Howard Aiken, George Stibitz, Harold Hazen, Samuel Caldwell, and Vannevar Bush.

"It is my perception," said Auerbach, "that . . . in almost every field the state-of-the-art will grow and provide a platform. That platform enables people to do things that five or ten years before they could not have done. Once that platform exists, it is possible that two, three, four, five people could get the germ of an idea, saying 'Holy Cow, if I do this, this, and this, this will result.' It's an invention. According to patent law, it's an invention."

' No one, including Mauchly, pretended that his work was completely original. In part of this testimony, he was asked about the harmonic analyzer.

"Will you agree that the harmonic analyzer . . . was not entirely of your own design but was a modification of a design used by MIT some years prior to 1940?" a Honeywell lawyer asked.

"This was not a flash from heaven," Mauchly responded, "a full-blown device without any prior suggestion as to how anybody could do anything, but neither were the mechanical type calculators and harmonic analyzers as far as I know. I have always used prior art where it seemed proper, and useful and appropriate." So does every other inventor. Flashes from heaven are very rare indeed.

Mauchly, however, declared repeatedly that he took nothing from Atanasoff. In a letter to Nancy Stern in 1979, he wrote:

I strongly maintain that I took no ideas whatsoever from Atanasoff. I tried to give him some, such as using the "scaling circuits" with which I was already acquainted to make his proposed device much faster, but JVA said that he couldn't get flip-flops to work reliably.

There is no evidence that Mauchly ever mentioned Atana-soff to anyone at the Moore School. Burks, who has since backed Atanasoff's position, filed an affidavit with the court in the *Honeywell* case stating clearly who he thought invented ENIAC.

Though Eckert and Mauchly were the chief inventors of the ENIAC, inventive contributions were also made by Shaw, Sharpless, and myself. Mauchly and Eckert gave us general plans, but these were mostly verbal and were not yet worked out, and hence constituted design problems. Sharpless, Shaw and I solved these problems in nonobvious ways and formulated and solved other problems as the work progressed. We did logical and electronic designs to the point where draftsmen and technicians could draw up and construct the units under our direction. We tested the constructed units and decided on and supervised the modifications needed to make the equipment operate correctly. . . . Eckert, Mauchly and I are clearly joint inventors of ENIAC; Sharpless and Shaw are also joint inventors; but there are no other joint inventors of ENIAC.

This was apparently written before Burks knew of Atanasoff and could reflect that Mauchly had never mentioned him.

But Atanasoff never considered himself to be the originator of the idea until years after ENIAC was revealed in 1946—when some lawyers suggested it. Several years later Atanasoff saw it working at Aberdeen.

"Wheels were moving; I don't know what was happening. If it had been a good machine, I would have been impressed," he recalled in a 1982 interview. "I didn't know very much about it. I didn't see any of the inner workings at the time. I wasn't even sure but what really that they had brand new ideas and they were far beyond me.

"There was an incident in 1954. I started a company of my own, and it was in Rockville [Maryland]. A man came to see me. He . . . says, 'I'm a patent attorney for International Business Machines Corporation.' He says, 'If you'll help us, we'll break the Mauchly patent because it's derived from you.'

"That was the first shock I had," Atanasoff said. "First time. Nobody had compared the two of us."[8]

Not even, apparently, Atanasoff himself. The inner work-

8. Interview with the author, 1982.

ings of ENIAC were hardly a secret by 1954. It is illogical to assume Atanasoff did not know how ENIAC worked or, by that time, how EDVAC or UNIVAC worked. Yet he saw nothing of his own work in those machines until a lawyer suggested it. The suggestion was reinforced in 1967 when Mauchly and a Sperry lawyer came to Maryland to see him. "The lawyer knew the suit was coming up and they had to face Atanasoff," Atanasoff said.[9] But between those times, and even after the visit of the IBM lawyer, Atanasoff made no claims that Mauchly had taken ideas from him and that his computer had led to ENIAC.

Auerbach, who worked on UNIVAC, was a witness in the trial, and "discovered" Atanasoff as the result of his trial work, said Atanasoff "didn't make any representation about what he thought he had done. Nobody else seemed to raise any question about what Atanasoff had done, and I guess if I hadn't instigated a search into his work, it is possible he would have never come to light."

Perhaps Atanasoff failed to see anything in ENIAC that was his because it contained nothing of his. Perhaps the Honeywell lawyers were just as surprised as everyone else when Larson accepted the Atanasoff theory. Perhaps Mauchly was enthusiastic about what he saw in Ames, but when he began to build his computer, he realized there was a better way of computing.

Obviously, Larson's decision has stirred great passions. One telling criticism comes from John Grist Brainerd, hardly an ardent advocate of Eckert and Mauchly. Brainerd wrote:

There is no question that Judge Larson was scrupulously honest, fair, conscientious, and intelligent, but there is a basic question as to whether he had enough background to arrive at the conclusions he reached in his opinion. (The basic invalidation of the ENIAC patent on a purely legal basis was practically a foregone conclusion.) Anyone wishing to look into the various opinions in the case must recognize two factors: (a) Judge Larson had about a month's tutoring in principles of computers, and (b) the various essentials which resulted in the ENIAC invention were unlikely to be covered because the man who did this preliminary work with Judge Larson would most probably not have understood the basic difficulties which faced the ENIAC personnel. The problems of

9. Ibid.

reliability, speed, complexity, and the achievement of a large computer were laced with technical obstacles of many kinds and of high difficulty.

Brainerd might have added that Larson was hampered by the failure of the Sperry lawyers to probe deeper into Mauchly's work at Ursinus and into his background in the laboratories of his father's friends.

Burks has become Atanasoff's (and Larson's) most vocal champion. He summarizes Atanasoff's innovations as follows:

He invented a novel form of serial store suitable for electronic computation.

True, but none of that appeared in ENIAC, which was, among other things, a parallel machine. EDVAC and UNIVAC were serial, but neither of them adopted Atanasoff's method.

He also conceived, developed and proved the fundamental principles of electronic switching for digital computation, principles encompassing arithmetic operations, control, base conversion, the transfer and restoration of data and synchronization.

Mauchly had already known most of that before he went to Ames. He had seen the switching work at the cosmic-ray research labs and had tinkered with the arithmetic controls while he was at Ursinus.

[Atanasoff's] was the first special-purpose electronic computer ever invented; indeed, it was the first electronic computer of any degree of generality ever invented.

Here the claim is at best debatable. If one considers an invention a machine that was never completed, then the ABC was indeed the first special-purpose electronic computer. Otherwise the honor of invention must go to the British who had COLOSSUS doing real work within a year after Atanasoff and Berry had abandoned their machine. The "degree of generality" is pushing things, however. Outside the limited scientific field, the ABC, had it been completed, would have been useless. It was Eckert and Mauchly who devised the first general-purpose computer, one that could conceivably find uses beyond the laboratory.[10]

Burks goes further. In his paper in the *Annals of the History of Computing*, he states:

The initial plan for the ENIAC arose from John V. Atanasoff's work at Iowa State College and an idea he had in 1941 for adapting his electronic digital computer to replace the differential analyzer, a mechanical analog computer capable of solving a wide variety of differential and integral equations. Atanasoff had pioneered in using vacuum tubes for digital computing, conceiving in about 1937 of an electronic digital computer to solve simultaneous linear equations. . . . We credit John Vincent Atanasoff with the invention not only of the first special-purpose electronic computer, as contrasted to the first general-purpose electronic computer, but also of the first electronic computer ever.

Except for the claim that Atanasoff was the first to use electronic tubes for computing, this just is not so. Brainerd says Burks exaggerates the importance of Atanasoff's attempt to produce an electronic version of the differential analyzer. As we have seen, there is nothing specifically Atanasoff's in ENIAC, and Mauchly arrived at the idea of a general-purpose machine independently at Ursinus, before he had ever met Atanasoff. Atanasoff's claim is still hampered by the fact that he abandoned the machine before it actually worked. The fact that it would have worked had he kept at it is immaterial. That the arithmetic part was functioning is a credit to Atanasoff and ensures him a place in the history of the computer, but not as the inventor of the computer. If the Wright brothers' plane had merely taxied around on the sand at Kitty Hawk but never taken off, would the Wright brothers deserve to be called the inventors of the airplane? Would their claim have been stronger if it had later been learned that

10. The reader will notice that many of these arguments are based on semantics. One rousing argument is over the term *general-purpose* as opposed to *special-purpose*. Bryan Randell, from the University of Newcastle upon Tyne, a leading British historian of the computer, thinks the first genuine general-purpose computer was EDVAC, because of its stored-programming capability. He also points half seriously to the IBM 1620, which used a table look-up system. Randell says that machine was known affectionately as CADET, Can't Add—Doesn't Even Try.

the plane would have taken off had they played around with it some more?

The evidence is unmistakable that Judge Larson and Arthur Burks are wrong. Atanasoff was a brilliant innovator who came very close to building the first electronic computer, but he did not contribute anything but enthusiam to the invention that won. He demonstrated to Mauchly that what Mauchly wanted to do was feasible. That is not a minor matter, and Atanasoff's achievement deserves recognition.

We are left with the semantic argument over the word *invention*. According to the dictionary, *invent* means "originate by experiment; to devise for the first time; as, Edison invented the phonograph."

Stern has summed it up this way:

But, as in other episodes in the history of technology, the inventors who demonstrate applicability as well as creativity, and who bring ideas to fruition are frequently the ones who gain recognition. Eckert and Mauchly's successful completion of the ENIAC was directly related to their ability to convince the government of the applicability of such a machine. Hence, the recognition to which they are entitled is based, in part, on the invention of the first fully operational electronic digital computer and their innovative ability to demonstrate its practicality for wartime use.

Who invented the modern computer? J. Presper Eckert and John Mauchly.

The decision in *Honeywell* vs. *Sperry Rand* left anger that persists to this day. Sperry Rand never appealed the decision. Having spent over $1 million on the suit, Eckert said, the company decided to give up. "What's the point?" he asked. "We were battling over a dead horse." Yet deprived of the money that would otherwise have been due to them, Eckert and Mauchly have spent the years after the Larson decision trying to establish their role in history. Eckert has become philosophical about what happened, but still refuses to appear in the same room with Goldstine or Burks. Every effort to get them to appear in scientific seminars on the history of the computer has failed. Mauchly, who died in 1979, let his anger become almost an obsession. "This issue, as far as I'm concerned, was part of Mauchly's death," Auerbach said. "It was an obsession with him."

Toward the end of 1982, Sperry Rand announced it was changing the name of its computers from UNIVAC to Sperry. The name UNIVAC will be taken off all its machines and replaced with the new one. The name invented in a converted dance studio over a clothing store in Philadelphia by Pres Eckert is dead.

11. **The Revolution**

"What if I tell you to paint purple pine trees? Would you paint purple pine trees just because the IBM company told you to? See, you wouldn't. And if you wouldn't put purple pine trees in a program just because IBM says to, then I can't trust you."
IBM EXECUTIVE RICHARD HANRAHAN TO BILL GATES

WHEN WE LEFT OUR SKETCH of the computer industry at the end of the 1960s, things were still fairly simple. Although IBM still dominated the field, other companies had staked out substantial, and profitable, territories on the periphery, filling specialized niches they developed by fitting themselves into gaps in the IBM product line or building machines that were compatible with IBMs but were better or cheaper, or both.

However, the revolution was on its way that would alter not only the nature of the business but also the nature of modern life. The result would be no less important than the Industrial Revolution more than a century earlier—it would just happen faster. Three technological advances were necessary, one of them also contemporaneous with ENIAC.

Eckert got ENIAC to work by overcoming the greatest obstacle to electronic computing, the unreliability and inconvenience of the vacuum tube. The tubes still used much too much power and produced too much heat; they took up a great deal of space, and there were practical limits to how small they could be. Trouble-shooting was a nightmare. The result was that vacuum-tube computers were erratic and gigantic. Unless some substitute for the tube was found, computers would remain exotic mathematical whales, restricted to very large institutions, limited by the size and expense of their care and feeding.

AT&T solved that problem with the almost-contemporary invention of the transistor, a semiconductor device that could do all the things the vacuum tube could do, but more reliably, while taking up less space and costing a fraction of the price. It was the ideal substitute for the tube and became the seminal device of the twentieth century. The transistor won the Nobel Prize for William Shockley, Walter Brattain, and John Bardeen.

The next step was to improve and shrink the transistors.

This development also began with William Shockley. Shockley left Bell Labs in 1954 to return to his hometown of Palo Alto, California, and, with Rockefeller money, to start his own electronic company to take advantage of semiconductor technology. Palo Alto was the ideal location for such a venture. The city is located forty miles south of San Francisco in the Santa Clara Valley. Palo Alto also was the home of Stanford University and its first-rate engineering school, which already had spun off several electronic companies, including Hewlett-Packard. The University of California at Berkeley, with its engineering school, was across the bay. Shockley's company essentially was the beginning of what is now called Silicon Valley.

Shockley had brought several very bright young men with him and hired more when he arrived. Some romance was missing, however; producing and selling transistors was not intrinsically interesting. It turned out to be difficult and tedious, and life at Shockley Semiconductor Laboratories at the Stanford Industrial Park was not pleasant. Shockley was not an easy man to work for—sure of himself, arrogant, and brusque.[1]

1. Shockley would later become infamous for his theories linking race with intelligence and eugenics, such as the notion that the brightest should be encouraged to reproduce and the least bright should be forbidden or discouraged. He would spend the last twenty years of his life in this field, essentially destroying his reputation.

Inevitably, in 1957, eight of the key employees, tired of being treated with what they considered disrespect, bolted. They received backing from an investment firm in New York and from Fairchild Camera and Instruments, which set them up in business in Mountain View, just south of Palo Alto. The firm was called Fairchild Semiconductor and almost every firm in Silicon Valley, until recently, derived from that small establishment.[2]

Bell Labs had made several improvements on manufacturing crystals of silicon or germanium with the built-in impurities needed to turn crystals of those elements into semiconductors, and the problem of improving electronics seemed to be a matter more of inventing new industrial techniques than of doing physics or engineering research.

The race was on between Fairchild and Texas Instruments to see who could produce chips of semiconductors that would replace hard-wired transistors. The two leading researchers were Robert Noyce and Gordon Moore, both Shockley defectors in Mountain View, and TI's Jack Kilby.

Kilby went first. He conceived of a manufacturing system that allowed the miniaturization of electronic circuits on semiconductor chips, called integrated circuits or ICs. He filed a patent in 1959. Kilby had reduced the transistor to the size of a match head. TI sold them for $450 each.

The first ICs, however, were clumsy to manufacture and had one basic problem: the transistors still had to be wired together. At Fairchild, however, Noyce adapted a system called "planar" manufacturing, in which all the transistors and resistors were formed together on a silicon chip with the metal wiring embedded in the silicon. He filed for a patent five months after TI.

Naturally, a lawsuit followed, as TI claimed patent infringement. TI lost, but any company planning to use ICs still needed

2. One of the objects of folklore in Silicon Valley was a genealogy table produced by the American Electronics Association in which almost every major firm in the area could trace its ancestry, at least in part, back to Fairchild. The only company that could give Fairchild competition was Hewlett-Packard. That is no longer true.

licenses from both companies. Hundreds of them applied. The planar IC became the basic component for the electronics industry. The chips became smaller and smaller as manufacturing techniques improved, and Moore soon developed what engineers know as Moore's Law, which holds that the amount of information storable on a chip doubles every year while the price remains the same. It quickly became possible to store more information on a chip smaller than a fingernail than Pres Eckert could get into a room full of mercury delay lines. They would use only a glimmer of electricity and operate for years, sometimes decades. They soon became so cheap the smaller ones were called "jellybean" chips and were put into everything from clock radios to washing machines.

That was the second crucial invention. The third would be the most remarkable yet.

First a little economic sociology: Noyce and the men who bolted from Shockley's company set an interesting trend.

Noyce was a physicist. Along with the engineers on his team, he suddenly found himself a wealthy man. No one goes into physics to become rich, and historically wealth was not the main motivation for engineers. But the patent on the IC earned each member of the Fairchild team $250,000 to begin with, and no end to the money seemed in sight. Noyce wound up general manager of Fairchild, which quickly became a $150-million-a-year firm. Yet, however wealthy you become working for other people, think of how much richer you could be working for yourself. Think of the money, the freedom. The scientists and engineers in the valley caught on fast. Innovation was worth quick gold, and a gold rush was on. Good engineering students from the best schools—Stanford, MIT, Caltech, Berkeley—found themselves besieged by recruiters; in a few cases actual fist fights were recorded. Venture capitalists, rich men who could pay money up front for equity positions, made capital available in a way never seen before. Conventional bankers went into shock even thinking about the risks—and missed what would become the greatest explosion of wealth since seventeenth-century Amsterdam. It was capitalism's Wild West.

The innovations came from new, small companies. Larger, more established firms either could not generate and nurture the kind of creativity that led to the advances, or couldn't market the discoveries they did make, and fell by the wayside. Many of America's best-known electronics companies did just that. Philco, GE, RCA, Emerson, to name just some of many that disappeared, were swallowed up by conglomerates or abandoned the business.

Key employees (physicists, engineers, programmers) would leave their old jobs and start their own companies. Those firms would flourish, become more conservative, and spin off more employees. It became a way of life; for a while the average engineer in Silicon Valley changed jobs every eighteen months, and several bars up and down the valley became meat markets where the recruiters and the recruited met for tortilla chips, margaritas, and career changes. Changing jobs sometimes became as easy as turning in the wrong driveway and knocking on the door. The big companies left behind, including Texas Instruments, spent their declining years suing for patent infringement.

Founding companies itself became great sport. Some men founded three or four. Eugene Amdahl had no problem with his newest company competing against Amdahl Computer, a company named after him, his first-born. Failure lacked the stigma it had in other environments. Make a good try, fail, try again. No problem. The capital was just sitting there waiting for good ideas.

Fairchild was the first to feel the pain of change. Noyce, Moore, and Andrew Grove left in 1968 to found their own company, Intel. Fairchild was gradually absorbed by a French company and vaporized. Intel devoted itself to making the newest kinds of ICs, random access memory (RAM) chips, which shrank the size of computers even further. That wasn't the real miracle.

Question: If you could put thousands of bits of information on a silicon chip, in essence reduce all those memory tubes UNIVAC stacked in room-sized cabinets, why couldn't you also reduce the "brains" of the computer, better known as the processor, into a chip as well? The chip would act as both logic board and traffic cop to the flow of data. On large machines that was called the Central Processing Unit or CPU.

Ted Hoff, a Stanford graduate student working at Intel, did it just a few steps ahead of TI, getting all that circuitry into one chip. Intel called it a "computer on a chip." When it was connected to the memory chips and input and output devices, that is exactly what it was. The new devices are more properly known as microprocessors.

With that, the computer age was born. With more sophisticated microprocessors, the computers went from room size to table size to hand held. Intel's first microprocessor was called the 4004 because it could handle four bits (ons or offs) of information at a time. It was soon replaced by the 8008, with double the capacity. Each piece of usable information—the computer equivalent of a letter or number—was eight bits (or a "byte") and the 8008 could handle a byte at a time.

At this point the corporations and the universities gave way to the people.

The first person perhaps to smell the change was an MIT graduate and former IBM employee named Kenneth Olsen. In 1957, he and Harlan Anderson founded the Digital Equipment Corporation (DEC) with $70,000 in venture capital from Georges Doriot.[3] Olsen and Anderson moved into an old wooden mill in Maynard, Massachusetts, after the two men had cleaned the place out, which included scrubbing the bathrooms. They hired a number of engineers, mostly from IBM, and turned them into salaried (not commissioned) salesmen.

Olsen believed in two things fervently: that computers ought to be easy to operate (fun if possible) and that they ought to be smaller and cheaper than the machines IBM and the dwarfs were selling. His first computer, the PDP-1, sold for $120,000. In 1965 DEC produced the PDP-8, the first com-

3. When Doriot sold his share in 1972, it was worth $350 million.

puter to use integrated circuits. It was an astounding success. Because of its size (it could fit in your average closet), Olsen called it a minicomputer.

The PDP-8 was important for several reasons. First, its success induced dozens of other companies to produce their own and the competition pushed the technology even further, which meant smaller, more powerful machines. An entire industry was created. Many of these companies were located on Route 128 outside Boston and for a decade Route 128 was the pot at the end of the rainbow.

Second, the machine was a perfect product. IBM had nothing like it and didn't understand the market. When the PDP-8 came out, only very large or very rich companies had computers, the hulking mainframes that IBM and its competitors sold. At universities, anyone wanting to use a computer, whether a physics lab or the economics department, had to find a way to work off the mainframe. Power struggles broke out between the data processing administrators and the faculty. The mainframe operators fought any attempt at independence in the labs partly because they philosophically believed in centralized computing and partly because decentralized computing eroded their power base. College campuses are very political places. On the other hand, faculty members across the country pushed the computer companies, especially IBM, to produce machines they could afford, computers that would fit in their labs. They wanted to do their own computing on their own time in their own way. IBM, getting rich with mainframes ($4 billion in profits a year) fought on the side of centralized computing, refusing to provide a product to fit the demand and supporting the data processing executives in the political wars. Because of IBM's reputation and clout, they rarely lost. The result was twofold: when DEC produced its first minis, university labs (and medium-sized companies) sucked them in as fast as DEC and its competitors could make them, usually using government grants and almost always going around the data processing administrators. Additionally, an animus toward IBM and its products grew and lasted for almost a generation on college campuses, particularly at engineering schools. When

IBM finally saw the light and the need to accommodate decentralization, it was too late: where their salesmen were welcomed as old friends in the Fortune 500 companies, they were almost physically ejected from college labs and departments.

Third, the DEC experience was the first unmistakable harbinger that the world was changing. They knew it and prospered along Route 128, and they knew it and would prosper by the next stage in the Santa Clara Valley. The one place they did not know it was Armonk, New York, at IBM's headquarters. Perhaps they were doing too well to pay attention; by the time IBM was finally hit by the changes, it was accumulating the largest profits in the history of capitalism. Nonetheless, through a combination of blindness, inertia, and blazing stupidity, IBM would make a series of tactical blunders almost unprecedented in American business. From a position of unassailed dominance—the company everyone envied and admired for its competence and profits—they would be brought to their knees by a kid from Seattle and put to shame by two young geniuses in Cupertino, California.

The drive was toward powerful computers small enough to fit on the desktop, giving *each individual* the computing power Eckert and Mauchly once dreamed of for large institutions. They would shrink even further and gain in power with no end in sight. Bill Gates in Seattle knew that; Steve Jobs and Steve Wozniak in Cupertino knew that. John Opel, then chairman of IBM in Armonk, appeared to have no clue what they were talking about.

You didn't even have to be in the computer industry to know it. An editor for *Popular Electronics,* Leslie Solomon, was urging the hobbyists who read his magazine to build machines that gave individuals power. The challenge was taken up in Albuquerque, New Mexico, by Ed Roberts, who cofounded a company called Micro Instrumentation Telemetry Systems (MITS), selling radio transmitters for model planes and kits for electronic calculators. The latter wasn't terribly successful; Texas Instruments could make and sell calculators for much less, and by 1974 MITS was hanging by its thumbs. Roberts decided to follow the wisdom of Solomon.

Intel was selling its 8080 microprocessor for $360 a chip. Roberts talked them down to $75 each. He had in mind a computer kit that could be put together by a knowledgeable tinkerer and could be priced under $500. Solomon's twelve-year-old daughter came up with a name for the machine, Altair, after the star.[4]

After his first model apparently got lost in the mail, Roberts flew to New York and in desperation he and Solomon photographed a fake machine for the cover of *Popular Electronics*. Then he flew back to Albuquerque and actually built one. The magazine advertised the Altair for $397.

Absolute hell broke loose. Checks by the thousands poured into MITS and the staff spent most of its time opening envelopes and making deposits. Roberts and Solomon apparently had tapped an explosive—and apparently unsuspected—market. Although they were providing kits, not complete computers, MITS couldn't build the kits fast enough. The popularity was odd because you really couldn't do anything with an Altair. Programming meant throwing switches one after the other, and if you made a mistake you had to start over. Readouts consisted of blinking lights. It served absolutely no useful purpose; there was nothing Altair could do that you couldn't do faster and easier another way. It was the principle of the thing.

Two young men in Massachusetts, however, had an idea. Paul Allen and William Gates III were part of a growing group of kids fascinated by computers. While students at a Seattle high school, they broke into Control Data's Cybernet system (something CD said couldn't be done) and crashed it by typing fourteen characters. They were just "hacking around," they said. They simply were bewitched by the machinery and the intellectual challenge. They became hackers.

Gates, the son of a prominent lawyer, was doing his pre-law at Harvard and Allen was working for Honeywell in Massachusetts, when Solomon's *Popular Electronics* edition with Altair came out. The goddess of history watched smiling while Allen

4. She was watching "Star Trek" at the time and Altair was where the *Enterprise* was going that week.

and Gates looked at the magazine and knew immediately what the Altair was good for. They began work on a version of the computer language BASIC which could be stored on paper tape and loaded into the Altair. With BASIC it would be possible to program an Altair to do actual—if stupidly simple—computing. The Altair only had a capacity of 2,000 characters. They wrote "Roberts" on the letterhead of a company they had formed as kids that no longer existed, claiming to have a BASIC that ran on all 8080 microprocessors, which wasn't true. Allen had programmed a DEC PDP-10 to act like an 8080 (a chip they had never seen) to work in an Altair (a computer they hadn't seen either). Understandably skeptical, Roberts invited them to Albuquerque. Gates stayed behind to further test the program and sent Allen off with a copy.

Allen arrived to find that MITS' offices were stacked between a laundromat and a massage parlor. After stalling for a day to hear if Gates had found any bugs, Allen fed the tape into an "advanced" (6k) Altair. The machine burped and printed out the word READY on the Teletype machine connection. Of such stuff are revolutions made. Allen was twenty-two, Gates twenty and looked sixteen.

Gates knew enough law to know he needed a legal entity to negotiate with Roberts, so he and Allen formed Micro-Soft in July 1975 to develop software for desktop computers, the first company of its kind in the world.[5] Micro-Soft licensed Roberts to sell their version of BASIC, while retaining ownership of the language, the model for software contracts today.

Meanwhile, MITS was going downhill; Roberts was no businessman. The kits he could produce were unreliable. He finally sold the company.

Gates and Allen began thinking of other horizons, finally hiring other programmers and a secretary and moving to an office of their own in downtown Albuquerque. Gates quit Harvard before graduation, to the consternation of his parents. He and Allen began selling their BASIC to other manufacturers, including Tandy, which had just launched its Radio Shack

5. The hyphen was dropped quickly.

TRS-80 machines, and the Canadian firm Commodore.

In March 1975 a group of San Francisco Bay "hackers" formed the Homebrew Computer Club in a garage in Menlo Park, just north of the Stanford campus. Many of them were engineers; many were refugees of the counterculture of the 1960s, generally from Stanford or Berkeley. They too were hackers. All they had to work with were Altairs and Altair clones. Meetings consisted of demonstrations of gadgets and discussions of problems. Nonetheless, by the third meeting the garage was too small and the club moved to a Victorian house.

Stephen G. Wozniak ("The Woz" forevermore) was a Homebrew member, a superb engineer, and another college dropout. Woz joined up with Steven Jobs, sharing his love for computers and for what were kindly called pranks. Following the lead of the legendary "Captain Crunch" (John Draper), Jobs and The Woz developed "blue boxes" designed to fool pay telephones into giving them free long-distance calls. Jobs then was working for Nolan Bushnell, the developer of the first computer game, Pong, at Atari; Woz was a programmer at Hewlett-Packard.

Woz had once built an improved Altair, which he called the Cream Soda Computer and thought he could do better yet. He took a new eight-bit microprocessor called the 6502, then selling for $20, and built a machine that could run BASIC. For no reason he ever could remember, he called it an Apple. Jobs was impressed. He sold his Volkswagen bus and Wozniak sold his two scientific calculators to raise capital and the two men went into business. Homebrew member Paul Terrell ordered fifty for his new Palo Alto computer shop. Moving into an apartment, Jobs and Wozniak founded the Apple Computer Corporation.

Still not satisfied with their machine, Woz and Jobs made modifications that leaped way ahead of anything on the market, adding a keyboard, a color screen, and built-in BASIC. The new machine was called the Apple II. In a few years, Apple became what was then the fastest-growing company in American history. The Apple II became the people's machine.

Because Jobs and Woz bought Gates's BASIC, teenagers

still fighting acne could sit in the basement of their suburban homes writing software and becoming richer than their parents. Writers wrote word processing software. Scientists wrote analysis programs. Teachers fell in love with the Apple II and moved the machine into their classrooms, frequently writing their own software as they went along. Everybody wrote games. Apple IIs began showing up at homes and offices, and the complexity of the software grew geometrically. They moved from toy to usefulness in a matter of a few years.

A Harvard MBA student, Dan Bricklin, developed an accounting system that transferred the accountant's worksheet onto the computer screen. Making a change in one cell in the worksheet automatically updated other pertinent cells, and because it was a computer, not a human, it never made arithmetic mistakes. He and his friends formed a company called Software Arts and signed an agreement with Dan Fylstra of Personal Software, Inc., to market the program Bricklin called VisiCalc.

Fylstra's first big customer was Apple. VisiCalc was so good—it actually did a better job and worked faster than the best accountant could with paper and pencil—people bought Apple IIs just to use VisiCalc; indeed, by September 1980, Apple estimated that one-fifth of its Apple II sales were driven by VisiCalc. The software eventually was written for other machines.

Companies rose and fell. Fortunes were made in months. In less than ten years after MITS's Altair, the microcomputer business became a $100 billion industry. Microsoft had grown into one of the largest software applications houses.

Programs were divided into applications and operating systems. Operating systems were the basic programs that turned a piece of metal, glass, and silicon into a computer. Applications were programs that ran on that computer, the ones that did the actual work for the user, such as VisiCalc. All the programs were written in one of several layers of language. In July 1977, Microsoft began selling versions of several languages, FORTRAN and COBOL. Because of the complexity of those languages, they were sold mostly for computers that ran an operating system called CP/M (Control Program for Microcomputer), written and sold by a small company in Monterey, California, called Digital Research, owned by Gary Kildall, another Seattle native.

CP/M could run on any computer using the 8080 microprocessor or its clones. It was tiny—3,000 lines of code—and could let applications do anything within the memory capabilities of the computer, a brilliant feat. Kildall made $60,000 the first year he was in business, and by the late 1970s CP/M was the dominant force, the so-called industry standard, in microcomputers.

In 1978, Microsoft was making more than $1 million a year and doubling sales. The firm had thirteen employees in its Albuquerque office. Allen thought they were in something of a geographic backwater and ought to move. Silicon Valley, where most of the customers were, seemed the obvious choice, but Allen wanted to go home to Seattle. He also thought Silicon Valley was too unsettled to be nurturing to stable businesses, what with engineers and programmers skipping from company to company. Gates was too busy to care. In the summer of 1978, Microsoft moved back to Washington, taking most of its employees with it.

In 1979, Microsoft's sales hit $2.5 million, with a million copies of BASIC out in the hands of paying customers. With the help of a high school student, Allen developed a card that would fit into Apple IIs that would let those machines, which then dominated the market, use CP/M and the newest BASIC. Microsoft sold 100,000 of them, making Apple the largest user of the operating system.

At that point, the giant stirred. Back in Armonk, somebody noticed that kids out west were making an awful lot of money with the cute little computers and thought it would be nice if their company got a piece of the action. IBMers, as they are called, didn't believe the machines would ever be major threats—nothing worked better than their mainframes—but a buck is a buck.

They naturally formed a committee. First they tried to buy Apple but Jobs and Wozniak wouldn't sell. So IBM decided to go it alone. The plan was to do as little actual development as possible. They would try to buy what they needed and "kludge" together a computer. Now, if you were thinking of getting into the microcomputer business, the two people you had to talk to were Bill Gates and Gary Kildall—Gates for the language to write your applications on, Kildall for the operating system to hang it on. An IBM executive named Jack Sams, one of the legions of middle-level executives that made IBM run, visited Seattle. Nothing definite is going on, he told Gates, who had borrowed a suit for the occasion, just want to talk about microcomputers in case IBM ever, well, you know. . . . Sams described a machine much less powerful than the one IBM wanted to build just to see what Gates said. Gates said it wasn't powerful enough. Thanks, Sams said, we may get back to you. Then again, we may not. He left.

After a couple of weeks of silence, Sams called again for another meeting. He said he was going to bring his legal team to talk to Gates's legal team, and a technical team to talk to Gates's technical team. Gates didn't have a legal team and he was the technical team, so he brought along four other employees so he wouldn't be outnumbered. Sams arrived with a lawyer and someone from "corporate practices" who was essentially a spy for upper management to report what the middle manager was doing and to keep the middle manager from saying things he ought not to say. Gates thought this was a wacky way to do business. Legal papers called non-disclosure agreements were signed to preserve the secrecy of the meeting.

By this time IBM was fighting a federal antitrust suit that was soaking up time and resources. Lawyers began dominating the company and almost nothing was done of any consequence without first clearing it with them. One of the mistakes IBM would make in the subsequent years was forgetting that you hire lawyers to give advice, not make decisions. Considering the antitrust suit, however, this mistake was understandable. What wasn't understandable was why anyone would agree to the legal restrictions IBM placed on anyone doing business with it. IBM had a horrible record of treating contractors poorly, raising some to heights of wealth they never dreamed of, then walking out when it suited Big Blue's purposes. The legal papers Gates was asked to sign essentially gave away the right to sue IBM, even when IBM deserved to be sued. Gates, however, was intrigued by the possibility of working with the world's largest computer company and agreed. He was right for the wrong reasons.

Microsoft and IBM agreed that Microsoft would consult on an IBM microcomputer. Sams asked about an operating system. Gates told them to talk to Kildall. He and Kildall had an informal agreement that Microsoft wouldn't do an operating system and Digital Research wouldn't do languages.

IBMers flew to Monterey to see Kildall, but Kildall was off flying his new glider and had no intention of cutting short his flight to meet with the easterners. His CP/M was raking in money and, as the industry standard, would do so for years, he felt. IBM could wait. So the IBM contingent had to deal with his lawyer-wife, who took one look at their non-disclosure agreements and threw the visitors out. She was wrong for all the right reasons.

IBM had one weakness even its executives admitted to: it couldn't write software. It was a combination of not having the best programmers (you had much more freedom and might make much more money working elsewhere), the fact their software didn't have to be brilliant (you want to use our computers, use our software), and a culture in which nothing was done without hordes of people flying all over the world, going to meetings, showing charts, and writing memoranda in lieu of actual work. Everything was done by consensus; individuality was discouraged as not being in "the IBM way." Writing great software is a highly individual process, requiring genius, daring, peace, patience, and courage. The IBM management was wise enough to know this. Sams called Gates and told him to get an operating system or the deal was off. Reluctantly, Gates agreed, knowing it would violate his agreement with Kildall, but it *was* Kildall's fault. Gates found a small Seattle company that had a rudimentary system called QDOS, for Quick and Dirty Operating System, and bought the rights for $175,000. It became the basis for MS-DOS.

IBM announced its first microcomputer on August 12, 1981, priced from $1,565 to $6,000, depending on the configuration. It was built around an Intel 8088, a 16-bit processor, and marked the beginning of a crucial relationship between the two companies. It could run VisiCalc or word processing and could link with data bases. The machine appeared in stores two months later and to the amazement of Armonk and everyone else was a gigantic hit. IBM also made a crucial decision that would rattle down its corporate history for a generation: the machine had open architecture, which meant that other companies could easily produce peripheral appliances or software that would work on the machine. The director of the product, Don Estridge,[6] pledged to provide anyone who asked the complete specifications. It ran Gates's MS-DOS, which was on the open market. That decision led to the dominance of the IBM-PC as a standard and ironically to the downfall of IBM.

Kildall took one look at what Gates had done and saw considerable similarities between CP/M and Gates's operating system. Most programs that ran on CP/M also ran on MS-DOS because several functions were deliberately copied from CP/M so that software would be compatible. Since his wife had refused to sign IBM's nefarious non-disclosure agreement, Kildall had not given away his right to sue—and did just that. IBM truthfully claimed it had no idea there were similarities in the code and made Kildall a very reasonable offer: if he dropped his suit they would agree to offer the 16-bit version of CP/M as well as MS-DOS to its customers when it was ready. Kildall accepted.

Kildall, who had already made one terrible mistake, now destroyed himself: he decided that CP/M would remain the industry standard and that he could price the operating system at any level he wished, say four times what Gates was charging for MS-DOS ($240 versus $60). It was CP/M, after all, and people would pay the price. He was wrong. By the time IBM could

6. Estridge, one of IBM's most brilliant managers, was killed in an airline crash in Dallas. Had he not, the history of IBM might have been different. As soon as he died, the bureaucracy in Armonk took control of his program and IBM's fall was unavoidable.

offer CP/M, Microsoft had established itself as the operating system for the IBM-PC. The difference in price—plus a six-month delay in the product—ended any chance of Kildall's recovering. Kildall and his company quickly disappeared, the victim of a *hubris* worthy of a Sophocles hero.[7] Within a few years the IBM-PC and Gates's operating system dominated the industry, helped by another financial program, Lotus's 1,2,3.

One problem with Estridge's open architecture policy was that other companies could buy the Intel chip, produce clones of the IBM machine, and often sell them cheaper than could Big Blue. Soon IBM found itself with the standard and a rapidly shrinking market share. Nonetheless for a time IBM, Microsoft, and Intel dominated the microcomputer industry.

The paradigm had one more shift, and that came from Jobs back at Apple. Jobs had to do something; the Apple II had been surpassed both technologically and in market shares. He was wise enough to understand that Apple had become a very large company and had all the symptoms of a coagulating bureaucracy. He took a group of programmers and designers out of the main office, set them up over a fast-food restaurant in Cupertino flying a skull and crossbones flag. He kept them totally isolated from the corporate structure. Their orders were to produce a computer dramatically unlike anything on the market. Their first design, Lisa (allegedly named after Job's illegitimate daughter), was an incredible 32-bit machine that used graphic icons instead of words and had an operating system controlled by a mouse that swooped around a metaphoric desktop. Lisa was awesomely slow, and writing software for it was mind-bending, but it begat the Macintosh in 1984.

Jobs insisted on several things for the Mac: it would be closed architecture so that no one could clone it; it would be easy to assemble (you cannot plug in peripherals incorrectly because the cables only fit in the right receptacles); and it carried the visual metaphor, now known as GUI or graphical user

7. Kildall died in 1994. His family and friends insisted that he never looked back at his failure, never read stories about Bill Gates, and never wondered whether he, not Gates, would have become the richest man in America. The author does not believe a single word.

interface, to the point where users didn't have to know a thing about computers and never had to type a command or write a program. Operating the machine was largely intuitive. Where MS-DOS was verbal, the Mac operating system was visual. Where it took days to assemble and then teach someone to use an MS-DOS machine, you could set up and be using a Mac in two hours. Because graphics can be easily incorporated into the operation, Macs essentially invented the desktop publishing industry and revolutionized publishing. By the end of the decade even IBM was using Macs for its publications. Software for the first Macs came from Gates.

Although Jobs's computer was several generations ahead of anything IBM and its cloners could produce, and developed a cult of "true believers," it never took a large enough market share to threaten IBM financially. IBM was still too powerful in the corporate culture. Yet the Mac heralded the future in a way IBM couldn't understand.

IBM never philosophically embraced what is called "distributed computing." As late as 1992, they were still designing micros that worked best when connected to a mainframe, which they touted as a virtue. Silicon Valley thought that hilarious. IBM could not compete on price with the clone-makers and quickly lost what technological edge they had. Computers became smaller, finally going to laptop to notebook size to hand-held, but rarely because of anything IBM did. The company was mired in bureaucracy, surrounded by legal and security concerns that would have sent Gilbert & Sullivan into paroxysms of laughter, was lawyer-ridden and disabled by a culture of meetings, overhead charts, and consensus. The differences were most apparent when IBM and Gates got together to write an operating system. Gates would put a few dozen people to work in one building and turn them loose. IBM had to use hundreds, perhaps thousands, spread out all over the world to keep all their division managers happy, then surround them with security people and lawyers. Programmers spent more time on airplanes and going to meetings than writing software. IBM even forced Microsoft through distracting security procedures.

The difference was largely generational. Silicon Valley (and Seattle) were hackers, products of the counterculture, partial to jeans and Birkenstock sandals, Friday afternoon beer bashes, all-night work orgies, and standing around in Fry's electronics store in Cupertino discussing processing speed, Star Trek, metaphors, and personal freedom. They played rock music in their labs, often smoked dope, and frequently burned out by the time they were thirty-five, wealthy enough to buy a place somewhere and start over when they recovered. IBM essentially was run by white-shirted salesmen and bureaucrats who couldn't be fired and were sure of a pleasant retirement when their risk-free careers were over.

Most important, however, was a philosophical chasm: only when it began losing gigantic sums of money did IBM understand where computing was going. The mainframe became the modern dinosaur, well on its way to extinction, and IBM came too late to understanding that. All of IBM's chairmen had come up through the oceans of in-house management, and all accepted the common wisdom of centralized computing through the mainframe. The chasm in understanding between those men and Gates, Jobs, and the engineers in Silicon Valley, who understood the power of distributed computing, was vast and daunting: while IBM was working from the big to the small—reluctantly shrinking mainframes—Gates and Jobs were working up, gleefully taking small computers and making them more powerful. IBM was trying to make desktop computers that made using mainframes more efficient; Gates and Jobs wanted workers free from what they considered the tyranny of mainframe computers and their administrators. Every time Gates negotiated another deal with IBM—and he spent a decade battling with them—he had two unassailable advantages: besides being the smartest person in the room, he knew something the others in the room did not—he knew the future. He never lost. Even the formerly successful manufacturers of minicomputers, such as Control Data and Digital, underestimated the paradigm and Route 128 became a ghost town.

Desktop computers became workstations, and by 1990 the workstations were as powerful as the minicomputers on the desktop, and the minicomputers, with architectures such as parallel processing (more than one microprocessor, sometimes thousands, working simultaneously), could outperform some mainframes. Designers also were seeing how small they could make the box; by 1995 they were producing computers so small that the size of the keys, which had to be struck surely by an adult human finger, were determining how small computers could be made, not the electronics.

By 1991, it all collapsed; a company that once bragged that it never laid off any employee let go 140,000. Entire towns surrounding IBM facilities were almost financially destroyed as tax dollars dried up and thousands of residents found themselves out of work. Hardest hit were the middle-aged, middle-level managers, people who generally could not find jobs elsewhere. IBM stock lost $75 billion in value, about the gross national product of Sweden.

After a succession of failures in the board room, IBM eventually hired from outside the company and outside the industry for the first time, taking a manager from RJR-Nabisco as its CEO. As of this writing, Louis V. Gerstner, Jr., had restored the grand old company to profitability, but it was only a ghost of itself, shed of half its employees and $5.6 billion in costs. As a final insult, IBM, like a fading aristocrat with an estate it could no longer afford, began auctioning its extensive collection of American art, first collected by Watson Sr. to improve the "human spirit."

The winners were the shock wave riders. Other companies that missed the shift, such as Wang, which produced a splendid word processor that did nothing else, or those that didn't play the currents right, such as Kaypro, came and went.

Even the riders had their problems. Jobs, unable to run the company himself, hired John Scully from Pepsi-Cola. It was not clear if Scully knew anything about computers beyond turning them on. The result was turmoil; Apple lurched from one technological path to another, executive turnovers came every six months (one of those was Wozniak, who couldn't stand Scully or the direction he was taking the company), reorganizations raged once a year. Apple, which became one of the worst managed companies in the valley, still has not recovered several years after Scully was fired. Further, Jobs had insisted on closed architecture that meant—unlike what was true for IBM—no one could clone an Apple, but also that no one else was pushing the technology, and the Mac lost its technological advantages while Scully chased after chimera.[8] In 1994, Apple agreed to permit clones but it may be too late.

Apple did win the philosophical war. Every year the software that ran IBM compatibles looked more like Macintosh. Gates, wise as usual, knew that Mac's technology was superior in most ways, and Microsoft devised a program called Windows that essentially sat in front of MS-DOS and pretended it worked like a Macintosh. It was much slower, not nearly as good—Mac enthusiasts dubbed it "Windoze"—but it was better than dealing with MS-DOS. Windows sold so many copies that it turned Gates, still the largest Microsoft stockholder, into the richest man in America.[9] Soon even laptops came with mouses, and the metaphors that began with the Macintosh[10] would become the dominant way of operating a computer as the machines became easier to use.

Eventually, both Apple and IBM would call a truce. Both companies joined with Motorola, the manufacturer of Apple's microprocessor, to produce a new processor for both companies' machines. Apple's PowerMacs have been successful; IBM's computers are just coming out at this writing. For Apple, it is a last ditch effort to remain a player in the computer business; for IBM it means freedom from Microsoft and Intel.

After years of battling with Gates over operating systems, IBM finally went on to try its own and free itself of Gates's domination. It took much too long, and by the time it came out

8. Jobs left to form his own company, Next, which produced a machine that dazzled users and an operating system far ahead of anything else on the market. It was a total failure. Microsoft had already won the operating system war. Scully was finally forced out but Apple has never recovered.

9. Paul Allen retired in 1983.

10. The metaphor and GUI were actually developed by Xerox's Palo Alto Research Center (PARC), one of the legion of firms with first-class research laboratories that proved completely incapable of marketing the results of that research. IBM is another. Jobs adopted what he saw at PARC for the Lisa.

in 1994, OS/2 was probably too little and much too late. IBM finally learned how to let people write good software. IBM returned to profitability, and, to demonstrate it was a new company after all these years, pulled off a hostile takeover of Lotus, apparently hoping to add its software and programming skills. Skeptics remain.

In June 1995, IBM licensed Apple's Macintosh OS to run on its PowerPC machines, along with OS/2, an acknowledgment it could not fight Microsoft alone. After spending a decade denigrating the Mac and doing everything possible to kill it off, they surrendered.

Things that go around do come around. Microsoft and Intel run the computer industry with 70 percent of the worldwide market, but even they can see the perils of flying high. Intel has been threatened by competitors who won law suits enabling them to produce clones of their most popular chips. Other competitors are beginning to dog them with advanced technologies.

Microsoft, which had control of 85 percent of the operating systems in personal computers, was hit by its very own antitrust suit, essentially for acting like the IBM of old. By controlling both the operating systems and the applications for computers, others in the industry charged the company had acquired too much power. If you wanted to write software for Windows, you had to deal with Microsoft, which meant that company knew what its own competitors were planning. The company adopted another page from the old IBM playbook with a practice known as "vaporware." If you see a competitor is going to produce something truly wizard, you promise your customers that you are working on something better even when in fact you have nothing even close that will be ready on time. IBM did that for years to keep mainframe customers from jumping to competitors. Microsoft did it with the latest version of Windows to keep potential buyers from jumping to Power Macs and OS/2.

Windows 95 finally came out in August of 1995, with Gates spending hundreds of millions of dollars on promotional stunts, including flashing the Windows logo on the Empire State Building and buying out the entire press run of the *Sunday Times* of London for advertising. A sycophantic media covered the event as the Second Coming. In fact, Windows 95 was merely an upgrade of an existing program and essentially turned Intel machines into imitations of slow, two-year-old Macintoshes. It also lagged behind OS/2 in pure power. Gates will probably make billions.

Microsoft was similar to the old IBM in other ways as well: it could get away with second-rate products because, as writer Steven Levy puts it, they owned both the railroad tracks and the trains. Microsoft's software rarely led, followed others' advances only with reluctance. If someone had a product that was too good, Gates bought the company.

The Clinton Justice Department settled the Microsoft suit in 1994, but a federal judge, listening to the howls of protest from Microsoft's competitors, rejected the settlement. In June 1995, a federal appeals court overturned the judge's decision, and to the dismay of Microsoft's competitors the settlement was upheld. Justice Department pressure that blocked Microsoft's purchase of Intuit—the seller of the most popular personal finance program—held, however, and the companies dropped merger plans. Competitors of Microsoft also feared that the company was trying to muscle into the lucrative Internet service, software that would allow users access to the world-wide computer network. At issue was the plan for Microsoft to set up its own computer network and build access program into Windows 95. That would directly compete against services such as America Online and CompuServe. The Justice Department was less concerned and also in June 1995 said it was not pursuing anti-trust action.

Nonetheless, the paradigm shifted, the revolution was in full steam, and the world changed. Computing had become totally decentralized. Everyone had the power on their desk or at home. The priesthood of the mainframe's information managers was dead. The people had won.

1996

Epilogue

"Any sufficiently advanced technology is indistinguishable from magic."
ARTHUR C. CLARKE

LELANI ARRIS IS THE EDITOR of the *Global Environmental Change Report,* a newsletter published by Cutter Information Corporation, in Arlington, Massachusetts. The only odd part of her job is that she lives nowhere near Massachusetts; she works from her home in Dunster, B.C., Canada, located between the metropolises of McBride and Valemount in the forested east-central part of the province.

While traveling in Canada several years ago she met a man in Jasper and fell in love. She parlayed a job with Econet, an ecology computer service in the United States, into a job with the newsletter and, because it really doesn't make any difference where she lives anymore, she moved to Jasper, married the guy, and bought property an hour and a half west of Jasper.

"From my house, I can look west across the Fraser River (we are near the headwaters) to the Cariboo Mountains, while just behind us to the east are the Rockies. Winters are long and summers short," she says, "but we are basically surrounded by wilderness and tend to worry about things like hitting a moose on the highway or meeting a bear in the bush, as opposed to getting stuck in traffic or mugged on the street. To me the trade-off is worth it."

Courier service takes at least two days from anywhere else, mail comes three times a week, and every business telephone call is long-distance. "Travel is the same—it's a full day trip to get anywhere, as the nearest airport is a three-hour drive and from there you can only fly to Vancouver or north." Communication, however, is instantaneous.

She is connected to the commercial computer service CompuServe and Econet, and she can use a local dial-up service in Vancouver called Mindlink. She can cruise the Internet, the mother of all computer networks, send and receive mail, send copy, download graphics. When she needs to travel, she takes her IBM-compatible laptop, which normally is plugged ("docked" is the word) into a monitor and keyboard at home, and plugs herself into the Internet to get her electronic mail. She can work anyplace that has a telephone with a jack. She doesn't even need electricity as long as the batteries hold out. She recently attended an environment conference in Berlin and kept in touch that way. Only the difference in time zones impinges on her freedom; if you have to call the North American East Coast you have to do it on their time. Arris is a classic example of the freedom computers bring. Time and space in the electronic age mean nothing. She wanted to live with the man she loved in a place she loved, and because of computers and her competence with them, she can.

In Sunnyvale, California, the Russian owner of a software company is having a serious generational problem within his family. As a result, he is building a cultural "time machine."

Stepan Pachikov's firm, ParaGraph International, is about to publish the first step toward their undertaking, AlterEgo, employing what they claim is the best 3-D, color multimedia graphics ever designed for a PC. It eventually will end as a phone-in service.

Pachikov seems to have an entrepreneurial gene. It was just

sitting around, waiting for the freedom to express itself. He founded his company in Moscow in 1987 as soon as *glasnost* arrived, opened a branch office in the U.S. in 1990, and moved his family here a year later. The firm is best known as the writers of the software that permitted Apple's Newton handheld computer to understand handwriting. The efforts at the time machine were inspired by Pachikov's thirteen-year-old son, Alex.

Alex immediately discovered the computer networks ("cyberspace" in the jargon) and now spends nearly all his off-school time cruising the computer nets. Pachikov sadly points out that Alex and his friends don't read books, especially the kind of books that warmed Pachikov's soul when he was a child, the greats of Russian and western literature. "The books he never reads, I read when I was six," Pachikov laments.

AlterEgo is Pachikov's way of teaching those values to Alex using Alex's preferred medium: his son can "jack into" western culture and be metaphorically transported back in time. Going back to first-century Rome, for instance, will mean living in a room just like one that a Roman would have, wearing authentic Roman garb, using Roman tools and utensils, being surrounded by Roman art and language, and dealing with other Romans on Roman streets, all in 3-D color with sound on the screen. Since every object in the room and on the street, as well as the other Romans, would have to be stored in the computer, the "context" will be enormous, but the technology already exists for that. Pachikov hopes his effort will eventually enable him to employ many of Russia's struggling intellectual elite to provide the context and make "historian the most popular and profitable profession in the world."

By 1998, ParaGraph International hopes to have developed its first "World," residing on World Player, a service to which "time travelers" will subscribe. "You could spend several days in ancient Rome and get bored. Nothing would happen," Pachikov said. World Player would provide "angels" or guides that would take you around to show you the sights and people of interest, explaining life in ancient Rome. Other worlds would follow. "You could meet Christ, talk to him, ask him questions.

If Alex wants to have a 'wonderful night,' he can have it with Desdemona. Now there's a reason to read Shakespeare!"

Up the Bayshore Freeway, Silicon Graphics, Inc., has donated four workstations and a network server to film director Steven Spielberg's Survivors of Shoah Visual Foundation to help preserve the memories of Holocaust survivors. Using $12 million of private funds—much of it Spielberg's—the foundation is attempting to record and videotape the testimony of as many of the 300,000 Holocaust survivors as are still alive. "It is the most important work I've ever done," he says. The high-tech project will help scholars navigate through masses of historical material. The Silicon Graphics computers will enable the documentation to be available through multimedia, which means pictures and sound, all interlinked to each other and to huge historical and statistical databases.

It was SGI's computers that created the dinosaurs in Spielberg's hit *Jurassic Park*.

In Seattle, the Boeing Company sent its first 777 jet off to United Airlines. The plane was designed entirely by computer. If the engineers wanted to see if a certain bolt would fit in a certain hole, the computer tried it out on Boeing's engineering workstations. If they wanted to see what adjustments they needed to make on the wing to improve lift, the computers told them. The computers could predict fuel efficiency and load. The entire plane existed as magnetic blips on disks before anything was actually built.

The plane itself will carry hundreds of computers.

Computers in aircraft aren't new. Lockheed's L-1011 could be landed with no hands in the late 1960s. The 777 would be almost totally computerized to the point where Boeing is locked in a philosophical battle with its competitor, Europe's Airbus, over just how much control computers should have over planes.

In conventional planes, the pilot uses a yoke or steering wheel and pedals connected directly to control surfaces on the wings and tail by hydraulic-powered cables. Airbus's jets use a fly-by-wire technique common with military aircraft. The pilot uses a joystick just like the ones used in computer games. The stick is connected electronically to a computer. The computer, using hydraulic cables, then adjusts the control surfaces. In the 777, the pilot uses a conventional yoke connected to a computer, but the computer fakes pressure on the wheels and pedals so it feels to the pilot as if he or she actually is flying the plane instead of the computer. Airbus's 320, 330, and 340 airliners also have computers that could overrule the pilots; if the pilot tried to do something the computer thought was dangerous—you cannot dive this plane at that speed without ripping off a wing—it would refuse the command. In the 777, the pilot has the last word—if I decide I need to dive this plane to get out of the way of another plane coming at me I will do so. Who is right in the argument remains to be seen. As of this writing, Airbus has had several accidents caused by disharmony between the humans in the cockpit and the computers. Either the computer proved wrong, or the human was reluctant to or incapable of ceding control. That the machines can be trusted to the point where the argument is even possible is testimony to how far we've come.

The famed Internet pornography section at the University of Delft in the Netherlands was voluntarily closed in early 1995 by its operator, Patrick Groeneveld, the victim of its own success.

Groeneveld said university officials were thinking of shutting down the collection of pornographic images because of the publicity and because the network server was accounting for more than half the network traffic out of the school. The site on the Internet's World Wide Web, known as the "Digital Picture Archive on the Seventeenth Floor," for its location in the electrical engineering department at Delft, was clocking more than 5,000 downloads a day, as many as fifteen a minute. The images had been collected from contributors around the world, gathered automatically every night by a small computer program at Delft. By the time Groeneveld pulled the plug, as many as 10,000 different people a day were accessing the file, he said.

"In one month we counted over 100,000 different sites accessing the archive."

"It started as a fun thing but it really got out of hand," Groeneveld said. "The publicity it created was not beneficial to my work and to my university, and technically our network could not support this kind of traffic."

The archives of other photos, including pictures of film stars, works of art, nature, and computer-generated art, remain active. The archive also includes a large collection of American lawyer jokes, and an on-line Bible.

Meanwhile Congress, full of American lawyers, passed a law banning pornography on the Internet. It can't be done; the system is too complex and too vast for anyone to control it.

You are a physician. You are at the bedside of a patient in the ICU. You have ordered lab tests and you need to know the results. You hold in your hand a palm-sized computer with a screen and buttons. Using a stylus, you query the lab and the results of the tests show immediately on the liquid crystal screen, accessed directly from the lab, even if it's across town or out of state. You also can get the patient's complete records from the hospital data bank or from his personal physican elsewhere. You can plug the handheld computer into a terminal and download graphics, including Magnetic Resonance Imaging (MRI), computer-generated 3-D color images of the patient's insides, or perhaps the results of a computerized axial tomography (CAT) scan, essentially an X-ray machine analyzed by a computer.

Then, if you wish, you may do a MEDLINE search, looking through the huge file of the National Library of Medicine at Bethesda, Maryland, to help you treat the case with the latest and most complete information. You can even call up a program based on artificial intelligence, a process in which a computer tries to emulate the knowledge and wisdom of a human expert, to help you decide what to do. You can update the records, or send a message to a specialist in another city.

All this can be accessed from the bedside with no wires, using the same technology you use on your VCR. The same information and communications would be available from your desktop computer in the office.

The films we see are now heavily influenced by computers, with many special effects, once done with clumsy models, are generated entirely by minicomputers. Forrest Gump, a fictional character, can be seen shaking hands with John F. Kennedy in the Oval Office. In a film about a castrato (a male singer castrated to keep his voice high), the ghostly singing was created by a computer. The roaring dinosaurs in *Jurassic Park* consisted of an amalgam of sounds, including screaming lions, to create a sound that no one has ever heard. New breeds of artists generate their work on computers, printing them out with microprocessor-driven color laser printers. The ability to alter photographs, called image processing, is so versatile that there is now a serious danger of doctored photos being mistaken for real ones. Music is recorded by computers and lasers on little disks that reproduce sound of sometimes awesome fidelity, and they never seem to wear out. The recording consists of minute pits on a shiny disk read by a laser, sampled millions of times a second by a computer and reconstructed into audible sound. Music often is composed on computers.

Much of the research for this edition of *Engines of the Mind* was done by hooking myself to the Internet, a network that started as a Defense Department attempt to create a communications system impervious to nuclear attack. I found Arris on CompuServe, downloaded much of the data used in this chapter from various sources on the net, including the archives of the *San José Mercury-News,* the *New York Times,* and *Time* and *Interactive Age* magazines, and through faxes hooked directly into my computer. Many interviews were done by e-mail. The chapter was written on a Macintosh Quadra 605 with a variant of a Motorola 68040 microprocessor with an effective 16 million bytes of memory and a speed of 20 megabytes per second, a relatively slow and weak system compared to what one of my sons uses. I wrote on a word processor (that is a new word in the language, one of hundreds computers have added to the dictionary) called Nisus that will automatically index for me. Even the way I write has changed, because computers allow me to play with words and structure eternally until I get it right or give up. No retyping, no physical cutting and pasting. A huge thesaurus and an unabridged English dictionary sit happily on my hard disk, ready to be called up with one botton stroke.

It's not just the computers you see, such as the one on Lel-ani Arris's desk or the display terminals in front of a 777 pilot, but the ones you don't see as well. Fax machines, which use microprocessors (computers-on-a-chip), represent probably the fastest technological conversion in business history. One year no one had one; three years later no one knew how they got along without them. It now is cheaper to send several pages of a letter by facsimile machines across the continent than it is to mail them, and they arrive instantly, thanks to the computers inside. We have computers containing millions of transistors in our cars. New luxury cars boast as many as nine. When I got my new car I was told my gas mileage with the second tank of gas would be much better than the mileage with the first tank, not because the engine was breaking in, but because one of the car's computers was adjusting the engine to my driving habits, and weather, road conditions, and speed. You can even plug your laptop into a telephone on an airliner and fax or transmit or receive copy while traveling at 40,000 feet, 500 miles an hour, thousands of miles from your office. The reason our VCRs are so versatile (and impossible to program) is that they contain microprocessors. Nonetheless, you can now watch television on your schedule, not a network's. The cameras that take videotape pictures, which have replaced home movies, are made possible by microprocessors. The newest television sets adjust the analog pictures with microprocessors and tune in the stations digitally. By the time you read this, the picture on your set may completely be digitized by computers and reassembled in our living rooms for spectacular pictures and sound. We bank using ATM machines that are nothing but simple-minded computers hooked to the bank's computer network, but you can withdraw cash from your bank in Omaha by using a cash machine in Florence, Italy. Some banks even are beginning to charge if you want to deal with a human teller. We have computers in our cellular phones, another technology that burst on the scene in a matter of two years, and the new ones will track you down no matter where in the world you are. Our phone calls are switched using computers, the quality of the sound monitored and improved by microprocessors that process them into binary digits and send them down fiber optic cables to be reassembled by microprocessors at the other end.

Thirty percent of our homes have home computers, ranging from old Apple IIs to computers with Intel Pentium or Motorola PowerPC chips that have power beyond the dreams of the inventors. In 1994, American consumers spent $8 billion on personal computers, close to what they spent on television sets. By the fiftieth anniversary of the invention of the computer, 1996, the computer industry may be bigger than the television industry. Virtually every business in America depends on them. The American space program basically was run on slower, dumber, and vastly larger machines than the PowerMac in my son's apartment. His computer comes with a CD-ROM, a computer version of the sound-recording devices that plays sound, pictures, and text, and one disk can contain an entire encyclopedia. Sound is in stereo and the screen can show more colors than the eye can discern. He lays out magazines on his machine, instantly and in color.

Not even the Industrial Revolution had the effect on everyday life the computer revolution has had. Of all inventions, perhaps the automobile and the telephone come closest, but they have reached the end of their curve—today's cars are not very much different from cars of fifty or seventy-five years ago, nor are telephones—and the microprocessor has only just begun. In fact, the telephone is about to be replaced by the computer.

The effects are not always obvious. One reason the Iron Curtain fell in the late 1980s and early 1990s was that the totalitarian governments lost their ability to control information. Computer networks were not yet a major factor, but fax machines were; students from Prague to Peking could keep each other informed and tell the world what was happening in a way never possible before. The next revolution, wherever it takes place, will use the Internet for communications, and no government can stop it. You can see it coming. Singapore, one of the most advanced countries on earth—and the most repressive—was trying mightily to keep ideas it disliked off the Internet while at the same time encouraging its citizens to take advantage of the computer network. Singapore will fail. So will China, which also is trying to limit access. No longer can information be controlled.

There are, of course, downsides to all of this. I was one of those science reporters who breathlessly predicted that computers would put an end to paperwork and paper in the office. Computers have, in fact, turned out to be better at *producing* paper than eliminating it. My untimely death will occur when all the papers piled on my desk fall on me as I sit at my computer. The Internet is being swamped by advertising, and message boards tend to revert to the rude and uncivil. The signal-to-noise ratio—the relationship between useful information and junk—is enormous and getting worse every day.

Every computer in business threatens the job of someone. That Chicago bank charging for human tellers already went through several periods of layoffs, first when computers replaced office work and second when ATMs replaced the first wave of tellers. Another wave will be sacrificed as ATMs grow. Secretaries have become an endangered species as executives with computers on their desks are expected to take over much of their own secretarial work. Never mind that they aren't as good at it and this is a less efficient way to spend their time; computers don't require salaries and benefits.

An entire generation of American worker has lost his or her job to computers and will never recover. Nothing can be done for these people. Their children have a better chance, but the fact remains that people who can use computers earn 15 percent more than people who don't, and not everyone gets the chance to learn. We are in the dire situation of creating a technologic underclass, a kind of information apartheid. Mitch Kapor, cofounder of Lotus Development, said that access to the information age of computers "will be highly correlated with the general have-nots. Early in the next century the [computer] network will become the major conduit through which we conduct our lives. Any disenfranchisement will be very severe." Of those 30 percent of American families who own computers, most are in middle or upper class homes. As computers get ever more important to the world, the chasm between those who can use them and those who cannot grows wider. Schools in economically well-off neighborhoods can afford computers and can produce workers who can use the devices, while schools in the inner cities and poorer sections of rural areas cannot. The graduates of the good schools will be able to cope with the challenges; the others haven't a chance.

The issue is not actually hardware. Computers get cheaper every year and already there is a robust second-hand market. The problem may be access to the Internet and the information contained therein.

Millions of jobs have been *created* by computers, but they are different jobs, held by different people.

Information has become the currency of our time, replacing gold. Now you can earn money by finding, manipulating, and using information. Even information can be a trap. There is a difference between data and information and those who can understand that difference have an advantage over those who will sink in data. New talents, new perceptions are being demanded by the electronic age.

No one could have predicted this any more than anyone can predict the future. If you go back to the old science fiction of the 1930s or even the 1950s, you will see how wrong it was. The future will not be the way it was predicted in the 1936 film *Things to Come,* based on the H. G. Wells novel, because Wells could not conceive of computers. Isaac Asimov's classic *Foundation* trilogy, written in the 1950s, now seems comical. As good as Asimov (and Wells) were, they could not have foreseen transistors, personal computers, and the effects of computers on society. The 1938 World's Fair, which tried to paint a tranquil, exciting, democratic future, missed as well. No computers.

So only a fool would try to predict the future. You cannot know what technologies are coming, or what advances in pure science will mean to applied science and technology. Einstein's work on the photoelectric effect, for which he won a Nobel Prize, led to radio and television, but he could not have known that, nor could anyone else. You can't predict what people will do with a technology once they get their hands on it. The telephone itself was designed as a business tool. When it was installed in people's homes, women turned it into a personal communicator and the telephone companies were in a business they had not predicted. Pres Eckert and John Mauchly produced ENIAC and EDVAC in a technological world without any hint that up the highway, less than 200 miles away, Shockley, Bardeen, and Brattain were working on the transistor. Their vision of what computers would be like was therefore wrong. It had to be. The people at Bell Labs were trying to make telephony more efficient and had no idea what was going on in Philadelphia.

No one can predict where all this will turn out. We only must be careful that the benefits are spread fairly, that as few people as possible are left behind, and that the technology of the computer, which is intrinsically neither good nor bad, is used for the good of all.

And the people . . . .

JOHN VINCENT ATANASOFF continued working in the Naval Ordnance Laboratory in Silver Springs, Maryland, through the last years of World War II. Toward the end, the navy decided that it, too, wanted a computer, and because Atanasoff had the most experience, they gave him $100,000 to build one. He said he did not have the time and asked Mauchly, who was still working part-time at ordnance, to draw up staffing specifications. The project petered out and Atanasoff was not heard from again in computer circles until the *Honeywell* suit.

Atanasoff went into business for himself as an engineer in the Washington area and eventually sold his company to Aerojet-General for a considerable amount of money. He retired to a gadget-filled house in Maryland. Iowa State University never tired of furthering his cause and his computer was eventually exhibited at the Smithsonian. He died on June 15, 1995, twelve days after Pres Eckert. He believed to his death that he was the inventor of the electronic computer.

CLIFFORD BERRY, Atanasoff's partner, left Iowa State and had an unremarkable career. In 1963 he was found in his bed with a plastic bag over his head. The official ruling was suicide. Atanasoff hinted several times he thought it was murder.

J. PRESPER ECKERT retired as vice-president of Sperry-Univac and lived well in the wooded hills of Gladwyne, Pennsylvania, and some of the time on his boat in Florida.

Eckert never fell victim to the deep bitterness that marked John Mauchly's last years—he confronted what happened with a certain degree of cynicism. Yet he carried on the feud against Goldstine. He believed that Goldstine's publication of von Neumann's "First Draft" helped keep him and Mauchly from getting the patent and von Neumann to get the credit for the machine.

"I saw computers as being very important," he told the author. "I don't think that anybody had foreseen them as having the importance that they achieved."

Eckert died at the age of 76 on June 3, 1995, less than a year before the University of Pennsylvania was to hold its golden anniversary celebration.

HERMAN GOLDSTINE left the Institute for Advanced Study and went to work for IBM and later became executive director of the American Philosophical Society in Philadelphia, one of America's oldest learned societies. Adele died in 1964; Goldstine remarried.

He remained von Neumann's most solid supporter, yet he was always puzzled that Eckert would not speak to him.

JOHN MAUCHLY left Remington in 1959 and set up his own computer consulting business, Mauchly Associates, which eventually wound up on the New York Stock Exchange as Scientific Resources.

"Then, through management, which I could not control, because I only had a minority interest at the time . . . [the company] lost $43 million, did a lot of other foolish things, not even furnishing reports to the stockholders," he told the author. "That's why, I think, it took so long for the $43 million loss to come out . . .

"I had $1 million worth of stock in that, and these other people got it delisted and off the board and so forth. I've been paying back debts and trying to collect a few things that somebody else owed me, and so we decided, well, we'd have to sell the acreage surrounding the house here: we're just lucky we can keep the house."

The acreage was in Ambler, twenty miles from Philadelphia, beautiful and wooded. His house was an old farm house, some sections going back to the eighteenth century.

His anger at Goldstine, Atanasoff, Brainerd, and von Neumann soured his last years and contributed to his physical deterioration. His blood disease got worse and purple blisterlike growths appeared on his nose, lips, and fingers. He became so sick that in his last years he sometimes had to tow an oxygen tank around behind him to help him breathe. He died in the late fall of 1980. Kay McNulty Mauchly remarried.

JOHN VON NEUMANN continued his career as one of America's preeminent scientists. He eventually was named to the Atomic Energy Commission and became one of the leading "Cold Warriors" of the time. He did, however, defend J. Robert Oppenhiemer in public, believing that Oppenhiemer had been treated unjustly.

One day in 1955, von Neumann fell in a corridor and injured his left shoulder. X-rays revealed that he had bone cancer and the cancer had already metastasized. He continued to work, although the cancer began to eat away his strength. His mind seemed to remain clear.

Few cancers hurt more. Eventually he was admitted to Walter Reed Army Hospital and surrounded by doctors and orderlies with security clearance lest he babble secrets. The terror began for him when his mind began to go. Edward Teller said he never saw anyone suffer so. Eugene Wigner wrote that the real terror for von Neumann was the possibility he would cease to exist, cease to think. He knew his fate was unavoidable, yet it was to him also unacceptable. He woke at night screaming with terror until finally he had to be drugged. As his biographer Steve J. Heims wrote, von Neumann, "who knew how to live so fully, did not know how to die."

He died on February 8, 1957. His reputation remains unblemished as one of the towering geniuses of the twentieth century. He is remembered for the real contributions he made to science, and they were many, and for at least one he did not make.

Santa Cruz, California
October 1995

Glossary

ABC Atanasoff-Berry Computer, built by John Atanasoff and Clifford Berry at Iowa State at the end of the 1930s. It was perhaps the first device to use vacuum tubes for mathematical computation.

Accumulator The part of a computer that compiles or accumulates numbers for use by the computer.

Algorithm A method of solving certain problems using mathematical formulas.

Amplifier A device that increases the strength of an electronic signal by means of tubes, transistors, or magnetic devices.

Analog Something that corresponds to something else; in computers, a device that computes by measuring one object by its relation to something else.

Analog computer One that computes by measuring the relative positions of things, the way a slide rule measures points on wooden bars relative to each other. It is rarely found outside specialized functions.

Analytical Engine Charles Babbage's second machine, built in mid-nineteenth-century London. It was a steam-driven mechanical device that would have been the world's first real computer had Babbage finished it.

Anode The positive electrode, the electrode toward which electrons flow, usually a vacuum tube or a transistor.

Atanasoff-Berry Computer See ABC.

Automatic Sequence Controlled Calculator (ASCC) Howard Aiken's electromechanical computer, built at Harvard between 1939 and 1944, which made use of IBM cards and did essentially what Charles Babbage wanted to do with his Analytical Engine. Also called the Mark I.

BINAC Binary Automatic Computer, built by Eckert and Mauchly for the Northrop Corporation to guide the Snark missile. BINAC was their first commercial sale. The first stored-memory computer built in the United States, BINAC is generally considered a failure.

Binary Referring to a numbering system using two digits, usually a 1 and a 0, the most common system used in computers. Quantity is usually determined by the position of the 1's and 0's in an eight-digit number (see Byte). For instance:

Digit	Binary Equivalent
1	00000001
2	00000010
3	00000011
4	00000100
5	00000101
6	00000110
7	00000111
8	00001000
9	00001001
10	00001010

Bit *Bi*nary digi*t*, a single binary digit, a 1 or a 0, one-eighth of a byte.

Boolean Algebra A system of mathematical logic using binary digits, 0 and 1, developed by the English mathematician George Boole.

Byte A cluster of eight binary digits, or bits.

Calculus A method of calculation using symbols, named for the stones used in early abaci.

Capacitor A device that stores electrical energy, also called a condensor, used to block the flow of direct current in electronic devices.

Central Processing Unit (CPU) The part of a computer that contains the "brains" of the machine, that processes the data according to instructions.

COLOSSUS An electronic special-purpose computer, probably the first in the world, built as part of the British ULTRA project to break the German code toward the end of World War II.

Decimal Referring to the numbering system based on ten numbers, 0–9.

Differential analyzer The analog computer developed by Vannevar Bush at MIT in 1930, making use of gears, wires, and wheels, which solved differential equations (see below). Models of this machine were built at the Moore School and at the Aberdeen Proving Grounds.

Differential equations Common mathematical equations that measure the infinitesimal difference between two consecutive values of a variable quantity. An example might be $x + x^2 = y$. The equations are particularly useful in electrical engineering.

Difference Engine Charles Babbage's name for two of his mechanical computing machines. Only the first one was ever built by anyone; none was built by Babbage.

Digital Using numbers expressed in digits, measuring discrete numbers.

Digital computer One making use of digits, usually 0 and 1. Almost all electronic computers are digital.

Diode A two-terminal device that conducts electricity better in one direction than in the other.

EDSAC Electronic Delay Storage Automatic Calculator, the first British electronic computer, and the first stored-program computer, built by Maurice Wilkes and a team at Cambridge University, based on EDVAC (see below).

EDVAC Electronic Discrete Variable Automatic Computer, the second machine designed by Eckert and Mauchly and the Moore School team, and the first computer influenced by von Neumann. It was a stored-program computer, the first with such a design, but was not built until after the original Moore School team had departed and Wilkes had built EDSAC in Cambridge.

ENIAC Electronic Numerical Integrator and Computer, the world's first electronic general-purpose digital computer, built at the Moore School during World War II, designed and built by the team headed by Eckert and Mauchly under a contract from the U.S. Army. It was completed in 1946.

ENIGMA The British version of the German encryption-decryption machine, part of the ULTRA project. The machine was a special-purpose electromechanical computer.

Flip-flops An electronic circuit that has two states, usually on or off, and remains in one state until it is commanded to change.

Integrated circuits Solid-state or semiconductor (see below) devices in which all the elements are contained on one chip instead of having each device separate and wired together. ICs are much faster and more reliable, are cheaper to build, and consequently have dominated electronics for the past fifteen years.

Logarithm The power to which a second number must be raised to yield the original number, usually based on 10. It is used to shorten mathematical computation and forms the basis for the slide rule.

Mainframes The large computers, usually the size of a room or a small building, that are dominant in business and large laboratories. The IBM 360 is the best-known example. UNIVAC was the first commercial mainframe.

Mark I See ASSC above.

Microcomputer The small, table-model computer, now used in offices and at home, making use of microprocessors (see below) and memory chips. Apples, IBM-PCs, TRS-80s are examples of microcomputers.

Microprocessor A solid-state device in which all the processing and control elements of a computer are housed on a single chip.

Minicomputer Smaller computers, usually for office work, which entered the market in the 1960s with the rise of solid-state or semiconductor technology.

Parallel architecture Computer design permitting the data to be handled in clusters, several bits at a time. ENIAC was a parallel machine, and so are many of the newest and fastest computers of the 1980s.

Peripherals Pieces of equipment, such as printers, that assist computers in doing their job.

Resistor A device that impedes the flow of electricity into a circuit.

Scaling circuits Electronic circuits that reduce large quantities of inputs to smaller, more manageable levels.

Semiconductor A group of materials that permits electric current to pass more slowly than a conductor but much faster than a resistor, usually made of silicon or germanium. It is the basis for almost all modern electronics.

Serial architecture Computer design in which the data are handled in sequence. Most computers are serial machines because of the ease of design.

Transistors Semiconductor devices that replace vacuum tubes.

Vacuum tubes Electronic devices that preceded semiconductor technology and consisted of electronic circuits housed in glass tubes from which air had been pumped out. ENIAC and all the early computers made use of vacuum tubes.

UNIVAC Universal Automatic Computer, the first commercial machine, produced first in the 1950s by the Eckert-Mauchly Computing Corporation and later by Remington Rand.

Bibliography

BOOKS

Alterman, Hyman. *Counting People: The Census in History.* New York: Harcourt, Brace & World, 1969.

Austrian, Geoffrey D. *Herman Hollerith: Forgotten Giant of Information Processing.* New York: Columbia University Press, 1982.

Babbage, Charles. *Passages from the Life of a Philosopher.* London: Longman, Green, Longman, Roberts & Green, 1864.

―――. *Charles Babbage and his Calculating Engines.* Edited by Philip Morrison and Emily Morrison. New York: Dover Publications, 1961.

Bernstein, Jeremy. *The Analytical Engine: Computers—Past, Present, and Future.* New York: Random House, 1964.

Boyer, Carl B. *A History of Mathematics.* New York: Wiley, 1968.

De Bono, Edward, ed. *Eureka!: An Illustrated History of Inventions from the Wheel to the Computer.* New York: Holt, Rinehart & Winston, 1974.

Durant, Will. *Our Oriental Heritage.* New York: Simon & Schuster, 1954.

Eames, Charles, and Ray Eames. *A Computer Perspective.* Cambridge, Mass.: Harvard University Press, 1973.

Fishman, Katharine Davis. *The Computer Establishment.* New York: McGraw-Hill, 1981.

Freiherr, Gregory. *The Seeds of Artificial Intelligence.* Washington, D.C.: Government Printing Office, 1980.

Goldstine, Herman H. *The Computer: From Pascal to von Neumann.* Princeton: Princeton University Press, 1972.

Hanson, Dirk. *The New Alchemists.* Boston: Little, Brown, 1982.

Hawkes, Nigel. *The Computer Revolution.* New York: E. P. Dutton, 1972.

Heims, Steve J. *John von Neumann and Norbert Wiener: From Mathematics to the Technologies of Life and Death.* Cambridge, Mass.: MIT Press, 1980.

Hollingdale, S. H., and G. C. Tootill. *Electronic Computers.* Baltimore: Penguin Books, 1967.

Hyman, Anthony. *Charles Babbage: Pioneer of the Computer.* Princeton: Princeton University Press, 1982.

Lavington, Simon. *Early Computers: The Story of Vintage Computers and the People Who Built Them.* Manchester: Manchester University Press (Digital Press, U.S.), 1980.

Lukoff, Herman. *From Dits to Bits: A Personal History of the Electronic Computer.* Portland, Ore.: Robotics Press, 1979.

Marshack, Alexander. *The Roots of Civilization.* New York: McGraw-Hill, 1972.

McCorduck, Pamela. *Machines Who Think: A Personal Inquiry into the History and Prospects of Artificial Intelligence.* San Francisco: W. H. Freeman, 1979.

Moore, Doris Langley. *Ada: Countess of Lovelace.* New York: Harper & Row, 1977.

Moseley, Maboth. *Irascible Genius: A Life of Charles Babbage, Inventor.* London: Hutchinson, 1964.

Pullan, J. M. *The History of the Abacus.* London: Hutchinson, 1968.

Sobel, Robert. *I.B.M.: Colossus in Transition.* New York: Times Books, 1981.

Stern, Nancy. *From ENIAC to UNIVAC: An Appraisal of the Eckert-Mauchly Computers.* Bedford, Mass.: Digital Press, 1981.

Turney, Catherine. *Byron's Daughter: A Biography of Elizabeth Wedora Leigh.* New York: Scribners, 1972.

Wulforst, Harry. *Breakthrough to the Computer Age.* New York: Scribners, 1982.

CORRESPONDENCE

John Mauchly to H. Holm Clayton, Nov. 15, 1940.
Mauchly to John Vincent Atanasoff, Feb. 24, 1941.
Atanasoff to Mauchly, Mar. 7, 1941.
Mauchly to Atanasoff (telegram), Mar. 22, 1941.
Mauchly to Atanasoff, Mar. 31, 1941.
Mauchly to Atanasoff, Apr. 22, 1941.
Mauchly to Clayton, Apr. 26, 1941.
Mauchly to Atanasoff, May 21, 1941.
Mauchly to Atanasoff, June 7, 1941.
Mauchly to Atanasoff, June 22, 1941.
Mauchly to Atanasoff, Sept. 30, 1941.
Atanasoff to Mauchly, Oct. 7, 1941.
Mauchly to Atanasoff, Oct. 15, 1941.
Atanasoff to Mauchly, Oct. 19, 1941.
Mauchly to Atanasoff, Oct. 20, 1941.
Atanasoff to Mauchly, Oct. 30, 1941.
Atanasoff to Mauchly, Jan. 19, 1942.
Atanasoff to Mauchly, Jan. 23, 1942.

INTERVIEWS

Atanasoff, John Vincent; Mt. Airy, Md., June 20, 1982.
Auerbach, Isaac; Penn Valley, Pa., June 20, 1982.
Brainerd, John C.; Philadelphia, June 1976.

Burks, Arthur; Ann Arbor, Mich. (telephone), Dec. 23, 1982.
Eckert, J. Presper; Gladwyne, Pa., 1976.
Eckert, J. Presper; Gladwyne, Pa., June 21, 1982.
Goldstine, H.; Princeton, N.J., Jan. 11, 1982.
Gorn, Saul; Philadelphia, Jan. 13, 1982.
Huskey, Harry; Santa Cruz, Calif., Dec. 16, 1982.
Mauchly, John W.; Ambler, Pa. 1976.
Mauchly, Kay; Ambler, Pa., Jan. 12, 1982.
Tropp, Henry; Arcata, Calif., Nov. 1981.
Weygandt, Cornelius J., Jr.; Philadelphia, Jan. 13, 1982.

ARTICLES

Andrews, E. G. "Telephone Switching and the Early Bell Laboratories Computers." *Bell System Technical Journal,* March 1963. Reprinted in *Annals of the History of Computers* (hereafter *AHC*).
"The Babbage Memorial Meeting; Report of Proceedings." The British Computer Society & The Royal Statistical Society, 1977.
Brown, Gordon S. "Harold Locke Hazen." *AHC* 3 (1981): 4–12.
Burks, Arthur W. and Alice R. Burks. "The ENIAC: First General-Purpose Electronic Computer." *AHC* 3 (1981): 310–400.
Chase, G. C. "Mechanical Computing Machinery." *AHC* 2 (1980): 198–226.
Higham, Norman. "John von Neumann." *McGraw-Hill Encyclopedia of World Biography,* 1973.
Hollerith, Herman. "An Electric Tabulating System." *School of Mines Quarterly,* 10 (1889): 239–56.
Huskey, Velma R., and Harry D. Huskey. "Lady Lovelace and Charles Babbage." *AHC* 2 (1980): 229–329.
"John von Neumann." *Current Biography.* 1955.
Kennedy, T. B., Jr. "Electrical Computer Flashes Answers, May Speed Engineering." *New York Times,* Feb. 15, 1946.
Kessler, Gary C. "Recollections of the Early Days of Machine Tabulating." *AHC* 2 (1980): 374.
Ledger, Marshall. "The Case of the E.N.I.A.C." *Pennsylvania Gazette* 81, no. 1.
———."The E.N.I.A.C.'s Muddled History." *Pennsylvania Gazette* 81, no. 2.
"Major Computer Patent Invalidated." *Patent, Trademark and Copyright Journal,* no. 162 (1974): A2–A7.
Metropolis, N., and J. Worlton. "A Trilogy of Errors in the History of Computing." *AHC* 2 (1980): 49–59.
Randell, B. "Annotated Bibliography of the Origins of Computers." *AHC* 1 (1979): 101–207.
Reinhold, Robert. "Vannevar Bush." *New York Times,* June 30, 1974.
Rucker, Rudy. "Master of the Incomplete." *Science 82,* Oct. 1982, 56–60.
Shallet, Sidney. "Electronics to Aid Weather Figuring." *New York Times,* Jan. 11, 1946.
Stern, Nancy. "John von Neumann's Influence on Electronic Digital Computing, 1944–1946." *AHC* 2 (1980): 349–61.
Tropp, Henry S. "Mauchly: Unpublished Remarks." *AHC* 4 (1982): 245–56.
Ulam, Stanislas. "John von Neumann, 1903–1957." *Bulletin of the American Mathematical Society* 64, no. 3, pt. 2 (1958).

Index

abacus, 22, 23–24, 27
  origins of, 23
  Roman, 24
Aberdeen Proving Ground, 99–102,
  119–20, 126
  EDVAC contracted by, 172, 182
  EDVAC patent and, 218–20
  electronic computer opposed at,
  144
  ENIAC construction and, 151, 157,
  167–68, 187–88, 206–7
  von Neumann at, 180–81
ACE (Automatic Computing Engine),
  211–12
ADA (language), 63n
Ada, countess of Lovelace, 54–56,
  58–63
  Analytical Engine and, 56, 58–62
  Babbage and, 53, 55–56, 58–63
  childhood of, 54–55
  Difference Engine and, 55
  illness and death of, 62–63
  marriage of, 58–59
  Menabrea translation of, 59–61
  personal problems of, 62
Adams, Henry C., 82–83

adding machine, printing, 94–95
addition, 21, 28
Ade, George, 248
Adelard of Bath, 26
Aiken, Howard H., 104–5, 181, 217n,
  226–28, 254–55
Airy, Sir George Biddell, 48
algebra, 25
algorism, 25–27
Al-jabr wa'l muqabalah (al-Khowar-
  izmi), 25–26
Al-Kashi, Jamshid ben Mas'ud ben
  Mahmud Ghiath ed-Din, 25–26
al-Khowarizmi, 25
Allen, Paul, 308–9, 312
Altair, 308–11
Alter Ego, 324–25
Amdahl, Eugene, 304
American Online, 322
American Totalizator Company, 234–
  36, 246
amplification, 132
  see also transistors; vacuum tubes
Analytical Engine, 56–62
  Ada and, 56, 58–62
  carries anticipated by, 57–58

Analytical Engine *(continued)*
  conditional operations of, 58
  described, 56–57
  funding for, 60–62
  library of, 58
  punch cards in, 57
Anderson, Harlan, 278–79, 305
Anderson, William, 276
Annals of the History of Computing, 288,
    297
Apple Computer Corp., 310, 316,
    319–20
  Apple II, 310–12, 316, 331
  Newton, 325
  Powermacs, 320
Arabs, 25–26
Aristotle, 20
arithmometer, 93
Armstrong, Edwin, 132*n*
Army, U.S.:
  ballistics research by, 100–102
  see also Aberdeen Proving Ground
Arris, Lelani, 323–24, 329–30
artificial intelligence, 54*n*
ASCC (Mark I computer), 104–5,
    254–55
  description of, 105
assembler languages, 210, 231*n*
Atanasoff, John Vincent, 93, 105–9,
    334, 336
  background of, 105–6
  ENIAC patent case and, 284, 287–
    98
  Mauchly and, 114–16, 190–91,
    289–92
Atanasoff-Berry Computer (ABC),
    107–9, 115–16, 288, 296
AT&T (American Telephone and
    Telegraph):
  transistor and, 301
  vacuum tubes and, 132
  see also Bell Telephone Laboratories
Atari, 310
ATM, 330, 332
audion, 132
Auerbach, Isaac, 108, 191, 222–23,
    229–33, 281, 287, 293, 298–99
  Atanasoff and, 295
  BINAC and, 229–31
  on EMCC, 232–33

Austria, 78–79
Austrian, Geoffrey D., 71, 77, 79, 83,
    91
Automatic Sequence Controlled
    Counter, Harvard-IBM (ASCC;
    Mark I), *see* ASCC
Asimov, Isaac, 333

Babbage, Charles, 37–65, 69, 73, 97*n*
  actuarial table of, 43–44
  Ada and, 53, 55–56, 58–63
  autobiography of, 64
  background of, 38–40
  curiosity of, 39
  dabbling by, 43–44
  death of, 64
  Difference Engine No. 2 of, 62–63
  education of, 40–41
  family life of, 43, 49
  inventions of, 43–44, 52, 63
  mechanical calculator of, 41–42, 44
  postal system changes suggested by,
    43
  social life of, 52–53
  street musicians and, 63, 64
  see also Analytical Engine; Differ-
    ence Engine
Babbage, Henry, 43, 51, 64
Babylonians, 20*n*, 22–23, 66
backups (duplicate tapes), 250
Baldwin, Frank Stephen, 95
ballistics, 99–101, 125
  calculations in, 127–31, 136–37
  firing tables in, 100–101
  mathematical vs. practical approach
    to, 100
  numerical integration and, 127
  Simpson's rule and, 128
  suicide angle in, 128–29
Ballistics Research Laboratory, U.S.
    Army, *see* Aberdeen Proving
    Ground
Bardeen, John, 301, 334
bases (radices), 20
BASIC, 309–10, 312
Bell Telephone Laboratories, 102–4,
    147, 158, 260, 276*n*, 287
  NDRC and, 145
  transistor and, 301–2, 334

Berry, Clifford, 107–8, 334
B5000 computer, 274
Bibby, Dause L., , 260
Bigelow, Julian, 215–17
Bilas, Fran, 127–28
Billings, John Shaw, 70–72
Billings, Kate Sherman, 71
BINAC (Binary Automatic Computer), 229–31, 237–42
    completion of, 239
    described, 229–31
    music from, 239
    Northrop dissatisfaction with, 240–42
    testing of, 237, 239–40
    UNIVAC and, 239–42
binary counters, 111–13
binary system, 20n, 34, 103, 107, 151
Birkenstock, James, 256–57
bits (binary digits), 141
Bletchley Park, 139–43
"blue boxes," 310
Boeing Company, 326
Boethius, 26n
Bond, George Mead, 82–83
Bonn, Ted, 237
Boole, George, 103
Boolean algebra, 103
Bowden, B. V., 63
Brahe, Tycho, 29
Brainerd, John Grist, 120, 130, 134–35, 200, 214, 336
    Eckert, Mauchly and, 166–70
    electronic calculator and, 134–38, 145–46, 148–49
    ENIAC and, 164, 172, 188
    ENIAC patent and, 169–70, 287, 297
    on Larson decision, 295–96
Brattain, Walter, 301, 334
Bricklin, Dan, 311
Briggs, Henry, 30
Brown, Wistar, 236, 245
Brunel, Isambard Kingdom and Marc Isambard, 52
Bucks, Arthur, 322–23, 326
Budapest, 173–76
Burks, Arthur, 98, 108, 120, 125, 135, 215, 284, 286, 289, 294
    on Atanasoff, 288, 296–97

ENIAC and, 149, 156, 165–65, 169n, 188, 195–97, 207
Burns, John L., 270
Burroughs, William S., 94
Burroughs adding machine, 94–95
Burroughs Corporation, 94, 221, 261
    computer business of, 273–74
Bush, Vannevar, 95–99, 144–45, 221
    importance of, 95–96
    product integraph of, 96–97
Bushnell, Nolan, 310
Business Week, 246
Byron, Anne Isabella Milbanke, Lady, 53–55, 62–63
Byron, George Gordon, Lord, 53–55
byte, 305

Cahill, Thaddeus, 133
calculators, desk-top, 93–94, 124, 126, 135–36
calculus, 24, 34, 41, 96–97
Caldwell, Samuel, 115, 145–46, 226–28
"Captain Crunch" (John Draper), 310
Carr, Esther, 123, 137, 150, 191–92, 195, 200, 205, 217
CAT (computerized axial tomography), 328
cathode-ray tube, 210–11, 238–39
CBS, 122
    UNIVAC and, 250–53
CDC, *see* Control Data Corporation
CD-ROM, 331
cellular phones, 331
Census Bureau, U.S., 191–92
    Hollerith machine and, 76–78
    machines researched by, 87–89
    Tabulating Machine Co., and, 85–89
    UNIVAC and, 221–22, 244, 253–54
censuses, 66–72, 82
    ancient, 66–67
    machines for, 69, 71–72, 76–79, 82, 83–84, 86–89
    religious resistance to, 67–68
    for taxation, 66–67
    U.S., 67–72, 77–78, 83–84, 86–89
central processing units (CPUs), 56–57, 310–11

Chambers, Carl, 114, 130, 199, 205
Chapline, Joe, 136
Chase, G. C., 22
Chedaker, Joseph, 155
Childe Harold's Pilgrimage (Byron), 54
Chuan Chu, 268
Civil Works Administration (CWA), 101
Clarke, Arthur C., 323
Clement, Joseph, 48, 50–51
Clute, Gene L., 233, 236
COBAL, 311
Code and Cipher School, Government (British), 139–43
  ULTRA and, 141–43
codes and code-breaking, 140–43
  machines for, 141–43
coding, 230, 250
Coleman, John, 273
COLOSSUS, 142–43, 296
  Mark II version of, 143
Columbia School of Mines, 70, 77
Commodore, 310
compasses, 28
Complex Number Computer, 103–4
Comptometer, 94
CompuServe, 322–24, 329
computational techniques, 21, 28–30, 44
computations, 21–22
Computer Establishment, The (Fishman), 271
Computer Research Corporation (CRC), 275–76
computers:
  analog, 26, 31, 97–102, 106, 129, 145
  digital, 31–35, 102–16, 141
  digital vs. analog, 31, 330
  electromechanical, 104–5, 143–44
  electronic, 108–16, 123–24, 131, 134–38, 142–43
  human, 42
  kits, 308
  need for, 96–97
  scientific, 95–116
  see also specific machines
Comrie, L. J., 95
Conant, James, 96, 255
conditional operations, 58
Congress, U.S., 67–69, 86

Constitution, U.S., 67–68
Control Data Corporation (CDC), 260, 263–68, 318
  advantages of, 263–64
  Commercial Credit acquired by, 266
  Cray computers of, 264–65
  Cybernet of, 267
  formation of, 263
  IBM document index of, 267–68
  IBM Service Bureau purchased by, 267
  IBM settlement with, 267–68
  IBM vs., 264–68
  Norris and, 260, 263–68
Coombs, A. W. M., 211
cost-plus contracts, 224–25
counting:
  decimal system for, 20
  development of, 19–20
CP/M (Control Program for Microcomputer), 312, 314–16
CPUs (central processing units), 56–57, 305
CRAY, 158n, 192n
Cray, Seymour, 264
Cream Soda Computer, 310
Cronkite, Walter, 251
CTR (Computing-Tabulating-Recording Company), 91–92
Cuneo, Ernest, 220–21
Cunningham, L. E., 148–49, 151, 157
Curie, Pierre and Jacques, 183
Curtiss, John, 223–26, 243
Cybernet, 267
cyberspace, 325

data processing, 78, 95
David, king of Israel, 66–67
DEC (Digital Equipment Corporation), 278–79, 306–7
decimal system (base 10), 20, 150–51
  fractions in, 26, 28
  zero in, 25
De Forest, Lee, 131–32
De Forest tube, 132
Dickens, Charles, 38n, 262, 268n
Difference Engine, 44–51, 55, 64
  Ada and, 55
  construction of, 48
  description of, 46

funding for, 47, 49–51
printing by, 46
technology and, 48, 51*n*
work ended on, 51
workshop for, 50–51
differences method, 44–46
differential analyzer, 97–102, 145,
290–91
accuracy of, 128–129
described, 97–98
electronic computer vs., 134
at Harvard, 130
modifications of, 98, 129
Moore School version of, 101–2,
119–20, 124, 128–31
second (MIT) version of, 99
set-up time needed for, 98–99
speed of, 129–30
differential equations, 96–97
Digital Equipment Corporation
(DEC), 278–79, 305–7, 309, 318
Digital Research, 312, 314
diodes, 131
Diogenes, 24
division, 21
logarithms and, 29
Donegan, L. Edwin, Jr., 271–72
Doriot, Georges, 305
Draper, Arthur, 252–53
Durand, Edward Dana, 88–89

Eckert, J. Presper, Jr., 93, 120–24,
139, 255, 260, 280, 323–24, 300,
303, 307, 334–35
attitude of, 123–24
background of, 121–22
Brainerd and, 166–70
EDVAC patent and, 184–87, 199–
201, 218–20
electronic calculator and, 123–24,
131, 134, 137–38
ENIAC and, 136–38, 148–72, 189,
196–97, 300
ENIAC patent and, 168–70, 184,
199–201
ENIAC programming problem
and, 171–72
IBM offer rejected by, 202–3
Mauchly and, 123–24, 131, 134,
167–70, 205–6
mercury delay tube and, 183–84

New York Times ENIAC leak and,
192–94
patent release rejected by, 199–201
on Remington Rand problems, 259
stored memory and, 171–72, 183–
87
Travis and, 198–201
UNIVAC patents and, 281–83
vacuum tubes and, 133–34
von Neumann and, 182–87, 204–5,
217–20, 285–86, 335
see also Eckert-Mauchly Computing
Corporation; Electronic Control
Company
Eckert, Wallace, 104, 181, 254
Eckert calculator, 254
Eckert-Mauchly Computing Corporation (EMCC), 231–53
board expansion for, 236
financial problems of, 241, 242–45
formation of, 231–32
modified BINAC and, 232–34
Nielsen buyout offer for, 244
Remington Rand buyout of, 245–
46
as Remington Rand subsidiary,
246–53, 259
Totalizator and, 236, 246
see also Electronic Control Company
Econet, 323–24
Edison, Thomas, 281
vacuum tube and, 131
Edison effect, 131
EDSAC (Electronic Delay Storage Automatic Calculator), 205, 209–10,
239
EDVAC (Electronic Discrete Variable
Automatic Computer), 172, 182–
87, 190–92, 214–15, 296, 334
funding problems for, 190–92
patent for, 184–87, 199–201, 218–
20
stored, programmable memory
needed for, 183–87
Subcommittee Z evaluation of,
226–28
von Neumann and, 182–87
von Neumann paper on, *see* "First
Draft of a Report to the EDVAC"
Egyptians, computations, 22
8008 microprocessor, 305, 308

8080 microprocessor, 308–9, 312
Einstein, 334
Electronic Control Company, 220–31
    financial health of, 223–25, 228–29, 231
    NBS contract with, 222–25
    security clearance problems of, 228
    see also BINAC; Eckert-Mauchly
        Computing Corporation;
        UNIVAC
1101 computer, 248
Eltgroth, George, 236, 245, 281, 287
EMCC, *see* Eckert-Mauchly Comput-
    ing Corporation
e-mail, 329
Emerson, 304
Encyclopédie (Diderot), 33
Engineering Research Associates
    (ERA), 213–14, 243
    Remington Rand buyout of, 263
Engstrom, Howard T., 213–14
ENIAC (Electronic Numerical Inte-
    grator and Computer), 148–72,
    187–90, 192–98, 206–8, 300, 342
    at Aberdeen, 206
    accumulators in, 156–58
    binary counting in, 151
    constant transmitter for, 158
    construction of, 149–66
    contract terms for, 148
    counting circuits in, 151–52
    as decimal machine, 150–51, 158
    description of, 166
    dismantling of, 207–8
    electrical pulses in, 158–64
    as fixed-decimal machine, 164
    flaws of, 171, 183
    function tables in, 157
    hard-wired circuits in, 164
    leaks concerning, 192–95, 198
    logic and, 149
    Los Alamos experiment on, 188–89, 285
    memory of, 171–72
    New York Times articles on, 192–94,
        196–97, 198
    numerical vs. programming circuits
        in, 158
    operation of, 156–58
    parallel architecture in, 158

    patent for, 168–70, 184, 199–201,
        281–99
    power needed for, 166
    programming of, 171–72, 183,
        188–89, 196, 206
    read-only memory in, 156–57
    reliability of, 151–53
    scientific use of, 197–98
    speed of, 151, 166
    standardization for, 152–53
    supplies for, 155
    team for, 149, 168–70
    testing of, 153–54, 165, 188–89
    total cost of, 197
    unveiling of, 195–97
    von Neumann and, 181–82, 188,
        198, 207
    see also Honeywell vs. *Sperry Rand*
ENIGMA, 141–42
Epimenides' paradox, 178
Estridge, Dan, 315–16
Evans, Christopher, 144
*Examples to the Differential and Integral
    Calculus* (Babbage, et al.), 41
exchequer table, 27
Eytocious of Ascalon, 23–24

Fairchild Camera, 276*n*, 302
Fairchild Semiconductor, 302–4
Farnsworth, Philo T., 122–23
Fax machines, 330
feedback systems, 152
Felt, Dorr E., 94
Fibonacci, Leonardo, 26–27
Field, Marshall, 84
Finke, Walter W., 268–69
"First Draft of a Report to the
    EDVAC" (von Neumann), 184–
    87, 198, 218–19, 285–86, 335
Fishman, Katharine Davis, 255*n*, 263,
    271, 274
Fleming, John Ambrose, 131
Fleming diode, 131–32
Flint, Charles Ranlett, 89–91
flip-flops, 103, 112, 116, 152
Flowers, T. H., 142, 211
Ford, Eugene Amzi, 83
Forrest Gump, 329
Forrester, Jay, 190, 248, 258, 278
Forster, J. Frank, 262

FORTRAN, 311
Fortune, 276
4004 microprocessor, 305
Frankel, Stanley P., 188–89, 197, 204
Franklin, Benjamin, 117–18, 190n
Fylstra, Dan, 311

Gabor, Dennis, 174, 175n, 176
Galileo, 28–29, 100
ganging, 124
Gates, William, III (Bill), 307–9, 312, 314–18, 320–21
Geheimschreiber (Fish), 142
General Electric, 198–99, 260, 281, 304
computer business of, 269–70, 277
geometry, 21, 23
Germany, Nazi, computers of, 143–44
Gerstner, Louis V., Jr., 391
Gillon, Paul, 120, 126, 172, 182
ENIAC and, 145, 147–49, 158, 193–97
Gödel, Kurt, 178
Goldstine, Adele, 126, 130, 149, 189, 196, 198, 206
Goldstine, Herman, 28, 97, 100–101, 103, 109, 125–26, 130–31, 176n, 210, 289, 334, 336
EDVAC and, 185–87, 218–20
ENIAC and, 148–72, 187, 196–97, 207
ENIAC patent and, 170
New York Times ENIAC leak and, 193–94
on post-war Moore School, 214–15
at Princeton, 207, 214–17
von Neumann and, 178–79, 181–82, 185–86, 188, 204, 207, 335
Grant, George Barnard, 93
Great Britain, 27–28, 37–38, 41, 211–12
ENIAC influence in, 209–12
see also Code and Cipher School, Government; ULTRA project
Greeks, 22, 23
Groeneveld, Patrick, 327
Grove, Andrew, 304
Groves, Leslie R., 239, 246

GUI (graphical user interface), 316–17
Hammond Novachord organ, 133
Hanrahan, Richard, 300
harmonic analyzers, 113–14, 293
Hartree, Douglas, 195, 197–98, 209, 211
Harvard University, 203, 254–55
Hazen, Harold Locke, 96–97, 145–47
Heims, Steve J., 337
Herodotus, 23
Herschel, John, 40–42, 44, 49
Hewlett-Packard, 301, 310
Hilbert, David, 176–78
Hindus, 25
Hoff, Ted, 305
Hofstdter, Douglas, 178, 231n
Holberton, Betty, 230
Holberton, John V., 187, 196
Hollerith, Herman, 66, 69–92
Billings and, 71–72
in Census Office, 70–71
CTR and, 91–92
diversification sought by, 79
education of, 70
electric adding machine of, 81
as employer, 79, 83
fame of, 75, 77
family life of, 74–75, 82, 91
Flint and, 89–91
health records systematized by, 73–75
honesty of, 84–85
Library Bureau and, 81–83
mechanical calculators of, 72–89
at MIT, 72
personality of, 69–70
punch cards and, 73–74
railroads and, 73n, 79–82
railroad tabulator of, 80–82, 85
Hollerith, Lucia Talcott, 74–75, 91
Hollerith Electric Tabulating System, 72–89
description of, 76–77
speed of, 76–78
tabulators on, 79
Hollerith punch card machine, 95
Hollerith punch cards, 80
Homebrew Computer Club, 310

Honeywell, 268–70, 277
  see also Honeywell vs. *Sperry Rand*
Honeywell 200 computer, 268–69
Honeywell vs. *Sperry Rand*, 281–99
  ABC in, 288, 296
  "First Draft" in, 285–86
  Iowa visit in, 288–91
  Los Alamos experiment in, 285
  ruling in, 285–88
  Sperry lawyers in, 286–87, 292–93
Hopper, Grace, 230
Humboldt, Baron Alexander von, 49
Hungarians, 173–76
Hurd, Cuthbert, 256–57
Huskey, Harry, 171–72, 206
Hyman, Anthony, 56, 58

IAS (Princeton computer), 217, 226–27
IBM (International Business Machines), 112, 249, 253–58, 261–79, 294, 300, 305–7, 312–15, 317–18
  antitrust suits against, 265–68, 282, 313
  ASCC (Mark I) and, 104–5, 254–55
  calculator research funded by, 254–56
  CDC settlement of, 267–68
  CDC vs., 264–68
  competition of, 260–79, 282
  computer industry dominated by, 261–79
  computers eschewed by, 245, 249, 255–56
  customer fear of, 242
  Eckert and Mauchly sought by, 201–3
  Electronic Data Machine Division of, 257–58
  integrated circuits and, 276–77
  laptop, 324
  losses, 319–21, 335
  management of, 271
  origin of, 92
  PC, 315–16
  Power PC, 321
  punch card readers of, 150, 158
  Remington Rand and, 257–58
  Remington Rand cross-licensing agreement with, 282–83
  Remington Rand patents challenged by, 282, 294
  sales team of, 254, 256, 258, 265–66
  tape machines rejected by, 256
  technological lag of, 257–58, 260–61
  von Neumann and, 256
  in World War II, 255
  see also CTR; Tabulating Machine Company
IBM 90 computers, 265–66
IBM System 360 computers, 265, 271, 276–78
  development of, 276–77
IBM 370 computers, 272
IBM 600 calculators, 256–58
IBM 650 computers, 265*n*
IBM 700 series computers, 256–58, 260
IBM 1401 computers, 268
IBm 1620 computers, 297*n*
ILIAC, 192*n*
Illinois Scientific Developments, 283–99
Industrial Revolution, 37
information economy, 313, 333
integrated circuits, 276–77, 279
  planar, 302–3, 306
integration, 97
Intel, 304–5, 320, 322
  8088, 315
  Pentium, 331
Interstate Commerce Commission (ICC), 85
Israel, 66–67
Italians, 27

Jacoby, Marv, 237
Jacquard, Joseph Marie, 57, 73
Jarvis, C. G., 48, 60
jellybean chips, 303
J. Lyons & Company, 210
Jobs, Steven, 307, 310, 312, 316–18, 320
Johns Hopkins University, 110
Johnson, T. H., 137, 145–46, 148–49
Journal of the Franklin Institute, 97
Jurassic Park, 326, 329
Justice Department, U.S., 88, 265–68, 305

Kapor, Mitch, 332
Kaufman, Paul, 315–16
Kaypro, 319
Kilby, Jack, 302
Kildall, Gary, 312–16
Knox, Dilwyn, 141
Korean War, 256

Lake, Clair D., 104, 254
Lardner, Dionysius, 42
Larson, Earl, 284–99
Learson, Thomas V., 255n, 257, 267
Leibniz, baron Gottfried Wilhelm
    von, 33–35, 41, 103
  scientific notation of, 41
Leigh, Augusta, 53–54
LEO (Lyons Electronic Office), 210
Levy, Oscar C., 245
Lewinski, Richard, 141
Liber Abaci (Fibonacci), 26–27
Liberator, 268
Library Bureau, 81–83, 249
life insurance industry, 93–94
Lisa, 316
logarithms, 29–31
logic, mathematics and, 177–78
Los Alamos, 204n
  ENIAC and, 188–89, 285
Lotus, 321, 332
Lotus 1, 2, 3, 316
LSIs (Large Scale Integrated Cir-
    cuits), 309
Lukoff, Herman, 153–55, 222–23,
    237–39

MacArthur, Douglas, 259
Macintosh, 316–17, 320–21, 329
  OS, 321
  Quadra, 305
McCulloch, Warren, 184–85
McDonald, Robert E., 262
McNulty, Kathleen, *see* Mauchly,
    Kathleen McNulty
Madison, James, 68
magnetic tape input-output, 228,
    237–39, 242–44, 250
mainframes, 262, 306, 318
MANIAC, 204n
Mark I (Harvard-IBM), *see* ASCC
Mark I, Ferranti, 211

Mark I, Manchester (MADM), 210–
    11, 239
Mark II (MEG; megacycle engine),
    211
Marx, Karl, 52
Massachusetts Institute of Technol-
    ogy (MIT), 72, 118–19, 201n,
    260, 277, 305
  computer conference at (1945), 168
  differential analyzer and, 99n, 145–
    47
  radar project and, 147
  Whirlwind computer of, 226–27
mathematics:
  development of, 21–22
  logic and, 177–78
  physical sciences and, 28–29
  written computations and, 21–22
Mauchly, John William, 109–24, 135–
    36, 255, 307, 334–36
  on ABC, 290–93
  Atanasoff and, 114–16, 190–91,
    289–92
  background of, 109–10
  Brainerd and, 166–70
  Eckert and, 123–24, 131, 134, 167–
    70, 205–6
  EDVAC funding sought by, 190–
    92
  EDVAC patent and, 184–87, 199–
    201, 218–20
  electronic calculator proposed by,
    123–24, 131, 134–38
  electronic counting devices of, 112–
    15
  ENIAC and, 148–72, 189, 195–97
  ENIAC patent and, 168–70, 184,
    199–201
  genetic disease of, 137–38, 336
  IBM offer rejected by, 202–3
  Iowa visit of, 115–16, 288–91
  memo of, 134–36
  meteorological research by, 110–
    11, 114
  at Moore School, 116, 119–25
  New York Times ENIAC leak and,
    192–94
  patent release rejected by, 199–201
  on Penn faculty, 125–38
  at Remington Rand, 246
  Sperry Rand and, 260

Mauchly, John William *(continued)*
    Travis and, 198–201
    UNIVAC patents and, 281–83
    vacuum tubes and, 133–34
    von Neumann and, 181–87, 204–5,
        217–20, 285–86, 335
    see also Eckert-Mauchly Computing
        Corporation; Electronic Control
        Company
Mauchly, Kathleen McNulty, 126–28,
    165, 188–89, 206–7, 247n, 292–
    93, 336
Mayans, 20n
Meader, Ralph L., 213–14
MEDLINE, 328
memory, 56
    cathode-ray tube for, 210–11, 238–
        39
    magnetic, 248, 258, 278
    on magnetic disks, 272
    mercury delay tube and quartz crys-
        tal combined for, 183–84
    random-access (RAM), 210, 304
    read-only (ROM), 156–57
    read-write, 156
    stored, programmable, 171–72,
        183–87
Menabrea, L. F., 59
mercury delay tube, 183
Merriam, William R., 83, 86
Metropolis, Nicholas, 188–89, 197,
    204n
microprocessors, 305, 311
Microsoft, 309, 311–14, 316, 321–22
Mindlink, 324
minicomputers, 279, 306, 318–19
MITS (Micro Instrumentation Telem-
    etry Systems), 307–9, 311
Monroe, Jay Randolph, 95
Monroe desk calculators, 95, 135–36
Moore, Alfred Fitler, 118
Moore, Gordon, 302–4
Moore School Lectures, 205
Moore School of Electrical Engi-
    neering, 99, 101–2, 114, 116–31,
    134–38
    computer project of, 137–38, 144–
        48
    Eckert and Mauchly fired from,
        200–201

EDVAC contract of, 172, 182–87,
    214–15
EDVAC patent and, 184–87, 199–
    201, 218–20
ENIAC patent and, 168–70
post-war breakup at, 214–15
radar project at, 135, 147
Travis at, 198–201, 204
war research at, 119–20, 123–31,
    135–38, 154
    see also EDVAC; ENIAC
Moore's law, 303
Moseley, Maboth, 43, 47
Motorola, 320
    Power PC Chips, 331
    68040 microprocessor, 329
Moulton, Forest Ray, 100
MRI (Magnetic Resonance Imaging),
    328
MS-DOS, 314–15, 317, 320
multiplication, 21
    logarithms and, 29
Munn, Charles A. and Gurnee, 235–
    36, 245

Napier, John, 29–30
Napier's Bones, 30
National Applied Mathematics Labo-
    ratory, 225
National Bureau of Standards (NBS),
    U.S., 205, 221–26
    UNIVAC and, 221–26, 242, 244,
        246
National Defense Research Commit-
    tee (NDRC), 96, 144–48
    electronic computer opposed by,
        144–48
National Library of Medicine, 328
National Physical Laboratory (Brit-
    ish), 211–12
National Research Council, 226
National Science Foundation, 96,
    167n
National Youth Administration, 111
Naval Ordnance Laboratory, 190–92
Naval Research Office, 221, 224
Navy, U.S., 213–14, 263
NBS, *see* National Bureau of Stan-
    dards, U.S.

NCR (National Cash Register), 146, 261
    antitrust suit against, 274–75
    computer business and, 273, 275–76
    Computer Research bought by, 276
neon tubes, 112
Newman, M. H. A., 142, 210
Newton, Isaac, 34, 41, 100
New York Central railroad, 80–82, 85
New York Times, 96, 192–94, 196–97
Nielsen, A. C., Jr., 243–44
Nielsen Company, 243–45
    UNIVAC contracted by, 244, 246
Nisus, 330
Norris, William C., 213–14, 249
    Control Data and, 263–68
    Rand and, 258, 263
North, Simon Newton Dexter, 85–88
Northrop Aircraft Company, 228–31, 239–42
Northwest Aeronautical Company, 213–14
Norway, 79
Noyce, Robert, 302–4
numbers, 19–21
    Arabic notation for, 25–27
    counting and, 19–20
    early uses of, 19–21
    group, 19–20, 23
    nine-digit system for, 25
    ordinal vs. cardinal, 21
    prime, 21
    words for, 21
    written, 21–22
numerical integration, 127

Old Testament, censuses in, 66–67
Olsen, Kenneth, 278–79, 305
On the Economy of Machinery and Manufactures (Babbage), 52
Opel, John, 307
operating systems, 274
Oppenhiemer, J. Robert, 217, 257, 336
organs, electric, 133
OS/2, 321–22
Oughtred, William, 31
Overhoff, Gerhard, 143–44

Pachikov, Stephan, 324–25
Palazzi of Nice, 28
Palmer, Ralph, 256–57
Palo Alto, 132, 301
pantograph, 76
Paragraph International, 324–25
parallel architecture, 158, 216, 296
parallel processing, 319
Paris Universal Exposition, 75
Parker, John E., 213–14
Pascal, Blaise, 32–33
Passages from the Life of a Philosopher (Babbage), 64
Patent Office, U.S., 72, 93, 284–87
Patterson, John, 274–75
PDP series (Programmed Data Processors), 279
PDP-1, 305
PDP-8, 305–6
Peacock, George, 40–41
Pender, Harold, 101, 125, 198, 200–201
    EDVAC and, 190, 218
    ENIAC and, 148, 164–65
    ENIAC patent and, 169–70
    Travis and, 198–200
Pennsylvania Railroad, 80–81
Pennsylvania Steel Company, 84
Pepys, Samuel, 30–31
personal computers, 314–15
Personal Software, Inc., 311
Philadelphia, 117, 121–23, 126
Philco, 260–61, 304
photoelectric cells, 129
physical sciences, 28
pi, 21, 26
Pilot ACE, 212
Pitts, Walter, 184–85
"planar" manufacturing, 302
plug compatible machines, 268–69, 271, 276
Polybius, 24
Pong, 310
Popular Electronics, 307–8
Porter, Robert P., 75, 78
Powers, James, 87–89
Powers puncher, 87–88
Powers Tabulating Machine Company, 95, 249
Pratt & Whitney, 76

Princeton Institute for Advanced
    Studies, 177, 194–95, 203–4, 207
    Electronic Computer Project for,
    215–17
    RCA liaison with, 215
Principia (Newton), 100n
Principia Mathematica (Russell and
    Whitehead), 177–78
printing adding machine, 94–95
printing press, 27
product integraph, 96–97
programmers, computer, 56, 272–73,
    317
programming, 216, 230
    development of, 210
    of ENIAC, 171–72, 183, 188–89,
    196, 206
prosthaphaereses, 29
Provident Mutual Life Insurance
    Company, 94
Prudential Insurance Company, 242–
    43
    UNIVAC contracted by, 243, 246
punch card calculators, 74–89
    vacuum tubes vs., 111–12
punch cards, 57, 73–74
    Hollerith, 80
    magnetic tape converters for, 250
    magnetic tape vs., 242–43
    paper tape vs., 73–74

QDOS (Quick and Dirty Operating
    System), 314
quartz crystals, 183–84

racetracks, computers and, 234–36
Radio Shack, 309–10
radio, triodes and, 132
railroads, 85
    Hollerith and, 73n, 79–82
RAM (random-access memory), 210,
    304
Rand, James, Jr., 245–46, 248–49,
    253, 258–59
    background of, 249
    Norris and, 258, 263
Raytheon Manufacturing, 224–25,
    262
    Subcommittee Z on computer of,
    226–28

RCA (Radio Corporation of
    America), 112, 122, 146, 147,
    260, 304
    computer business of, 269, 270–73
    computer research at, 194–95, 201,
    204, 302
    counting systems researched by,
    152
    Princeton liaison with, 215
    Selectron of, 238
    von Neumann and, 204–5
rectifiers, 303–4
Rees, Nina, 189–90, 221
Reeves Instruments, 221
Remington Rand, 89, 112, 239, 245–
    53, 258–59
    competitive advantage of, 248–49
    EMCC bought by, 245–46
    ENIAC patents and, 281–83
    ERA and, 248, 263
    IBM as competition to, 257–58
    IBM cross-licensing agreement
    with, 282–83
    sales force at, 258–59
    St. Paul-Philadelphia dispute in,
    258
    UNIVAC patents and, 281–83
Roebling, Ferdinand W., 82–83, 90
ROM (read-only memory), 156–57,
    304
Romans, 22
    abacus of, 24
Roosevelt, Franklin Delano, 96, 119
Roosevelt, Theodore, 88
Royal Astronomical Society, 44–49,
    51
Russell, Bertrand, 177–78
Russia, 82

SAGE computers, 278
Sams, Jack, 313–14
Samuel, Arthur, 261, 302
Sarnoff, Robert, 271–73
scaling circuits, 151–52
Scheutz, Georg, 51
Schickard, Wilhelm, 32
School of Mines Quarterly, 72
Scientific Research and Development
    Office, U.S., 96, 167
Scully, John, 319–20

Seaton, Charles W., 69, 72
Selectron, 238
semiautomatic tabulators, 87–88
semiconductors, 302
Senkereh tablet, 22–23
serial architecture, 158n, 216, 249–
    50, 296
servomotors, 129
Sharpless, Kite, 149, 164, 169, 214,
    289, 294
Shaw, Robert, 154–55, 164, 169n,
    199, 204, 222, 284, 294
Sheppard, C. Bradford, 199, 215
Shockley, William, 183, 301, 303, 334
Shockley Semiconductor Labora-
    tories, 301
silicon, 302
silicon chips, 302–5
Silicon Graphics, Inc., 326
Silicon Valley, 301–4, 312, 317–18
Silver, Jack, 237
Simon, Leslie, 120, 137, 145, 169, 172
1604 computers, 264
6600 computers, 264–65, 277
slide rules, 30–31
Sobel, Robert, 260–61, 264n
software, 271
    compatibility of, 268–69, 276
    computer design and, 273–74
Software Arts, 311
Solomon, Leslie, 307–8
Somerville, Mary, 55, 61–62
sonar, 132
Soviet Union, 198n
Specimens of Logarithmic Tables (Bab-
    bage), 52
Spectra 70 computer, 271–72
Sperry Rand, 89, 259–63
    ENIAC patent case and, 284–99
    Illinois Scientific and, 283–99
    Norris defection from, 260
    RCA computer division bought by,
        273
    UNIVAC patents and, 281–83
Spielberg, Steven, 326
spin-offs, 310
Stanford Industrial Park, 307
Stanford University, 132n, 201n, 301
statistical analysis, 78
statistical piano, 77

Stern, Nancy, 144, 147, 169, 182,
    203, 227–28, 234, 240–41, 244,
    287, 293, 298
Stibitz, George R., 103–4, 145, 147–
    48, 181, 223–24
    on Subcommittee Z, 226–28
stone counters, 20, 23
strange loops, 178
Straus, Henry, 234–36, 245
STRETCH, 264–65
S-2000 computer, 261
Subcommittee Z on High-Speed Com-
    puting, 226–28
subroutines, 210
subtraction, 21
Swain, George F., 82–83
switching circuits, 133–34
Szilard, Edward, 174, 176–77

table look-up, 157
Tabulating Machine Company, 79,
    82–91, 95
    Census Bureau as competition to,
        85–89
    Flint buyout of, 90–91
    incorporation of, 82–83
    monopoly image of, 85–86
    1900 census and, 83
    Powers' puncher and, 87–88
    punch cards as profit-maker for, 84
    Tabulating Machine vs. *Durand*, 88–89
Taft-Peirce, 83–84
Talcott, Mrs., 74–75, 82
tally sticks, 27–28
Tandy, 309
Teleregister, 244
television, 122–23, 193n
Teller, Edward, 174
    on von Neumann, 188, 327
Terrell, Paul, 310
Tennyson, Alfred Lord, 52–53
Texas Instruments, 276n, 277, 302,
    304, 307
Thayer, Harry Bates, 82–83, 86
Thermionic valves, *see* vacuum tubes
Thomas, Charles, 35
torque amplifiers, 97–98
transistors, 260–61, 265n, 301–2
translator languages, 210
Travelers' Insurance Company, 81

Travis, Irven, 114, 124–25, 198–201,
        204, 221, 273
    patent release sought by, 199–201
Treasury, U.S., 94
trigonometry, 26
triode, 132
Trowbridge, William, 70
Turing, Alan, 140–42
    ACE and, 211–12
    binary computer envisioned by, 141
    eccentricities of, 140
    ULTRA and, 141–42

ULTRA project, 141–43
UNIVAC (Universal Automatic Com-
        puter), 221–53, 265n, 269–70,
        296, 299, 304
    BINAC and, 239–42
    contracts for, 242–45
    description of, 249–50
    early IBM computers vs., 257–58
    Forster and, 262
    magnetic tape input-output of, 228,
        237–39, 242–44, 250
    in 1952 election, 250–53
    patents for, 281–83
    peripheral devices for, 250
    speed of, 249–50
    subcommittee Z evaluation of, 226–
        28
Univac division (Sperry Rand), 260
University of California at Berkeley,
        301
University of Delft, 327
University of Pennsylvania, 99, 113–
        14, 117–18, 136
    origins of, 117–18
    see also Moore School of Electrical
        Engineering
Ursinus College, 109–11, 114, 125,
        135–36
user friendly, defined, 150n

vacuum tubes, 107, 111–12, 115–16,
        123–24, 129, 131–35, 144, 260–
        61, 300–1
    in COLOSSUS, 142
    development of, 131–32
    Edison and, 131
    electronics industry and, 132–33

inconsistency of, 133–34, 300
    limitations of, 133–34
    transistor and, 302–3
    voltage level and, 133
Varian, Sigurd and Russell, 307–8
Veblen, Oswald, 100, 117, 125–26,
        137, 138, 177, 189, 203
Vickers, Harry, 259–60, 262
VisiCalc, 311, 315
von Neumann, John, 140, 173–98,
        201–7, 213–15, 238, 335–37
    background of, 174
    as computer spokesman, 216–18
    Eckert and, 182–87, 204–5, 217–
        20, 285–86, 335
    education of, 174–77
    EDVAC and, 182–87
    EDVAC patent and, 218–20
    ENIAC and, 181–82, 188, 198, 207
    IBM and, 256
    mathematical world of, 177–78
    Mauchly and, 181–87, 204–5, 217–
        20, 285–86, 336
    mental prowess of, 178–79
    New York Times ENIAC leak and,
        192–94
    personality of, 179–80
    at Princeton, 177, 194–94, 203–4,
        207
    Princeton-RCA project of, 215–17
    as prodigy, 174–75
    research offers to, 203
    stored memory and, 184–87, 218
    on Subcommittee Z, 226–28
    war research of, 180

Walker, Francis A., 72
Wang, 319
War Department, U.S., 75
Warren, Reid, 168, 170, 185, 214
Washington, George, 68
Waterman Products Company, 238
Watson, Arthur, 277
Watson, Thomas, 91–92, 158, 245,
        249, 254–57, 274, 319
    Eckert, Mauchly and, 202–3
    Mark I and, 254–55
    NCR and, 274–75
Watson, Thomas, Jr., 255–57, 264–
        65, 277

Watson Labs, 244
Weather Bureau, U.S., 191–94
Weaver, Warren, 167, 181, 190
Wellington, duke of, 49–50
Wells, H. G., 333
Western Electric, 76, 158
Westinghouse, George, 73
Weygandt, Cornelius, 102, 119–20, 128–29, 154
Wharton School, 136
Whirlwind, 226–27
Whitehead, Alfred North, 177–78
Whitmore, Georgiana, 43
Wiener, Norbert, 203
Wigner, Eugene, 174–77
Wilkes, Maurice, 64, 205, 209–10, 212
Williams, F. C., 210, 212
Williams, Samuel B., 104, 169
Windows, 320
Windows 95, 321–22

Winterbotham, F. W., 142
word processing, 314–15
World War I, 175–76
  ballistics in, 100–101
  research in, 132
World War II, 255
  Moore School, research in, 119–20, 123–31, 135–38, 154
Wozniak, Stephen, 307, 310, 312, 319
Wulforst, Harry, 250–52

Yale & Towne Manufacturing, 85

zero, 25
Z3 computer, 143
Z4 computer, 143–44
Zuse, Konrad, 143–44
Zuse Apparatebau, 143–44
Zworykin, Vladimir, 190, 192–95, 201, 204